AND STILL WE RISE

Interviews with 50 black role models

Barbara Reynolds

USA TODAY Books
Gannett Co. Inc., Washington, D.C.

And Still We Rise: Interviews with 50 black role models
© 1988 by Gannett New Media Services, Inc. No part of
this book may be used or reproduced in any manner what-
soever except in the context of reviews. For information,
write USA TODAY Books, P.O. Box 450, Washington,
D.C. 20044, or call (703) 276-5978.
  Printed and bound for USA TODAY Books by Arcata
Graphics Co. in Kingsport, Tennessee, the United States of
America.

Library of Congress Cataloging-in-Publication Data

Reynolds, Barbara A.
  And still we rise

  1. Afro-Americans — Interviews. 2. Afro-American
leadership. 3. Success — United States. I. Title.
E185.96.R49   1988   920'.009296073   (B)   88-57
ISBN 0-944347-02-9

CONTENTS

Foreword ix
Introduction xi
Dedication xv

MARIAN WRIGHT EDELMAN

"We want every young person to think they can be something. We know that they can — if we give them the opportunity."

73

WALTER FAUNTROY

"If I went South, I had to pack a bag lunch because they wouldn't feed me at a restaurant. I was outraged."

77

KIM FIELDS

"I am a very private person. I am very shy. I am more of an observer."

81

JOHN HOPE FRANKLIN

"This country is what it is because of the blood, sweat, toil and tears of blacks. And to deny them their rights is unconscionable."

85

MARY HATWOOD FUTRELL

"I wanted to emulate those who had a tremendous influence on me."

89

NIKKI GIOVANNI

"Life is fun. I recommend laughter. And I say this to the kids too."

93

DICK GREGORY

"If I ever came close to being crazy, it was when I was in those nightclubs abusing my body."

97

ROSEY GRIER

"I see an incredible opportunity. I see all these people. Some are broken down on the highway of life, needing a push."

101

ALEX HALEY

"As my writing and research led me to the point where Kunta Kinte is going to be captured . . . I talked to him."

105

DOROTHY HEIGHT

"We are a people with a past, a present, a future. We have a heritage, a strong cultural base, a strong religious base."

109

JENNIFER HOLLIDAY

"In many cases, we are trying so much harder to prove something to ourselves. Not to anybody else."

113

LENA HORNE

"I never thought I'd have this kind of attention. I've been around long enough to collect three generations."

117

JOHN JOHNSON

"If you can sell, you can succeed. . . . You can think only in terms of what the other person would like to have."

121

BISHOP LEONTINE KELLY

"Some people who were dear friends felt it was foolish for a black woman to consider running hundreds of churches."

125

CORETTA SCOTT KING

"In the achievement of economic justice we still have a mighty long way to go."

129

MARTIN LUTHER KING SR.

"When we vote our strength, we are demonstrating power."

133

MARTIN LUTHER KING III

"Once we became an integrated society, we became selfish and we tried to forget the past."

137

CARL ROWAN

"I want people to remember me as a journalist who was never afraid to write or to say what he believes."

169

SUGAR RAY LEONARD

"I might have acted like I was crazy. But it was the desire to win that drove me onward."

141

WILMA RUDOLPH

"When my parents were away, I would take the braces off and try to walk without them. I . . . attribute that motivation to my mother."

173

JOSEPH LOWERY

"I believe that all black folks live with the edict that they must enter the movement or perish."

145

DAVID SATCHER

"One of the things I worry about is whether young people are finding the kind of role models I had."

177

MELBA MOORE

"It is up to me to try to make the neighborhood safe. . . . If you don't do something about it, it won't be done."

149

NIARA SUDARKASA

"How can you possibly know how far you can go if you have no sense of how far you have been?"

181

ETHEL PAYNE

"We have retrogressed in some respects. But in others we have become wiser."

153

SUSAN L. TAYLOR

"I wanted to create a product that would touch people, that would talk about . . . issues I didn't feel any magazine was looking at."

185

PHYLICIA RASHAD

"People usually think that when you meditate you get all doe-eyed and you get all slurpy. No. You get peaceful."

157

CICELY TYSON

"I cannot do things just for money. I have to have some inner gratification."

189

LOU RAWLS

"I used to think I was real slick. I was smarter than everyone else. I found out that slick ain't nothing but a word."

161

MALCOLM-JAMAL WARNER

"Kids want to be famous. They want to be celebrities. That's not what it's all about."

193

RANDALL ROBINSON

"As long as African-Americans see themselves as something disconnected from Africa, we never will be her heirs."

165

HAROLD WASHINGTON

"A viable society must have new blood churning constantly. We should always be proud of the franchise, the right to vote."

197

FOREWORD

On Sept. 15, 1982, USA TODAY was founded on a commitment "to serve as a forum for better understanding and unity" across the USA, and the editors of The Nation's Newspaper pursue that goal in every edition.

The daily Opinion and Inquiry pages of USA TODAY play a key role in this pursuit and so does Barbara Reynolds, editor of the Inquiry page and a member of the Opinion page editorial board.

This book, *And Still We Rise*, represents a special segment of Ms. Reynolds' share in the USA TODAY commitment — a collection of her interviews with 50 black men and women whose achievements make them strong role models for everyone.

The success stories of these 50 leaders provide the facts and some of the frustrations. They offer ideas and inspiration. They share words of warnings and examples of courage for all who care to follow these footsteps of achievement.

USA TODAY is proud of the contributions to its pages by Ms. Reynolds and is pleased to share these selections of her work.

—John C. Quinn
Editor, USA TODAY
Chief News Executive, Gannett Co. Inc.

BARBARA REYNOLDS

LIVING THE DREAM

Struggle and creativity pay triumphant rewards

Born in Columbus, Ohio, Barbara Reynolds was graduated from Ohio State University with a bachelor of arts in journalism in 1967.

Her first newspaper job was with *The Columbus Call & Post*, her hometown newspaper serving the black community. She went to a metropolitan paper, the now-defunct *Cleveland Press*, in 1968 and became assistant editor of *Ebony* magazine the same year.

She later worked for *Chicago Today* and the *Chicago Tribune*. While at the *Tribune*, Reynolds began airing radio commentaries for WBBM-AM and started free-lance writing for *Essence* magazine, *Playboy*, *The New Republic* and *Black Family*. She co-founded *Dollars & Sense*, a magazine for black professionals.

In 1975, Reynolds published *Jesse Jackson: The Man, The Movement and The Myth*. She updated the book in 1985 under the title, *Jesse Jackson: America's David*. In 1976, she was named a Nieman Fellow at Harvard University; she studied constitutional law.

Reynolds became a Washington correspondent for the *Chicago Tribune* in 1979.

She joined USA TODAY's editorial board and became Inquiry page editor in 1983.

Among her many honors are the 1987 Southern Christian Leadership Conference Drum Major for Justice Award.

Reynolds lives in Washington, D.C., with her 6-year-old son, John Eric.

I am proud to introduce *And Still We Rise,* conversations with 50 black role models in the areas of education, entertainment, science, sports, civil rights, politics, business and religion. All have appeared on or have been interviewed for the Inquiry or Opinion pages of USA TODAY. The interviews have been updated and refocused especially for this book.

Many of the people whom I have interviewed for this book I have known and respected for many years. At USA TODAY, I shared stories about the people whose personal struggles had uplifted me — like Coretta King, my mentor, who persevered to teach me the power of non-violence and love; and like Marva Collins, who advised that when life deals you lemons, make lemonade.

It was my joy to find that the stories I had kept private, once shared, were motivating a lot of people around USA TODAY, especially a vice president — Nancy Woodhull — and USA TODAY Editorial Director John Seigenthaler. And it was quickly concluded that many of the people in this book are role models not only for black people, but for the nation.

These are human stories. These are stories of pain and triumph, of each person's strength and struggle, of examples of amazing creativity, such as how John H. Johnson raised $500 by mortgaging his mother's furniture and parlayed it into a multimillion-dollar publishing company.

The men and women in this book are achievers, despite great odds. They are people like Wilma Rudolph, who overcame polio to become an Olympic champion; Ray Charles, who despite being blind, helps the world to see the beauty of music and love; and Mary Frances Berry, who began her early life in an orphanage and now is a lawyer, professor, author, scholar and human rights activist.

MARTIN LUTHER KING III: Carries on father's dream.

Role models like these show amazing abilities to bounce back, not only from extreme circumstances but also situations that could confront us all. For example, Rosey Grier, former football star and one of the old Kennedy crowd, tells what it took to begin the long climb back after he hit bottom mentally, physically and financially. Alex Haley, a literary giant, tells in riveting detail how his relatives from the grave kept him from jumping overboard to his death when he was depressed over the progress of his book *Roots*. Melba Moore, star of screen and stage, talks about how she almost self-destructed, picked herself up and now has the strength to help save the national black family.

In the past, so much of the nation's attention focused on blacks as problems. Here, for once, is a refreshing look at 50 black achievers who offer promise and solutions for changing their lives and that of the nation as we march toward the 21st century.

DOROTHY HEIGHT: Protege of Mary Bethune.

With a sense of urgency, many of the black thought-leaders offer recipes for change, running the gamut from self-help to economic alternatives to opening the window of opportunity through politics, civil rights or an enlightened Third World foreign policy.

The voices here are Republicans, Democrats, Independents, a Communist. The voices are of the very young, such as teen-ager Malcolm-Jamal Warner from *The Cosby Show,* and of more seasoned world travelers, such as journalist Ethel Payne, one of the nation's first black female war correspondents.

The voices are of many who have made their mark on Earth and one, astronaut Guion Bluford, who has soared into space.

Many of the people from the pages of *And Still We Rise* are household names, such as Bill Cosby, Lena Horne, Sugar Ray Leonard and Cicely Tyson. What are they really like? This book helped me — and I hope will help you — see behind the glitter of celebrities and feel their pulse and see what really counts in their lives.

It is fitting that this book comes in the 20th anniversary year of the death of Dr. Martin Luther King Jr. Most of the voices and views in this book were either part of the King movement or were touched by it, and they have personalized the values of love, commitment and resolve for which Dr. Martin Luther King Jr. stood.

I feel comfortable and comforted as I listen to the people from *And Still We Rise.* "The Dream" did not die, but lives on through the examples of people like conservative Robert Woodson, who is infusing black communities nationwide with new ideas for economic self-respect. And through Chil-

GUION BLUFORD: Pioneer in space.

dren's Defense Fund President Marian Wright Edelman and people like Rep. Walter Fauntroy and Joseph Lowery, who marched with King. People like Mary Futrell, the nation's most visible teacher. They are updating, revising and continuing his work.

What better time than now to take inventory of where we are as a nation 20 years after the Dreamer has gone. Among those who are taking stock are talk-show star Oprah Winfrey, who says, "I am living the dream," and poet Nikki Giovanni, who concludes that "now is a time to celebrate a job well done."

Maya Angelou encourages us with a note of optimism in her wonderful poem, *And Still I Rise*, from which the title of this book was taken. She indicates that the long nights of disrespect, violence and abandonment are ending. Daybreak is coming. She writes:

MARVA COLLINS: 'When life deals you lemons, make lemonade.'

Leaving behind nights of terror and

MARY FUTRELL: Leader of nation's teachers.

fear; I rise; Into a daybreak that's wondrously clear; I rise; Bringing the gifts that my ancestors gave; I am the dream and hope of the slave; I rise; I rise; I rise.

Still, the lesson must not be lost. The role models in this book are different from most people.

They began life further back and expended twice as much energy to go half as far as others whose paths were not barricaded by bigotry and unfairness.

John Hope Franklin, one of the nation's best-known historians, reminds us that there are still places in the USA where he is not welcome. Bishop Leontine Kelly, the nation's first and only black woman bishop, talks about how racism and sexism in religion add unnecessary baggage.

Also often alluded to in this book are self-inflicted wounds blacks suffer. For example, David Satcher points to an issue that is little known outside the black family — color prejudice that many blacks harbor toward each other. This color bias, as well as a "selfishness" that Martin Luther King III talks about, also hinder black progress. They must be overcome.

Equally as enlightening are the people whom many of the role models in this book look to as their role models:

▶ Mary McLeod Bethune, educator and activist who played a key role in the Roosevelt administration and was founder of the National Council of Negro Women in 1935. Her protege, Dorothy Height, still heads that organization.

▶ Jackie Robinson, who suffered boos and jeers on the playing field in 1947 when he became the first black person to play major league baseball.

▶ Walter White, a former NAACP executive secretary, who because of his light skin could wit-

SUGAR RAY LEONARD: Tells of life out of the ring.

ness and report on the lynchings of blacks in the South.

▶ Harriet Tubman, who escaped slavery in 1845 and went on to become a leader of the underground railroad that helped thousands of slaves make their way through the South to freedom in the North.

▶ Sojourner Truth, a preacher, abolitionist and lecturer.

▶ A. Philip Randolph, whose black union, the Brotherhood of Sleeping Car Porters, was instrumental in improving the wages and working conditions of black employees.

▶ Paul Robeson, a labor and civil rights activist as well as an athlete, singer and lawyer. A magnificent actor, he played *Othello* and *The Emperor Jones.* In 1950, the government canceled his passport, denying his travel abroad because of his friendship with people labeled communists.

▶ W.E.B. DuBois, the first black to get a Ph.D. from Harvard University and one of the founders of the NAACP.

▶ Pat Harris, who in the Jimmy Carter administration became the only woman ever to serve in two cabinet posts. Harris, with whom I traveled up and down the Mississippi Delta researching health care problems of the poor, was also a role model for me.

Their success stories should be as well known as those of their white counterparts, such as Patrick Henry or Susan B. Anthony. But to most readers — both black and white — their names are not familiar.

This is because blacks in the USA have an image problem, primarily because the media, the textbooks, the information industries have not been doing their jobs. For too long, blacks were forever asking. "Mirror, mirror on the wall, why aren't we there at all?"

When we were included, we were often defined by the lowest common denominator. Our image

JOHN H. JOHNSON: Creative.

LENA HORNE: Tells what really counts in her life.

from Hollywood on down — a fact that journalist Tony Brown and Cicely Tyson address — was welfare client, victim, destroyer and pillager of society. How could there ever be equitable results with those kinds of stereotypes? As author Angelou says, "Only equals can be friends."

As with their role models, the achievers are making strides in erasing the disparities and improving the image. For example, three characters from TV's *The Cosby Show* family featured here have become symbols of wholesome family life.

In introducing this book, I believe the Gannett Co. has taken another step toward beginning a correction. Moreover, this book ensures that the struggles and achievements of these 50 black role models will not be buried, lost or overlooked into oblivion.

In selecting these 50 interviews for inclusion in *And Still We Rise,* we are not trying to anoint new leaders or dethrone the old. Thousands of people across the USA are deserving of mention in these success stories. This book is just one step in the right direction. I am sure there will be more. Many more black sources, views and perspectives have been sought after and included on the Opinion and Inquiry pages of USA TODAY.

In each chapter, you'll read my impressions of each of the 50, along with edited question-and-answer conversations and biographical information.

It is our hope that this living black history will bring us one step closer to one truth, one reality and a more complete history of the USA.

—**Barbara Reynolds**
1988

AND STILL WE RISE

A veteran editor and a child have super-special roles with writer

This book is dedicated to the two men in my life named John — John Eric Reynolds and John Seigenthaler. John Eric Reynolds, my 6-year-old son, represents my future. John Seigenthaler, USA TODAY editorial director, represents how futures are made.

John Eric, when you're old enough to read better, you'll find within the pages of *And Still We Rise* role models, people to point the way, to show you how they became winners, heroes and overcomers.

No matter what obstacles block your rise, John Eric, there are heroes and "sheroes" in this book who have laid body and soul on the line to show you and all the world how to see challenges instead of roadblocks, how to see temporary interruptions instead of failure and how to hold on to faith when lesser souls despair.

Life for the people in this book was "no crystal stair" as Langston Hughes wrote. And it won't be for you. But the one message these black achievers deliver is that if we put our faith in God and work hard, there is the blessed assurance that even if we fall: And Still We Rise. We as a people always have. We have risen through slavery, Jim Crow laws, lynchings, segregation, self-hate, poverty, substandard living conditions, police brutality, double standards, job discrimination. And through it all, We Still Rise.

John Eric, I hope you can view this book as soul food, substance for the soul, something to digest into your marrow, sinew, brain and soul. This book shares with you how to have the last word when the world rejects you; how to value the lessons of our elders as a blueprint for the future and how important it is to give of ourselves to continue Dr. Martin Luther King Jr.'s Dream. These role models are winners, but they are also expanding the winner's circle so that success can one day become a reasonable expectation rather than an accident, like lightning striking on a snowy day.

John Seigenthaler is also super-special. There never would have been a Barbara Reynolds at this juncture in journalism if there hadn't been a John Seigenthaler. In 1983, he hired me as a member of the editorial board and an editor of the Inquiry page. And it went without saying that he did so with a mandate for openness to all views and voices across the USA.

It is important to know that in the USA, blacks are not normally on editorial boards. In fact, blacks as supervisors and managers in the newspaper industry are still far too rare. Minorities represent only 3.9 percent of the 12,000 personnel in newspapers' supervisory positions; 56 percent of USA newspapers have no minority journalists.

In the people he hires and by ensuring that their views are shared on the Editorial and Inquiry pages, Seigenthaler is setting a standard for the industry. If the USA is ever to be a truly open society, his example must be emulated. Gannett and USA TODAY have become the first major media institutions to discover that blacks, browns, yellows, reds, women and children live in the USA, too, and make a positive contribution.

Seigenthaler and others at USA TODAY have found that fairness — hiring and promoting minorities and opening the nation's newspapers to everyone — improved the product and is bringing the country closer together as a national family.

This is not the first time Seigenthaler has stood out from his peers. Here is a man, a white Southerner, who was accosted and beaten on the head in the civil rights movement trying to protect the freedom riders in the South. He is a man who remains an enemy of bigotry and a friend of fairness.

I am proud to have John Seigenthaler as a friend and role model.

Barbara A. Reynolds

MAYA ANGELOU

Her full life gives her many voices
to sing out about love and forgiveness

ANGELOU: 'Life loves the liver of it. Life loves to be taken by the lapel and be told: "I am with you kid. Let's go." '

IMPRESSIONS

Maya Angelou is a special person whose voice I will remember when I'm old. Her voice replicates the wind, the trees and civilization. Her prose reads like poetry. Her poetry, like music. Her music sounds like magic. It brings together self and love. Her voice shows that she has suffered pain, but speaks of joy. She has passed along to me a sense of no regrets, of forgiveness.

— **Barbara Reynolds**

Hailed as one of the greatest voices in contemporary literature, Maya Angelou has seen life from many viewpoints. By her early 20s she had been a Creole cook, a streetcar conductor, a cocktail waitress, a dancer, a madam and an unwed mother. She speaks French, Spanish, Italian, Arabic and Fanti, an African dialect. Over the decades, the world has seen her emerge as a successful singer, actress, playwright, editor and civil rights activist. She is the author of five autobiographical works. Angelou currently is Reynolds professor of American studies at Wake Forest University, Winston-Salem, N.C. An interview with her appeared on the USA TODAY *Inquiry page March 5, 1985.*

USA TODAY: Your poem, *And Still I Rise*, inspired this book. How did the poem come about?

ANGELOU: I can hardly ever tell exactly the moment that a poem strikes me. It is a gradual conditioning. Some years ago I was in Pine Bluff, Ark., and I heard a preacher speak on Mother's Day to a church group. He pointed to the women in particular and said: "Mothers I want you to know that the state of Arkansas is building more prisons. Who do you think they are building the prisons for? Your children." Then he said: "Mothers I have even some worse news. The state is buying a new gas chamber. Will that little boy sit in it or that little boy?" It just turned me upside down.

USA TODAY: What did you do?

ANGELOU: I came home to California and with Ruth Love, who was superintendent of schools in Chicago, started a school for black children who were said to be ineducable. This was in Oakland. In one year our children started to compete with the kids in the top 10 percentile. In one year! I looked at those children's faces turning bright and the curiosity to learn growing in them and I thought: "Despite being thrown away by a larger society, ignored by their own and brutalized by their mothers, these children are rising. They are rising!"

USA TODAY: That inspired the poem?

ANGELOU: I began to write that poem then. But there are so many other incidents.

USA TODAY: The poem is peppered with the promise of hope. Is hope the right response when there are so many problems for blacks in the USA?

ANGELOU: I am hopeful, yes. However, I do think that we are on a social level now which makes us more endangered than we have ever been because the avenues of hope seem to be evaporating from our community. Unfortunately, a number of the black "haves" — those who have money, education, those who have hope, those who have a way out — are forgetting the "have-nots," allowing a separation from the bulk of the community. And we will all die if that happens. There is no way that we can survive. Unfortunately, a number of blacks in the "haves" camp take on the mediocrity of the whites. Not the enterprise, but the posturing of the larger society. And therein we lose.

USA TODAY: Are people innately talented?

ANGELOU: I believe that every person is born with talent. We come from the Creator, as the poet Wordsworth says, "trailing clouds of glory." We are all creative, but by the time we are 3 or 4 years old someone has knocked the creativity out of us. Some people shut up the kids who start to tell stories. Kids dance in their cribs, but someone will insist they sit still. By the time creative people are 10 or 12 years old they just want to be like everybody else.

USA TODAY: Why don't we fight harder for our right to be creative?

ANGELOU: Some of us are timid. We think we have something to lose so we don't try for that next hill or that next rise. The truth is we have nothing to lose — nothing. Shakespeare said that we would "rather bear those ills we have than fly to others that we know not of." Thus, conscience does make cowards of us all because we would rather just stay right here and not dare. Yet the young person who knows and is informed dares enough to understand that life loves the liver of it. Life loves to be taken by the lapel and be told: "I am with you kid. Let's go."

USA TODAY: I grew up hearing, "Children should be seen and not heard." Isn't the reluctance to take risks a result of growing up in a society where blacks were treated as inconspicuous?

ANGELOU: White children were told that as well. But slavery exacerbated it for us. That was already in the social thinking. And also: "If it's good to you, it's probably a sin. . . . Shut up and flagellate yourself in some way. . . . Be poor and don't talk." That was all a part of what was brought to these shores in the 17th century. Being black and a part of the underclass and working class, we had to be quiet and as inconspicuous as possible. So what was going on in the larger society was intensified for us.

USA TODAY: How did you develop your style?

ANGELOU: Years ago when I was very young I had the affliction of muteness for five years. I listened to everything and I memorized. I memorized Shakespeare, Paul Lawrence Dunbar, James Weldon Johnson, Edgar Allan Poe. Those four writers influenced my early years. And the Southern black preacher speaks in such music and such poetry that I still laugh out loud in church. The black American Southern minister influenced and informed my ear.

USA TODAY: How is the South different now?

ANGELOU: Black children and white children go to school together now. Black youngsters and white youngsters are seen staring into the same shops in malls, sometimes walking together on field trips. The mystery between the races is not as prevalent as it was in my day. I really thought that white people were not real.

USA TODAY: What do you mean?

ANGELOU: I thought we were people but white folks were "white folk." And that if any person put his hand on a "white folk" their hands would go right through them. I mean they were so mysterious to me. I just couldn't believe that "white folk" had livers and hearts and all this stuff that we had inside us. It is a different world entirely. Not that racism isn't still prevalent. It is as prevalent in the South as in the North. As it is often said, "Savannah, Ga., is down South and New York City is up South."

USA TODAY: Is there still a need for Black History Month?

ANGELOU: I am sorry to say we still need it. I long for the time when we won't have it at all — when black history, Native American history, Asian history and all history dealing with these yet-to-be United States are included in the American history text books. Until that time we desperately need at least a month.

USA TODAY: Is it important for today's young people to know the history of blacks in the USA?

ANGELOU: Young black men and women need to be informed about our history — the dreams fulfilled and those deferred, the promises achieved and broken — that's for the young black people. The young white people desperately need to be informed about black American history.

USA TODAY: Why is that?

ANGELOU: Because only equals can be friends. Any other relationship made between peers will topple. It will be a paternalistic, maternalistic,

ANGELOU PROFILE

Born: April 4, 1924, in St. Louis; name originally was Marguerite Johnson.

Family: Divorced; a son, Guy Johnson.

Education: Graduated from Mission High School in San Francisco; studied dance and drama with Pearl Primus.

On life: "I try to address each person as a fellow child of God. Now I blow it a lot. I am not proud of that, but I do forgive myself and try to ameliorate my actions."

Home: Winston-Salem, N.C.

Role model: Her mother, Vivian Baxter.

MILESTONES

1954: Appeared in *Porgy and Bess* on 22-nation tour.

1957: Appeared in off-Broadway play, *Calypso Heatwave;* recorded *Miss Calypso.*

1959: Northern coordinator for the Southern Christian Leadership Conference.

1963: Started four years as assistant administrator of the School of Music and Drama, University of Ghana.

1970: First volume of best-selling autobiography, *I Know Why the Caged Bird Sings*, published.

1971: *Just Give Me A Cool Drink of Water 'Fore I Die* published.

1972: *Georgia, Georgia* published.

1973: Broadway debut in *Look Away.*

1974: *Gather Together In My Name* published; directed film *All Day Long.*

1975: *Oh Pray My Wings Are Gonna Fit Me Well* published.

1976: *Singin' and Swingin' and Gettin' Merry Like Christmas* published.

1981: Returned to the South to live and work; *The Heart of a Woman* published.

1983: *Shaker, Why Don't You Sing?* published.

1986: *All God's Children Need Traveling Shoes* published.

philanthropic relationship. Not that those can't be good relationships, but you cannot make friends from those unequal positions. If those white students knew black American history and knew how the struggle had been waged and knew the achievements, they could look at young black people in an informed light. Then it would be easier to make friends, and out of friendship comes support.

USA TODAY: What must the black community do to continue to rise?

ANGELOU: You have to have enough courage to admit where you are. It is imperative not to jive, but to really say, "This is where I am." That is the first thing. And the second thing that is necessary is to evaluate: "Do I really like it here? Is this what I want? Is this how I want to see myself and be seen?"

USA TODAY: What if the answer is no?

ANGELOU: The third immediate necessity is to forgive yourself. It is imperative to say: "I did what I knew to do and it was stupid, but that's all I could do. So now that I have forgiven myself I'll make a change. And it's all right." You are the only person who can forgive yourself. Once that forgiving has taken place, you can then console yourself with the knowledge that a diamond is the result of extreme pressure. Less pressure is crystal, less pressure than that is coal, less than that is fossilized leaves, or just plain dirt. The pressure can make you into something quite precious, quite wonderful, quite beautiful and extremely hard.

USA TODAY: Looking back on your life, what do you feel you have contributed?

ANGELOU: What I really would like said about me is that I dared to love. By love I mean that condition in the human spirit so profound it encourages us to develop courage and build bridges, and then to trust those bridges and cross the bridges in attempts to reach other human beings. I would like to be remembered as a person who dared to love and as a very religious woman. I pray a lot. I am convinced that I am a child of God. And that everybody is a child of God. I try to address each person as a fellow child of God. Now I blow it a lot. I am not proud of that, but I do forgive myself and try to ameliorate my actions.

ARTHUR ASHE

He volleyed his way past whites-only rules to open tennis opportunities for blacks

ASHE: 'If one is very persistent but does not have the talent to follow through to one's dream, that's being unrealistic.'

IMPRESSIONS

He is the Jackie Robinson of tennis, a man who has soaked up a lot of pain for being "the first." In 1979 at age 36 and at the height of his career, Arthur Ashe suffered a heart attack. But in his early retirement he continues to reach for new challenges. He has an inspiring interest in black athletes. And he has completed a book that he says is the first definitive history of the Afro-American athlete. I have always wondered whether the stress of racism contributed to his almost fatal illness. Ashe answers, "No." I give him great credit for not folding up and allowing a bad break to deter him.

— **Barbara Reynolds**

Arthur Ashe became the first black to win the men's singles at Wimbledon when he defeated Jimmy Connors in 1975. He first gained national tennis stardom in 1968 when, as an amateur, he won the U.S. Open Tournament at Forest Hills, N.Y., the tennis club that once denied membership to United Nations Undersecretary Ralph Bunche. Ashe was the first black man to become a member of the U.S. Davis Cup tennis team. After a series of heart attacks in 1979, he gave up his No. 7 world ranking and later became captain of the U.S. Davis Cup team. He is outspoken about South African apartheid and entertainers and sports figures who appear before segregated audiences in South Africa. He has been a regular columnist for the Washington Post and his articles also have appeared in The New York Times and People magazine. An interview with Ashe appeared on the USA TODAY Inquiry page Sept. 24, 1985.

USA TODAY: As one of the first blacks to successfully play professional tennis, you were first to face a number of racial barriers. Does one stand out?

ASHE: Because of my race I was denied the chance to enter a U.S. Tennis Association tournament. I was 12. When my mentor and tennis instructor at the time, Ron Charity, tried to enter me, the official looked us in the eyes and said: "Gee, I would like to have you play, but you just can't. It's the rules. This is a white park. We know you are one of the best 12-year-olds around here, but we just can't do it 'cause those are the rules." He wasn't nasty. In fact he was very nice about it.

USA TODAY: How did these policies affect your ability to compete?

ASHE: I only played one junior tournament in my whole life. They didn't allow blacks to play in the official tournaments. So we had to play in all-black tournaments. I couldn't enter a lot of tournaments in my home state, even in my home city of Richmond, Va. I missed five years of those tournaments. I finally got to play in a mixed "official tournament" when I was 18.

USA TODAY: What are your thoughts about the way segregation held you back?

ASHE: On one hand, you think of it as kind of natural because it happens to all blacks. You say, "I am not the only one who had that situation to work against." On the other hand, you learn about equality in your public school history and civics classes, but you find out life is not really like that.

USA TODAY: What do you regret most about segregation in tennis?

ASHE: I am really disappointed for the others — those players who came before me like Jimmy McDaniel and Reginald Weir. They were some of the great black players from before World War II. The segregated system denied them their rightful shots at the honors and accolades they may have won. If they had been allowed to play in the so-called official tournaments, their names would have been in the record books. Because they could not, their names were only in the black record books.

USA TODAY: With the obstacles you faced, why didn't you give up?

ASHE: The idea of giving up did not enter my mind. It was not even an alternative. But my talent plays an important part in how I deal with that. If one is very persistent but does not have the talent to follow through to one's dream, that's being unrealistic. Along with enthusiasm, dedication and persistence, you've got to be realistic.

USA TODAY: Who were your role models?

ASHE: Jackie Robinson, the first black to play major league baseball, was a role model for all of us black kids in the South in 1948 or so. He was at the height of his popularity. We all wanted to be Jackie Robinsons. We all wanted to play second base. We all wanted to wear his number, 42. Jackie Robinson was it.

USA TODAY: Why did you choose tennis over a more traditional sport?

ASHE: I lived 10 yards from tennis courts located in what was the largest black playground in Richmond. It had everything — four tennis courts, a pool, a basketball court and a football field. Everybody played a little bit of everything. Although tennis was not among the top four most popular sports, I chose to play it. I took some kidding from the guys but that never stopped me from playing.

USA TODAY: You have won the U.S. Open, the U.S. Clay Court Championships and the World Tennis Tournament. In 1975 you became the first black player to win the men's singles at Wimbledon, defeating Jimmy Connors. How did you psyche yourself up for that match?

ASHE: My winning wasn't a matter of psyching

myself up. If I had psyched myself up, I might not have won. On that day I was the better player.

USA TODAY: What was the most disappointing loss of your career and how did you handle it?

ASHE: In 1967 I lost two Davis Cup singles matches against players from Ecuador. That's the lowest I ever felt. I took awhile to get over it like anyone would. Then I literally climbed back into the saddle. Some people may have considered quitting. But not me. Strangely enough, the following year was the best year I ever had until I defeated Connors in 1975.

USA TODAY: Are drugs a problem in tennis?

ASHE: We are not completely immune to drugs. But in tennis if anyone did use drugs, we would know rather quickly. You are out there on the court all by yourself with no substitutions, no time outs and no coaching. If you are fooling around with drugs, you are just not going to play very well.

USA TODAY: In 1979, at age 36, you suffered a heart attack. How has your life changed?

ASHE: I watch what I eat and watch the stress. I eat fish. Then once or twice a week I eat turkey. I don't eat any red meat.

USA TODAY: What is important to you now?

ASHE: My health first. My family second.

USA TODAY: What message do you think your life has for the rest of us?

ASHE: I have led a rather balanced life. I did not equate my self-worth with my wins and losses on the tennis court. I didn't feel less of a person when I didn't play very well. I came to professional tennis after graduating from college and serving two years in the Army. I wasn't some young rookie coming on the pro tennis tour. I had a fair idea of just how good I was. My yardstick for judging my wins and losses on the court was applicability and preparation. If I were to prepare, try as hard as I could and still lose, well, that's just bad luck.

USA TODAY: You have traveled the world as a professional tennis player. Has exposure to different countries and cultures changed your ideas?

ASHE: Yes. I was brought up in the Christian church. After traveling so much around the world and seeing other religions up close, I am not nearly as much of a die-hard Christian as I was before. Now, I'm maybe a little bit of everything. It is difficult to see all of the other religions of the world and to come back to Christianity thinking that it has all the answers.

ASHE PROFILE

Born: July 10, 1943, in Richmond, Va.

Family: Married to Jeanne Moutoussamy Ashe; one daughter, Camera Elizabeth.

Education: Bachelor of science from UCLA.

On life: "I did not equate my self-worth with my wins and losses."

Homes: Miami and New York City.

Role models: Jackie Robinson and Andrew Young.

MILESTONES

1950: Began playing tennis at age 7 at a segregated playground.

1958: Reached the semifinals in the junior national tennis championships.

1960: Won the National Indoor Junior Tennis Championship, first time a black player captured a national men's tennis title.

1961: Entered UCLA on a tennis scholarship; won the National Indoor Junior Tennis Championship.

1963: Named to the U.S. Davis Cup team.

1965: Won the national championship played at Forest Hills, N.Y.

1967: *Advantage Ashe* published; began two years of service in the Army.

1969: President of Players Enterprises Inc.

1975: Defeated Jimmy Connors at Wimbledon, becoming the first black man to win the singles title; *Arthur Ashe: Portrait in Motion* published.

1977: *Getting Started in Tennis* published.

1979: *World Tennis* magazine called him "the most significant male tennis player of the open era."

1980: Retired from tournament tennis because of recurrent heart trouble.

1981: Named captain of the U.S. Davis Cup team; *Off the Court* published.

1985: Inducted into the International Tennis Hall of Fame.

USA TODAY: What do you think the future holds for blacks in professional tennis?

ASHE: I think there are endless opportunities out there for anyone who wants to learn the game. But the black community is just a bit more interested in some of the other sports — basketball, football and baseball — because that's where we have had historical success. But it does not mean we won't catch up in tennis one day. In a decade or so there will be at least five or six black Americans in the top 30 seeded players.

USA TODAY: You work with young players?

ASHE: I tutor them. And sooner or later almost all of them come to me for advice, which I give.

USA TODAY: When you look at the nation, are you pleased with the progress you see?

ASHE: I would like to see much less emotional dependence on the government to solve problems for us. We are much too dependent. We are sometimes too quick to blame racism for our problems. The examples are everywhere. Just look at the Vietnamese who came over here. The son of a Vietnamese family that came over here graduated first in his class at one of the military academies. None of them asked the U.S. government to teach the Vietnamese language in public school. Their parents just sat their children down and said, "Listen, you must learn English." Now while Hispanics are demanding that Spanish be taught in school, blacks are saying we need to lower standards for some schools and universities.

USA TODAY: How do you think blacks should handle that problem?

ASHE: What they really need to do is to buckle down with some local groups and churches and grind out the work. It's a matter of putting your nose to the grindstone and getting the work done. It has nothing to do with racism. Just get the job done and stop blaming the man for our problems.

MARY FRANCES BERRY

Wide-ranging education prepared her for role as a leader in thought and change

BERRY: 'My mother . . . told me to remember that whenever you go into any room always be more educated than anybody in the room.'

IMPRESSIONS

Mary Berry prefers a life of quiet, writing and playing tennis, but she often has to take time out to lead. When the USA and the struggle in South Africa were minus a connector, she helped provide it by agreeing to be jailed in the first anti-apartheid protest at the South African Embassy in Washington, D.C. That was the spark that helped start the Free South Africa movement. She has fought back at President Reagan's move to destroy the U.S. Commission on Civil Rights. And she has shown the USA that one does not have to seek glory for self to be effective in changing our society.

— **Barbara Reynolds**

Mary Frances Berry, a *scholar, lawyer and educator, stands out as an advocate for the rights of blacks and poor people. As a member of the U.S. Commission on Civil Rights, she has taken on conservative presidents and members of Congress to continue the fight for equal rights for all. She also has been in the forefront of the protest against apartheid in South Africa. Comments by Berry appeared on the* USA TODAY *Inquiry and Opinion pages June 1, 1984, and Sept. 15, 1987.*

USA TODAY: You and your brother, George, once were in an orphanage in Nashville. What kind of a life was that?

BERRY: My mother made so little money around the time I was 4 years old that we stayed at an orphanage funded in part by a local charity. During that period we were very hungry. We almost starved. My mother did not know. The guy who ran the orphanage would eat pork chops for dinner and then sell the kids the bones. I never will forget that.

USA TODAY: What else happened?

BERRY: They would also take milk and add water to it to dilute it. They would go to the store and get food that was being thrown out by the supermarket, like chicken necks and wings. They cooked it with lots of black pepper to cover the fact that it was almost spoiled. They would make the kids stand up — holding this little diluted glass of milk with this little plate of this rotten food on the table — and sing, "Thank you Lord for this food." But my mother got us out of there. After she acquired some skills at beauty school, she managed to get a job as a beautician and she could feed us.

USA TODAY: What did your father do while all this was happening?

BERRY: I am a classic example of somebody who came from poor class to middle class as a result of the civil rights movement led by Dr. Martin Luther King Jr. My mother and my brother raised me. My father deserted us. He was a laborer. It's one of those cases of a poor black family with a man who couldn't find a job after he came back from the war. He had great difficulty finding employment and became very depressed. He went on the road and never came back.

USA TODAY: Were you ever on welfare?

BERRY: We never had welfare. There wasn't any discussion about us having it. We lived on what my mother and the other relatives had. She had a lot of brothers and sisters who had their own children. All came from the same poor background that she did, but they tried to help each other.

USA TODAY: You started working at age 10. What did you do?

BERRY: I worked in white people's houses cleaning up, ironing, anything I could do. I always had a job. The idea was you work, you go to school, and you work. And that happened with my cousins. Everybody was supposed to save some money and then go to Tennessee A&I in Nashville. The families all moved to Nashville or near it. And they could go there and the tuition was very cheap.

USA TODAY: Were you put down because of poverty?

BERRY: Oh, yes. Kids at school were always taunting us, but my mother was always telling me I could be anything I wanted to be.

USA TODAY: Was your family religious?

BERRY: We were very religious. My mother made sure we always read inspiring things about overcoming adversities. She would always quote the 37th Psalm, the one that says, "Fret not thyself because of evildoers." The part I really like is when it says that when you see the evil person in power spreading himself like a bay tree, he will be cut off. My mother used to pause when she read that.

USA TODAY: What else made an impression?

BERRY: My teachers. I was lucky enough to find empathic teachers at a very difficult period in my life. I had at least one or two teachers who said: "Hey, you are smart. You could do something. So what if you are kind of raggedy." My teachers treated me as a diamond in the rough, someone who needed smoothing. Also they had a larger vision of the world than my parents. Although my mother knew about education she didn't know the options in the larger world.

USA TODAY: How did you end up in the North?

BERRY: My high school teacher, Minerva Hawkins, said I might want to consider going to college in the North. I didn't even know what the North was. I went to Fisk University in Nashville for a year because Minerva had gone to Fisk and because she got me a scholarship. And then I went to Howard University in Washington, D.C.

USA TODAY: What was life like at Howard?

BERRY: I worked all the time. If I could change something, I might change that. Most of the things that happen to students when they are in college didn't happen to me. I didn't have time to do anything except breathe and work and send my mother some money to help her.

USA TODAY: You have Ph.D. and law degrees from the University of Michigan. Is that unusual?

BERRY: Yes. My mother told me to be over-educated for everything you do. And if somebody says you should get whatever kind of degree there is, go get it. Once you get it you may have too many of them but they are yours. She also told me to remember that whenever you go into any room always be more educated than anybody in the room. She said: "Let them say anything they want about you. But when you look around the room make sure you know more than anybody there."

USA TODAY: How did you become chancellor of the University of Colorado?

BERRY: I agonized over that because at the same time people were asking me if I wanted to be president of Spelman College in Atlanta. Most of my friends told me I had to take the chancellor job because no woman was running a major university in this country. And Colorado is a major university with a big football team and everything.

USA TODAY: Why did you leave the education field to accept a position on the U.S. Commission on Civil Rights?

BERRY: I took the appointment because I thought it was going to continue to be this quiet little agency where we did some things on civil rights that might be helpful. It wouldn't take up a whole lot of time. I could basically be out of the public eye, and still be making a contribution.

USA TODAY: Things weren't quiet. In fact you became Ronald Reagan's most vocal critic on the commission.

BERRY: I got my back up like Frances Berry Wiggins' daughter is supposed to. I said: "Wait a minute, this guy is doing something that I think is illegal. Therefore, he's not going to get away with it. Not only that, I don't agree with his policies. And this little agency which has its independence and has been here all this time without anybody trying to take that away is about to be violated. I am not going to sit here and let it happen." So I fought it.

USA TODAY: You have risen over so many bar-

riers. Why are many others not making it?

BERRY: I made it much further than my mother. And by comparing us, one can tell some differences. It is not that I am smarter than my mother. It is not that I worked harder than my mother. No one can work any harder than my mother. It is that my work paid off for me more than her work did for her. My being smart paid off more for me than hers did for her.

USA TODAY: You're saying if your mother had had the opportunities, she might have surpassed you?

BERRY: It was the civil rights changes that made it possible for me to do some stuff my mother couldn't do.

USA TODAY: What does that mean for others?

BERRY: The window opened a little bit and some people got through. A whole lot of us got through. Then the window closed up a little bit. What you have to do is open the window again. When you open the window it does not mean that everybody will get through. There are people of my generation who didn't get through. But a whole lot of people did get through. So if you want to increase the odds that more people get through what you do is create the same kind of emphasis on opportunity.

USA TODAY: What message do you hope your life bears for others?

BERRY: My life illustrates that solving the problems of poor people or black people by a one-dimensional approach isn't going to work. I was lucky enough that all the pieces came together. There is going to come a time in the next few years that these pieces come together again. And a few more of us — some of my younger cousins and others — are going to get through the window.

GUION BLUFORD

With achieving parents as models, he knew he would realize his dream to fly

BLUFORD: 'I was fortunate because I decided very early what I wanted to do. I had a reason for working hard and persevering.'

IMPRESSIONS

The USA's first black person in space, Air Force Col. Guion Bluford symbolizes an end to some man-made barriers on Earth. Though he says his life adventure has no special significance to his race, he's being modest. He's a first in a very special area of human endeavor. I know that significance when I look at my 6-year-old son, John Eric. Because of Bluford, my son's dreams can soar. A role model has knocked down another barrier and shown the way in space.

— **Barbara Reynolds**

His direction came from his father, and Guion Bluford knew early he would spend his life involved in aerospace. His interest in engineering — his father's profession — and his interest in airplanes became a winning combination. As a pilot in the Air Force he served in Vietnam. Later he became one of the first blacks accepted for astronaut training. He flew his first mission aboard the 1983 space shuttle Challenger on its first night launch from the Kennedy Space Center in Florida. That flight made him the first black person from the USA to travel in space. (Arnoldo Tomayo Mendez, a Cuban of mixed heritage, was launched by the Soviets Sept. 8, 1980, and is considered by some as the first black in space.) An interview with Bluford appeared on the USA TODAY Inquiry page Feb. 1, 1983.

USA TODAY: In 1983, you became the first black person from the USA to travel in space. On that mission you were in orbit for six days. You went up again on a seven-day mission in 1985. What is space like?

BLUFORD: I'm an engineer. While I was amazed at the view, I was also impressed by the capability of the vehicle. Yet I am awed at man's ingenuity and what he can achieve. I recognized what a beautiful and fragile planet we live on. Seeing Earth from 170 miles out in space is not like standing on Earth and looking at the moon.

USA TODAY: How does Earth look from space?

BLUFORD: Similar to the way it looks from the window of an airplane. But things are much, much smaller and you can see a greater expanse of land and the gentle curve of the blue horizon.

USA TODAY: How does space look from an orbiting spacecraft?

BLUFORD: You can only see out into space from the dark side of the Earth, the side away from the sun. From there you can't see the moon. It's much like looking at the sky on a very dark clear night — except you are not standing on Earth. You're in the middle of the sky.

USA TODAY: Shortly after liftoff, things become weightless. How does that feel?

BLUFORD: You don't notice it until between eight and 10 minutes after liftoff. Then things begin to float. You really notice it when you get up. It's like swimming under water without the water. You float around pushing off the ceiling and walls to propel yourself in the direction you need to go. And you learn to do that gently.

USA TODAY: In light of the malfunction that led to the Challenger disaster on Jan. 28, 1986, do you ever worry that something could go wrong on one of your flights?

BLUFORD: No. I'm more convinced of the success of the space program because we fly the vehicle very carefully and cautiously. We spend a great deal of time examining the vehicle and learning how it flies.

USA TODAY: What did your space flights mean to you?

BLUFORD: The flights were a realization of a long-established dream. I had trained for an awful long time. When I went up I was emotionally up, ready to fly, looking forward to the experience.

USA TODAY: Why did you become an astronaut?

BLUFORD: I've always had an interest in how airplanes fly and how spacecraft operate. Flying in space is just a combination of those strong interests. I didn't start off being an astronaut. My interests were aviation and airplanes. When I grew up I developed an interest in model airplanes. I did a lot of reading and decided relatively early that I wanted to be an aerospace engineer. My father is an engineer and I knew that meant going to college to get a degree in that area. Once I got into it my interest broadened into flying airplanes and working with space systems. From an initial interest in airplanes, my interests have evolved.

USA TODAY: What were your duties during your flights?

BLUFORD: I was a mission specialist. During the '83 mission, I also worked as a scientist. We worked 24 hours a day. I processed experiments with various furnaces, grew crystals and, taking advantage of the vacuum in space, made medicines that are very difficult to make on Earth. During the '85 mission I was the Orbiter systems expert and helped the pilot and commander. On that mission we deployed a satellite for India. We took a look at how man adapts to zero gravity because we were trying to understand why some astronauts get sick in orbit.

USA TODAY: Who were your role models?

BLUFORD: My role models growing up were my parents. Especially my father because he was an engineer. My mother was a teacher.

USA TODAY: What was your childhood in Philadelphia like?

BLUFORD: I was very fortunate. I was raised in an integrated situation. I had what I consider a normal childhood. I was raised in a middle-class family and went through the public school system.

USA TODAY: How important was it to your parents that you attend college?

BLUFORD: It was assumed that my two brothers and myself would go to college. Both of my parents insisted that we do our homework and do well in school. They took a very strong interest in how we did in school from the first grade on. When I went to Pennsylvania State University, my parents paid for most of my college education. I had to work during the summer to provide additional funds for spending money and school books and all. I usually worked on campus after classes.

USA TODAY: Was growing up in an integrated environment a help or a hindrance?

BLUFORD: It helped me because I never looked at the world and thought I couldn't do something I wanted to do. I never felt handicapped by race. I never felt being black made me less capable of doing anything.

USA TODAY: Were you ever affected personally by racism?

BLUFORD: While I was growing up I never really experienced racism. I never knew there was a serious problem with racism until 1957 when efforts began to integrate schools in Little Rock, Ark. The first place I felt the sting of segregation was in the Air Force. I had problems finding a place for me and my family to live in Tampa, Fla., and Selma, Ala. I was distressed and angered but I picked myself up and kept going. I haven't had any problems since.

USA TODAY: What would you tell others who encounter unfair treatment because of race?

BLUFORD: I would tell people to work and aggressively solve the problem. Thanks to the civil rights movement of Dr. Martin Luther King Jr., we have mechanisms in society that can address issues of racial inequity. Our society does not tolerate that any more. If I saw a problem at NASA I could file grievances. I would advise people to work through

BLUFORD PROFILE

Born: Nov. 22, 1942, in Philadelphia.

Family: Married to Linda Tull Bluford; two children, Guion Stewart Bluford III and James Trevor Bluford.

Education: Bachelor of science from Penn State University, University Park, Pa.; master's from the Air Force Institute of Technology, Dayton, Ohio; Ph.D. from Air Force Institute; master's in business administration from the University of Houston, Clear Lake, Texas.

On life: "I learned to work hard for success. It was the only way I could achieve what I wanted. I also learned to be persistent and not let intermediate failures deter me from achieving a long-term goal."

Home: Houston.

Role models: His parents, Lolita Harriet and Guion Bluford Sr.

MILESTONES

1965: Received pilot's wings; assigned to the 557th Tactical Fighter Squadron, Cam Ranh Bay, Vietnam.

1967: Assigned to 3630th Flying Training Wing as flight instructor; received Vietnam Service Medal and Vietnam Cross of Gallantry with Palm.

1978: Chosen for USA's astronaut corps.

1979: Named Distinguished National Scientist by National Society of Black Engineers.

1983: Mission specialist on the first night launch of the space shuttle Challenger from Kennedy Space Center in Florida, becoming USA's first black astronaut in space; received Ebony Black Achievement Award; received NAACP Image Award.

1984: Awarded Pennsylvania's Distinguished Service award.

1985: Mission specialist aboard Orbiter Challenger, USA's first spacelab mission.

systems where those structures exist.

USA TODAY: What, other than inspiration from your parents, helped you succeed in becoming an astronaut?

BLUFORD: I learned to work hard for success. It was the only way I could achieve what I wanted. I also learned to be persistent and not let intermediate failures deter me from achieving a long-term goal. I learned to accept failures and successes along the way.

USA TODAY: What do you do when times get tough and you want to quit?

BLUFORD: As one gets more successful, the mind washes out the hard times. I was fortunate because I decided very early what I wanted to do. I had a reason for working hard and persevering. I'm a persistent fighter, particularly when I have a clear idea of what I want. My religion helped me considerably during college and the early part of my military career. I always went to church. I am of the Christian Science faith. I practice my religion by living it, by reminding myself of the principles of it and recognizing that I am not alone.

USA TODAY: What do you say to encourage others to become astronauts?

BLUFORD: Hard work and perseverance. Our society is very rich in opportunities. There are plenty of careers they can choose from. I encourage more minority students to pursue careers in science and engineering. Hopefully they too will become astronauts. It is something that more minorities should pursue.

USA TODAY: What is important for the world to remember about you?

BLUFORD: When people look back I'd like them to say they are proud of the job I did in the space program and in the aerospace field. I want to be remembered for my accomplishments and how well I performed my job. I hope that I can leave a legacy of excellence. I want them to say: "Wow, he did a great job. Wow, I think I could do it. Let me follow in his example, setting high goals and following a sense of excellence."

TONY BROWN

'Green power' is the way to freedom, says this multifaceted communicator

BROWN: 'Black people for the most part worship whites too much. We have to learn to love ourselves.'

IMPRESSIONS

What makes Tony Brown most angry? Barriers, especially in the communications industry. He was angry that the USA had no syndicated news talk shows with a black host. Angry that few movies showed positive images of blacks. Angry at the lack of black participation in the production of television documentaries. His anger forged solutions: He's helping to correct all three inequities himself. Brown — a peppery idea man — proves you can use journalism not just as a mirror to reflect, but as a motor to speed progress.

— **Barbara Reynolds**

Tony Brown *writes a syndicated column that appears in 150 black newspapers across the USA. He publishes* Tony Brown's Journal, *a quarterly magazine, and is the host and executive producer of a public affairs program — also called* Tony Brown's Journal — *which airs on public television. He also is the producer of a collection of documentaries,* The Library of Black History. *His latest project is producing a feature-length film,* The White Girl. *Brown is the founding dean of Howard University's School of Communications in Washington, D.C. His national "Buy Freedom Campaign" encourages black economic development throughout the USA. An interview with Brown appeared on the* USA TODAY *Inquiry page Oct. 22, 1985.*

USA TODAY: From your vantage point as a journalist, filmmaker, producer and former university dean, what is needed to knock down remaining racial barriers?

BROWN: The race problem will never be resolved so long as the black movement insists that white people give up a percentage of their standard of living. If we continue to do that, whites will always oppose us — not necessarily out of racism, but out of self-interest. The bottom line is that the color of freedom is green.

USA TODAY: You are now introducing your green power philosophy into the film industry. Is this your attempt to counter claims that Hollywood historically portrays blacks in a negative light?

BROWN: Yes. I have produced the film *The White Girl*, which addresses drugs in our society and the self-hatred so prevalent in the black community. *The White Girl* has a double meaning. It is the street name for cocaine and it is how the young black woman in the movie sees herself.

USA TODAY: What else does the movie do?

BROWN: The movie also serves as a vehicle for black economic development — it will create opportunities for black entrepreneurs. The average black movie earns about $15 million. Blacks spend $1.5 billion on movie tickets yearly, one-half of the $3 billion earned by the movie industry each year. They never share in these enormous profits. Entrepreneurs and organizations will be offered a role in marketing *The White Girl*.

USA TODAY: Where did you get the resources to produce your movie?

BROWN: The money came from Tony Brown Productions. In the past three years I have made 100 to 130 speeches. I earn $3,000 to $5,000 for each speech. I put all of my speaking fees into my company. I have not paid myself a salary for the past three years. What salary I had coming was reinvested in my company. I wrote the script, which saved about $150,000. I also directed the movie, which saved about $300,000. My two producers deferred payment. Through our own resources we have invested about $2 million in the movie. That is how we got it done.

USA TODAY: What was life like growing up in Charleston, W.Va.?

BROWN: I was born in the middle of the Depression. In the black community we had one black doctor, one black dentist, one black photographer, maybe two black lawyers. Schoolteachers and the postman basically rounded out the black middle class. No one had the stigma of poverty because no one had that much. I was taught that God would take care of you. I was taught that if you work hard, study hard and you are honest, whatever you want in life you'll have — within reason.

USA TODAY: What was family life like?

BROWN: Several of my brothers and sisters were farmed out to relatives for financial reasons so we were split up. But we all played together. We all knew we were Browns. We had a very functional extended family.

USA TODAY: Did you live with relatives?

BROWN: Some of us were living with people who were not blood relatives. Many were living with blood relatives who were not our parents. My older sister was raised by my maternal grandmother. My oldest brother was raised by my paternal grandparents. The sister right ahead of me was raised by a college professor. I was raised by two women we would call domestics. They worked in the kitchens, in the hotels. Whatever happened, every child in our community was taken care of.

USA TODAY: You once told me that your parents showed you how to make bricks without straw. What did you mean?

BROWN: We always had very little, but we shared whatever it was. I was the first boy on the block to have a wagon. I played in the high school band with a $35 drum that today I guess would cost

$600. I had music lessons when I was in the fourth grade. The women who did this for me were women who were washing pots and pans in a hotel.

USA TODAY: You graduated from Wayne State University in Detroit with a degree in social work. Why didn't you study journalism?

BROWN: When I went to college if you were black and you studied journalism, they would have wrapped you up in a mental institution. Where would you have gotten a job? I have never studied journalism. Remember, as blacks, all of us in college were job oriented.

USA TODAY: How did you get into journalism?

BROWN: I always had this interest in communication arts. When I got my master's degree in psychiatric social work, I went to the black newspaper in Detroit, the *Detroit Courier*. I asked the editor if I could write a drama column. He said yes. He said, "We don't have any money but if you want to come here and write, we will teach you." And he did. Over five years I moved from writing drama columns to news stories to feature articles. Then I became a stringer for the *Pittsburgh Courier* newspaper. Other people noticed my ability to write. And then I got involved in civil rights.

USA TODAY: Your activist nature led you to challenge the licenses of TV stations in Detroit. What did you accomplish?

BROWN: I discovered the Communications Act of 1934 and realized that through it black folks had a right to have access to television. That could mean jobs. I started suing local TV stations, including the public TV station where I worked in Detroit, to force them to allow community access to the stations. Then I became executive producer of *Detroit Black Journal*, the only national black TV show at that time. The following year, 1971, Howard University in Washington, D.C., contacted me and asked me if I wanted to be considered for the position of dean of the new School of Communications.

USA TODAY: How did you get *Tony Brown's Journal*, your syndicated talk show, on the air?

BROWN: I had a grant from the Public Broadcasting Corporation. It took everything I could muster to stay on the air because some officials in the Nixon White House pulled some strings and my grant was pulled. The black community picketed. If the picketing had not happened, Tony Brown would not have been on TV. I had done everything I could do to get some money and I was sinking. One day a guy called from Pepsi and said they had

BROWN PROFILE

Born: April 11, 1933, in Charleston, W.Va.

Family: Divorced; a son, Byron.

Education: Bachelor of arts in sociology and master's in psychiatric social work from Wayne State University, Detroit.

On life: "I was born in the middle of the Depression. In the black community we had one black doctor, one black dentist, one black photographer, maybe two black lawyers. Schoolteachers and the postman basically rounded out the black middle class. No one had the stigma of poverty because no one had that much. I was taught that God would take care of you. I was taught that if you work hard, study hard and you are honest, whatever you want in life you'll have — within reason."

Home: New York City.

Role model: Ruth Norman, his high school English teacher.

MILESTONES

1961: Hired as *Detroit Courier* writer.

1970: Became executive producer and host of *Black Journal*, a national public affairs program aired on public television; nominated for an Emmy for the show.

1971: Founding dean of Howard University's School of Communications, Washington, D.C.

1972: Received Media Workshop Award.

1976: Named Communicator of the Year by the National Association of Market Developers.

1977: *Black Journal* TV program renamed *Tony Brown's Journal*.

1980: Started Black College Day to aid black colleges and universities.

1985: Started the Buy Freedom Campaign to aid black businesses.

1987: Wrote screen play, produced, directed *The White Girl*. Movie was in editing stage at the end of the year.

been watching my program and asked if I was interested in being sponsored by the company.

USA TODAY: What issues are important?

BROWN: I started Black College Day in 1980. I am still involved in fighting to keep black colleges open. Fifty percent of blacks with college degrees graduate from black colleges. Seven out of 10 of us don't finish white colleges. So if all of us were forced to go to white colleges and didn't have black colleges as a choice, as an alternative, we wouldn't have many black people graduating from college.

USA TODAY: Are blacks discouraged from attending predominantly white colleges?

BROWN: White colleges don't want the majority of black students. They only want those who score in the top 3 percent or 4 percent on SAT scores. So, the vast majority of blacks wouldn't have much chance for education. I got very involved and that's one thing I feel good about.

USA TODAY: What about your economic development crusade?

BROWN: I feel very good about my Buy Freedom Campaign, which is helping black people understand that the only way to be free is to have power. The only way that you can have power is to use your wealth to develop it. Presently the black community has an unstable economy because blacks only spend 6.6 percent of their money with black-owned firms or professionals. We spend about 95 percent of our money with non-black groups that spend about 5 percent with us. We're saying it's time to correct that.

USA TODAY: How will it help blacks if they spend their money at businesses owned by blacks?

BROWN: Blacks earn more than $200 billion a year. No matter how many programs blacks get to bring them into full employment, unless blacks retain a larger percentage of their money in their own communities and stimulate businesses to create jobs, then blacks will never catch up with whites.

USA TODAY: How do you see yourself?

BROWN: If I were white, I wouldn't be unusual. I'm black and that makes me very unusual. I am not afraid of white people. I believe most black people are scared of white people. I don't think there is anything there to fear. They are no better than I am. I don't think some of them are as good as I am. Black people for the most part worship whites too much. We have to learn to love ourselves.

SHIRLEY CAESAR

She preaches, sings and dances to tell the good news she heard at age 12

CAESAR: 'Women have a way of treating people more softly. We treat souls with kid gloves. We have a more tender outreach.'

IMPRESSIONS

I remember tracing Shirley Caesar's past through the streets of Durham, N.C., one summer. As we rode in her red, phone-equipped Mercedes, she showed me her grade school, the house where she was born and the yard where she jumped and shouted after she was "born again" at age 12. We made a final stop at the cemetery where her mother, Halley Caesar, is buried. We returned to the Durham Civic Center where hundreds were gathered to celebrate the 17th anniversary of her ministries. Though barely 5-foot-2, including her spike-heeled shoes, she's a giant in and out of the pulpit.

— **Barbara Reynolds**

Shirley Caesar could be considered the queen of gospel music. She has won five Grammy Awards and earned three Gold Albums. Her songs often top the gospel charts. An evangelist, she was the 1987 spokesperson for McDonald's Salute to Gospel Music. She heads the Shirley Caesar Outreach Ministry to aid the poor in Durham, N.C. She and her husband, Bishop Harold Ivory Williams, are pastor and co-pastor of Mount Calvary Church in Winston-Salem, N.C. An interview with Caesar appeared on the USA TODAY Inquiry page Oct. 1, 1987.

USA TODAY: Your career started with the Caravans in the 1950s. What was life like on the gospel circuit then?

CAESAR: I was a teen-ager and was on the road all the time. All of us — six women — used to pack our bags and get into an old Buick. We would get on the road and travel all day to get to a concert to make $30 apiece. Discrimination kept us out of finer hotels and restaurants. And even if we had had that right, in those days we did not have the money.

USA TODAY: What was it like growing up?

CAESAR: We did not have a whole lot. We did have food to eat. We did have a roof over our heads. And the majority of my clothes — since all of my brothers and sisters were like stair steps — were just handed down from one to the other.

USA TODAY: When were you born again?

CAESAR: I was only 12 years old. I was on my way home from school one day, and I stopped at a grocery store. As soon as the man in the store turned his back, I got me an armful of Popsicles and put them under my coat. I walked through the graveyard so I wouldn't have to give anybody any. I was selfish. When I got home I had grape, cherry, orange all down my dress, all on my mouth. I walked in the house. Momma said, "Stick your tongue out." It was all on my tongue. She asked me what was it. I said Popsicle. She asked where did I get the money because she knew I never had any money. I told her that somebody had given me the money. Momma knew I was lying. I admitted to her that I had stolen them. She whipped me.

USA TODAY: Then what happened?

CAESAR: After school the next day, my sister Annie, my brother Solomon and I went out into the back yard to play church with Solomon as the preacher. We had an old Bible, no back on it. And we would sit out on the bottom step just like we were in church. And we would jump up and we would shout. We had a funeral for the dog, the cat. I jumped up and shouted "Jesus!" Then we all jumped up and shouted "Jesus!" We did it again.

USA TODAY: And on the fourth try?

CAESAR: I jumped up and I started shouting "Jesus!" Annie, my sister, said, "Come on Shirley, I'm tired of playing church now." But I kept on praising God and I kept on dancing, praising God and crying. The will of the Lord did something for me in the back yard. I went to church that Tuesday night after school. I heard a knock at the door of my heart and I ran to the window of my soul, looked out, Jesus was standing there. He said "I called you with the holy calling." That's why I believe God called me to preach.

USA TODAY: You heard the voice of the Lord?

CAESAR: Yes. I was sitting right in church. I heard the voice of God speak to me. He said, "I have called you with the holy calling." That's when I jumped up, ran to the altar. I fell at the pulpit with my hand stretched out just kicking my feet. And I stayed on the altar, crying.

USA TODAY: Did the Lord speak to you again about your call to the ministry?

CAESAR: Later, when I was in college, he told me that I had been sanctified from my mother's womb. I never tried to be different. All I know is that I wanted to be whatever the Lord wanted me to be. Whether preacher, singer, teacher or whatever. I never ran from my ministry.

USA TODAY: Gospel music has the spice of the blues and the flavor of spirituals, yet it is neither. How do you define it?

CAESAR: Gospel music has many messages. It encourages. It uplifts. One line in a song can say more in gospel music than a whole song can say in most other music. It is just like the Bible. Gospel music teaches us to love, respect, to uphold. It might speak of hell, damnation and fire. But it also speaks of the bright side. That the Lord is faithful, and he is loving, kind and forgiving. Gospel music will tell you that when you pray, God listens.

USA TODAY: What about the music itself?

CAESAR: Professor Thomas A. ("Tommy") Dorsey introduced gospel music to us in the early

'20s when blacks migrated from the South to the North. So many of them found their deliverance in singing gospel music — with musical accompaniment. By contrast, spirituals are sung without music — just hand claps and maybe a drum.

USA TODAY: Does the rise of gospel music make a statement about religion?

CAESAR: A lot of people are no longer hanging their hopes on jazz and rhythm and blues. They're coming back to the church. I'm finding there is a turning back to the church all of a sudden. Singing and preaching go together like ham and eggs. Young women and young men are becoming more aware of their singing ministry. And the doors are opening up for them to record through a choir or their own singing group.

USA TODAY: You have an outreach ministry, feeding and clothing people in Durham and Winston-Salem, N.C., and in Paterson, N.J. Why?

CAESAR: My father died when I was little, leaving my semi-invalid mother to care for me and my 12 brothers and sisters. We were very poor. When the Lord blessed me to become a singing evangelist, that enabled me to take care of my family. Then I began to see how many other mothers were struggling alone. Out of that grew the ministry to help needy families.

USA TODAY: What do you think about denominations barring women from being ordained?

CAESAR: That barrier is coming down. For many years, churches in my denomination — Church of God in Christ — wouldn't allow us to be called minister or preacher. We had to be called missionaries or teachers. When the Lord called me to preach at age 17, I chose the title evangelist — someone who would travel and not be stationary at any church.

USA TODAY: What difference does it make whether women are allowed to be pastors?

CAESAR: Women have a way of treating people more softly. We treat souls with kid gloves. We have a more tender outreach. We are less boisterous as we reach out to people. Although I feel women ought to be in the pulpit, there are other ministries that I feel are important. The church is composed of five ministries: the teachers, the pastor, the evangelist, the prophet and the apostle or bishop. And women are involved in all of these ministries. Remember, Jesus didn't have a pulpit at all. He preached from a mountain top.

USA TODAY: You are a Pentecostal minister in

CAESAR PROFILE

Born: Oct. 13, 1938, in Durham, N.C.

Family: Married to Bishop Harold Ivory Williams.

Education: Bachelor of arts from Shaw University, Raleigh, N.C.

On life: "Gospel music teaches us to love, respect, to uphold. It might speak of hell, damnation and fire. But it also speaks of the bright side. That the Lord is faithful, and he is loving, kind and forgiving . . . A lot of people are no longer hanging their hopes on jazz and rhythm and blues. They're coming back to the church . . . Singing and preaching go together like ham and eggs. Young women and young men are becoming more aware of their singing ministry."

Home: Durham, N.C.

Role models: Albertina Walker and Mahalia Jackson.

MILESTONES

1958: Began gospel career with the Caravans.

1966: Left Caravans to form her own group, the Caesar Singers.

1967: Best Gospel Music Award from Hob Records.

1969: Started the Shirley Caesar Outreach Ministry.

1971: Grammy for Best Gospel Single, Female.

1975: Best Female Gospel Singer Award from *Ebony* magazine.

1979: Performed at White House for President Jimmy Carter.

1981: Grammy for Best Gospel Album, Female.

1985: Grammy for Best Gospel Album; Grammy for Best Gospel Duo, performed with Al Green; won NAACP Image Achievement Award.

1986: Grammy for Best Gospel Single.

a denomination with 4 million members nationwide. Members often dance or shout, which some critics ridicule. What is your view on that?

CAESAR: The majority of our black churches are dancing in the spirit, and a lot of the white ones are too. They are seeing the goodness of God in their everyday lives. The dance is given to people who have the victory over their lives. They have been through the fiery furnaces, and God brought them out of their affliction, sickness, poverty. That is enough to make you want to dance and shout. The other day I did a few steps in the street. I stopped my car, pulled over to the side, opened the door, and cut me a few steps. I had just got the message that a man who we had been praying for was recovering. Initially, the doctors were going to pull the plug. But his wife called me, and I told her not to do it because as long as there is life in a body, it is a candidate for a miracle. Now the man is out of a coma. Isn't that something to dance or shout about and thank God for?

USA TODAY: What is "the dance?"

CAESAR: It is called the holy dance. Now you don't relate the holy dance to the funky chicken or the twist. They're dancing to another kind of music. We're singing a different music, and we have a different partner.

USA TODAY: You are often compared to Mahalia Jackson, who refused to sing any kind of music but gospel music. Would you sing crossover music, such as the blues?

CAESAR: No! Since I'm dancing with this new partner who I found at the age of 12, why should I go over and sing with somebody else, and then come back over and sing and dance with Jesus? That's just like trying to mix water and grease.

USA TODAY: Often you sing and then you stop and preach. Why?

CAESAR: I do it because I'm a preacher. And I like to paint pictures. If I can't pull that picture out of a song then I paint that picture with words. I want them to see what my song is saying.

HORTENSE CANADY

Innovative leader of more than 100,000 proves that 'sisterhood' can get results

CANADY: 'I am an organization person. I believe in individuals banding together. I don't believe in unilateral actions.'

IMPRESSIONS

She's an example of amazing grace under pressure. As the leader of Delta Sigma Theta sorority, Hortense Canady is pulled in myriad directions as she provides leadership on such issues as single-parenting, health care in West Africa, the Reagan agenda, affirmative action and South African apartheid. I've watched her convene conferences from Dallas to Detroit to Washington to the Bahamas, and she is aflame with new ideas and programs. In leadership circles that are so dominated by males, it is refreshing for me to see the cause of black women raised with such force and elegance.

— **Barbara Reynolds**

The 18th president of Delta Sigma Theta sorority, Hortense Canady leads more than 100,000 women throughout the world. Not just a social organization, the Deltas are active in such pressing national issues as housing, education and health care for blacks. She is a mother and university administrator and has been active in community affairs for decades, including attempts to desegregate the school system in Lansing, Mich. She was a member of the Lansing Five, a group that eventually won that integration fight. An advocate for black women and education, she has served in executive positions on the board of directors of the United Negro College Fund, Lansing Board of Education and the Michigan Women's Commission. An interview with Canady appeared on the USA TODAY *Inquiry page March 12, 1984.*

USA TODAY: Under your leadership, Delta Sigma Theta sorority has won a lot of praise. But some people look at sororities and fraternities as frivolous. How do you respond?

CANADY: I resent the defining of Greek organizations as though they are a homogeneous group. They are not. It's as if you would describe all churches, all denominations as the same. How could you say the Baptists are like the Methodists or the Catholics? But whenever there is an article about Greek organizations there is a tendency to lump them together. I resent it. As for Delta Sigma Theta, it's the sisterhood. I don't know of another group anywhere in the world with quite as much talent. They are imaginative and creative. They don't let obstacles defeat them.

USA TODAY: What has been one of your most challenging issues?

CANADY: The work of the Lansing Five in Lansing, Mich., in the early 1970s. We persuaded the Board of Education to desegregate the junior and senior high schools. But this left the elementary schools rigidly segregated. I had worked with the NAACP Education Committee for seven years, so I ran for the Board of Education and won. We drew up a plan to desegregate the elementary schools and voted it in. We subsequently were recalled.

USA TODAY: Couldn't you have used a different strategy?

CANADY: Everybody has one point where you are willing to take your stand. And it was very important to me to take a stand like that at that time.

USA TODAY: Wasn't the reaction to your efforts partially reflective of the climate in the USA?

CANADY: This all happened during the presidential election year that brought in Richard Nixon. It was a terrible time to have an election because it was a very conservative sweep. The Lansing NAACP took the new board decision to rescind our desegregation plan to court, but the courts upheld the plan. And so the plan we had voted in did hold.

USA TODAY: How would you describe your leadership style?

CANADY: I am an organization person. I believe in individuals banding together. I don't believe in unilateral actions. Some people don't like organizations. But it is always awesome to me when you can pool a lot of talent and a lot of people who have so many talents. That is when you really can make your program move. I have been involved with many organizations throughout my adult life. It was good preparation for the presidency of Delta Sigma Theta.

USA TODAY: You were born in Chicago. What was your family like?

CANADY: My father was a pharmacist. My mother was a social worker. When my father died we moved to Tennessee where we had relatives. My grandfather was a fireman on the railroad and my grandmother owned a restaurant. They lived across the street from Lane College.

USA TODAY: What do you remember about Jackson, Tenn.?

CANADY: We had to learn a whole set of mores. We had to sit at the back of the bus. The schools were rigidly segregated. I had to go across town to high school. I repeatedly encountered racial slurs. If you were a nice-looking girl, you were fair game for inappropriate comments from whites as you walked to school.

USA TODAY: Was there anything in Jackson's black community to counter this?

CANADY: Lane College. It attracted great orators, singers and musicians. This was a time when there was no television. This was a time when they had segregated movies. My mother, Essie Golden Perry, refused to go to the movie theater in Jackson. And she liked the movies, particularly ones with Bette Davis. It was a matter of principle. We would have had to sit in the balcony. But Lane College would sometimes bring films to the college. And Lane had a library. I spent a great deal of my youth in those stacks. We read all summer long, all winter long.

USA TODAY: How did your experiences in a segregated environment shape you?

CANADY: It gave me an opportunity to concentrate on many things that perhaps I would have been distracted from and would not have done in another environment.

USA TODAY: You seem to consider your childhood a pretty good one.

CANADY: I would think so compared to what most blacks seem to have had at that time. My dad's father was a landowner. Upon his death he willed all of his children about 110 acres of land apiece. So they had land. I went to college from the sale of that land. We had something to sell. We had some assets. My mother was also a college graduate. She had a degree in social work from the University of Chicago.

USA TODAY: Did you consider yourself pretty lucky growing up?

CANADY: I can answer you the same way my mother answered one of her friends who said my mother was lucky because she had never had a difficult time. My mother went into a litany: "Aren't I lucky that my husband died in his 30s? Aren't I lucky to have had to give up my home after his death to make a way for my children. Aren't I lucky!"

USA TODAY: Did your mother prepare you for his death?

CANADY: My father died after a long illness. My mother entrusted me with the knowledge of business. I knew about the property. I knew about money she had in the bank account. I knew about all her insurance. She wanted me to be knowledgeable in case something ever happened to her. She wanted me to know that there was enough money there for me to go to college. And she would be counting on me to help my brother who was four years younger.

USA TODAY: Why did she do this?

CANADY: She was giving me information so there would never be anyone who could tell me there wasn't the money to do certain things. We would review the monthly bank statements and the bank accounts. Most children don't have the va-

CANADY PROFILE

Born: Aug. 18, 1927, in Chicago.

Family: Married to Clinton Canady Jr.; four children, Clinton, Alan, Mark and Alexa.

Education: Bachelor of arts in biology from Fisk University, Nashville, Tenn.; master's degree in college student personnel administration from Michigan State University, East Lansing.

On life: "When someone argues that they know how to do something better than I do, I usually agree. That's probably the best way I know. Because they are probably right."

Home: Lansing, Mich.

Role models: Her mother, Essie Golden Perry; Mary McLeod Bethune, W.E.B. DuBois and Patricia Roberts Harris.

MILESTONES

1968: Sojourner Truth Award, Negro Business and Professional Women's Association.

1969: Named to Michigan State Women's Commission.

1971: Secretary, Lansing Board of Education.

1976: Elected to six-year term on YWCA National Board of Directors.

1977: Elected to Lansing Symphony Association board of directors.

1979: Presidents Award from the National Dental Association.

1980: Citizen of the Year award, Lansing branch of NAACP.

1983: Elected president of Delta Sigma Theta Inc.

1984: New York Urban League's Whitney Young Award.

1985: Elected to second term as president of Delta Sigma Theta Inc.

1987: Convened global single-parenting conference in Nassau, Bahamas.

guest idea of how much money their family makes, how much money they have or where the money is. But she thought it was important that I know that. So I guess I was lucky.

USA TODAY: How have you put your imprint on Delta Sigma Theta?

CANADY: I would like to be remembered for the revival of programs that were already there as much as for any new programs that might have originated under my administration. As an example, reaffirmation of the distinguished professor's chair. We have an educational foundation. We hope to leave that with a feasible endowment so that it can be independent and stand on its own. The African Diaspora project tries to create a bond between people of color throughout the world. We still have the legacy of racism here. We tend to think of our history as beginning with slavery. The African Diaspora program attempts to give a longer view of history and also to impart the idea that blacks are not defined by slavery. That was only one incident in the great long history of people of African descent and their contributions to the cultures of the world.

USA TODAY: Do you feel that women are well represented by male-led organizations?

CANADY: When you look generally at most of the groups in this country — whether they are black or white — they tend to be male-dominated. But in Delta Sigma Theta, the women are in the leadership role. So it is a great training ground. Hopefully they will be stepping forward to take their rightful place in society. But in the interim this is an opportunity for black women to define their own style of leadership and promote their own programs.

USA TODAY: You have been applauded for your grace under pressure. What advice do you have to help others effectively handle criticism?

CANADY: When someone argues that they know how to do something better than I do, I usually agree. That's probably the best way I know. Because they are probably right. If you don't realize there is always somebody who knows how to do something better than you, then you don't give proper respect for others' talents. You are always going to get criticized. You are not perfect. You are going to forget some things from time to time that are very important. The best way to deal with that is if you make a mistake, admit it. You have to allow the other person room to disagree with you. You have to allow him or her to save face.

RAY CHARLES

Though blind, he's far from handicapped;
he clearly sees the beauty of music and love

CHARLES: 'Naturally, I love music. If you love something, you automatically want to learn more about it.'

IMPRESSIONS

America, the Beautiful was never my kind of song until Ray Charles sang it. With the riffs, the flourishes, the soul he added, the song said something more than those words had ever said before. He communicates that sense of belonging, caring. I was drawn to the song of the USA's beauty and bounty. Ironically, the portrait of the USA that this great artist paints for others is a scene his eyes can't see. But except for his trademark dark glasses, very little about him signals his so-called limitation. We all have a lot to learn from Ray Charles about doing for others the things we cannot do for ourselves.

— **Barbara Reynolds**

*T*hough blind since age 6, Ray Charles became a music superstar. A versatile musician, his career spans country, pop, rhythm and blues, and gospel. Considered the "High Priest of Soul," his music has crossed traditional boundaries, mixing the secular with the tone and sound of gospel music. He is credited with creating the demand for black music that led to crossover play for many black artists. In 1973, he cut an unprecedented deal with ABC-Paramount records giving him control of his master tapes — unheard of in the industry at that time. He now owns two record labels — Crossover Record Co. and RPM International — and a production facility. Interviews with Charles appeared on USA TODAY Inquiry pages Nov. 1, 1985, and June 23, 1986.

USA TODAY: You are so independent and have mastered so many tasks. How has being blind affected your accomplishments?

CHARLES: Blind people can do 98 percent of anything that sighted people can do. There's nothing wrong with saying, "I wish that person could see like I can and can do all the things I can do." But after saying that to yourself then let it go, drop it. Then say, "He certainly can't see but he certainly has a healthy mind and he can think." I know blind people who work as jewelry salespersons, as lawyers, in computer programming.

USA TODAY: Didn't you learn to play music before you became blind?

CHARLES: I started playing songs before I lost my sight. When I was around 3 years old a neighbor would stop to show me how to play little piano melodies with one finger as opposed to hitting on all the keys with your whole hand. That's what I was doing. I didn't know the difference. But he took the time and showed me. Naturally, I love music. If you love something, you automatically want to learn more about it. So that is what happened in my case.

USA TODAY: You have often talked about how important education and information have always been to you from an early age. Are today's children equally as inspired?

CHARLES: It's different now. Children are coming out of school and they spell city S-I-T-Y. They can't read. Believe me, when I was 5 years old I could read my ABCs. I could count before I even got to school. Guess who I got it from? My mother. A lot of parents put the kid in front of the TV. I witness cases where the teacher is having a problem with the kid, and the parent comes to school and curses the teacher in front of the child. When I was coming up people understood not to do things like that. Today's children are left a bit too much to their own devices.

USA TODAY: You sing different types of music — from country to blues and spirituals. How did you develop such a wide range?

CHARLES: I guess it was like starting at the beginning. All of my life I knew what a tone was or a sound was. Being raised in the South, I heard blues and rhythm and blues. Yet on the radio they had mostly country stations. I was a great fan of the Grand Ole Opry. And of course I would listen to people like Count Basie, Tommy Dorsey, Benny Goodman, Artie Shaw and others.

USA TODAY: Did your singing country music alienate fans?

CHARLES: A lot of people were annoyed that I was doing country music. I felt that was unfortunate because I'm not a blues singer, a jazz singer or a country singer. I am a singer who can sing the blues, who can sing country music, who can sing jazz music. When I first told ABC Records I wanted to make a country album, the guy said, "What's the matter with you?" He thought I was going to lose a lot of fans. I said, "I may lose some fans, but I'll gain more fans than I lose." That's exactly what happened. We put out *I Can't Stop Loving You* and *Born to Lose* and the rest is history.

USA TODAY: Do you ever want to perform today's rock music with the sexually suggestive lyrics?

CHARLES: Although my song *What'd I Say* was frowned upon years ago, my mother would have killed me if I had recorded something like today's rock music. It is just a matter of taste. I don't think that it is necessary. I am one of those people who came up from the old school and the things that my mama didn't like just never got done. That's the way I came up. A lot of parents just don't have any control over their children and they want to make other people responsible. That's unfair.

USA TODAY: I heard you sing your version of *America, the Beautiful,* at the Republican National Convention in 1984. What goes through your mind when you are singing that song?

CHARLES: In my mind America is a very beautiful place. We have a little bit of almost everything you can think of — oceans with beaches, mountains, deserts, rich farmland. That song talks about the beauty of the country and the people who were brave, who stood up for their country. I like that.

USA TODAY: Do you think of the other side — racism or poverty — when you sing that song?

CHARLES: I will tell you something, I don't know of any country that is set up as glorious as this one. That's what makes us look so bad with racism, sexism, poverty, because we're so great that most of this stuff we really don't need.

USA TODAY: A song you are famous for is called _Drown in My Own Tears_. What experiences in life have caused you the most tears?

CHARLES: The death of my mother was the most traumatic thing in my life because I was very close to her. I was an only child. I was very young, but I was old enough to remember it. My brother's drowning bothered me. Even losing my sight was a pretty bad thing. But I think the worst thing of all was the loss of my mother.

USA TODAY: You were addicted to heroin for 20 years, and were arrested on drug charges in Boston in 1973. What made you kick the habit?

CHARLES: My oldest kid, Ray Jr., was in Little League and they were giving the kids little rewards and honors for doing certain things. On a particular night all the fathers were supposed to be there. I had to leave because I was doing a song for the movie _The Cincinnati Kid_ with Steve McQueen. I had to go to the recording studio. He was a big boy, about 12 or 13 years old, and he started crying. That hurt me so bad. And it really hurt me so much until I started to think my kid loves me so much that he cries because I can't be here for his award. I knew then how much it would hurt him if someone would ever have to call his father a jailbird.

USA TODAY: And that was the turning point?

CHARLES: I started to think that since my children were getting up in age and I wasn't getting any younger myself, it was just time to hang it up. It just wasn't worth it. The kind of hassle you had to go through — ducking police and all this kind of foolishness. I was just so overwhelmed by my son's love for me I didn't want anything coming between us.

USA TODAY: Why do you think drug use is so widespread?

CHARLES: I'll tell you something. I got involved as a matter of wanting to belong. I was the youngest among a lot of grown people. And I

CHARLES PROFILE

Born: Sept. 23, 1930, in Albany, Ga.; name originally was Ray Charles Robinson.

Family: Divorced; three sons, Ray Jr., David and Robert.

Education: State School for Deaf and Blind Children, St. Augustine, Fla.

On life: "A lot of people were annoyed that I was doing country music. I felt that was unfortunate because I'm not a blues singer, a jazz singer or a country singer. I am a singer who can sing the blues, who can sing country music, who can sing jazz music. When I first told ABC Records I wanted to make a country album, the guy said, 'What's the matter with you?' He thought I was going to lose a lot of fans."

Home: Los Angeles.

Role model: Mother, Aretha Robinson.

MILESTONES

1935: His 4-year-old brother, George, drowned accidentally.

1937: Lost his vision from glaucoma.

1945: His mother, Aretha Robinson, died.

1948: First record, _Confession Blues_.

1952: Atlantic Records bought out his contract with Swing Time label for $2,000.

1960: Pop Grammy for _Georgia On My Mind;_ signed with ABC-Paramount.

1961: Rhythm and Blues Grammy for _Hit The Road Jack_.

1962: Country Grammy for _I Can't Stop Loving You_.

1973: Kicked 20-year heroin addiction after Boston arrest; stopped performing for one year.

1981: Star added on Hollywood Boulevard Walk of Fame.

1984: Performed at the Republican National Convention; _Brother Ray_ published.

1986: Kennedy Center Honors Award for Lifetime Achievement.

wanted to be like they were. And I wanted to do what they did. And I eventually got involved in drugs. But I feel that a lot of the dope and the crime is a direct result of the lack of parental guidance. We are the ones destroying us. I can't see myself going out and destroying my own neighborhood or robbing my own people.

USA TODAY: You have been married three times and you have had plenty of girlfriends. Do you find it difficult to maintain stable relationships?

CHARLES: I've always been wild when it comes to women, and I can see how my long line of love affairs finally busted up my marriages. But I believe that women have been the victims of society's oppression. They've been waiting on us men like slaves. I see the shame and pity of it all.

USA TODAY: Are you against marriage?

CHARLES: I have no interest in getting married anymore. Ever. I am not knocking it. I feel about marriage like I feel about cabbage: It is a good product but it ain't good for everybody. I have tried it and it made me sick, along with a few other people I was involved with. I would not make somebody else's life miserable, not to mention my own.

USA TODAY: You received a lot of criticism for going on a concert tour to South Africa. Was the criticism justified?

CHARLES: In my contract it was guaranteed that we would not — under any circumstances — play for a segregated audience in South Africa. These black people who are protesting the visit, they don't remember this. I was fighting segregation before a lot of them were even born. I was going down there with the busing and having bombs put under my stage when Dr. Martin Luther King Jr. was going through his stuff. And they are going to start telling me about going to South Africa?

USA TODAY: What do you plan for the future?

CHARLES: If God lets me, I want to continue to play my music, stay healthy and help some youngster along the way. I can't teach but I can certainly coach. I can take a kid who has talent and show him things to help him along. I have been very fortunate, a very blessed man. I have many awards and Grammys and decorations. I have talked with three presidents of the most powerful country in the world. My version of *Georgia on My Mind* is a state song. I think I have done pretty good for a little boy who came out of the South in short pants, with patches on his clothes.

SHIRLEY CHISHOLM

'Elder stateswoman' keeps eye on political progress for black women

CHISHOLM: 'You can't accept defeat. Realize that defeat should never be a source of discouragement but a stimulus to keep plotting.'

IMPRESSIONS

In 1972 I was the hostess of a Chicago TV talk show where unbossed, unbought Shirley Chisholm was the guest. I was awestruck. She was running for president. As I followed her campaign, I marveled at the way she would disappear for a 20-minute nap and awaken refreshed for the next speech. She wrestled with black male egos that were damaged by her independence. She endured to the bitter end despite the impression that her campaign was "symbolic." She was a trailblazer for blacks and women in politics. And she continues as a catalyst on the political scene today.

— **Barbara Reynolds**

The first black woman elected to Congress and the first black person to seek the presidential nomination from a major political party, Shirley Chisholm spent 26 years in politics. Since her retirement from Congress in 1983, she has written books, become a professional lecturer and is among the founders of the National Political Congress for Black Women. That group encourages black women to become involved in elective politics. Interviews with Chisholm appeared on USA TODAY Inquiry pages Oct. 6, 1982, and Aug. 26, 1987.

USA TODAY: You have been analyzed a lot by the media. How do you see yourself?

CHISHOLM: As a person who has shown you can do anything that you want to do.

USA TODAY: What role are you playing in politics since your retirement?

CHISHOLM: An elder stateswoman. I spent 26 years in the political arena. I still get a lot of letters from people all over this country — black and white. They say: "You are a trailblazer, you are a role model for women. You dared to do it even though you were a bearer of a double jeopardy — being black and female. And Shirley Chisholm, you helped me."

USA TODAY: What impact did your 1972 presidential bid have on the USA?

CHISHOLM: Many women come to me and tell me I was a role model for them in terms of having the nerve and determination. They said that if Shirley Chisholm — a black female — can do it, why can't we do it? From that standpoint I am regarded as a role model by women, particularly beginning with the '60s and on up until today.

USA TODAY: Does it bother you that political pundits describe your presidential bid as symbolic but called Jesse Jackson's 1984 run serious?

CHISHOLM: One has to realize that people were shocked that a black woman was making a bid for president. They said I really couldn't be serious because I didn't fit the traditional role of a person seeking the highest office of the land. Years later Jackson began to run. First of all he is a man, so that sexist attitude crops up again. Second, he came from a real base in terms of being a disciple of Mar-

tin Luther King Jr. And Jesse was much better known than I was when I made my bid.

USA TODAY: Did not being as well known give you a feeling of isolation?

CHISHOLM: I felt the press very often left me out as they discussed politics since the black woman has always been pictured at the bottom of everything. For a black woman to have the nerve to say she is going to run for the presidency — it just blazes in people's minds that she is half-crazy. If I was not serious, why would I knock myself out and go all the way to the end of the convention? I believe I am the only person in the USA who ran a presidential campaign and went all the way to the convention on a shoestring. I spent approximately $500,000 on that campaign. Unbelievable.

USA TODAY: Did white feminists desert you during your campaign?

CHISHOLM: I always say that and a lot of people don't like it. But if it was not for the women in the South — white women and black women — I would have fallen flat on my face at the convention. In my home state of New York, where I had expected to get support, some of the outstanding feminists who had worked with me through the years and who had encouraged me to run deserted me.

USA TODAY: Did this support from Southerners carry over to the Democratic convention?

CHISHOLM: At the convention, Mississippi gave me approximately eight of their 17 votes. Louisiana gave me nine of their votes. New York gave me three votes out of around 250. New Jersey gave one vote out of around 190. I make no bones in telling everybody that it was the South that really helped put me across and gave me a showing. They don't like to hear this in the Northeast, but history must be written truthfully. So I need to set the record straight. In Mississippi three white women lost their jobs because of backing Shirley Chisholm. The political structure in Mississippi told them, "Don't you see she's black?" And these women said, "We are not blind, but we believe there's something about this woman."

USA TODAY: At the 1972 Democratic National Convention I heard you tell a group of black male politicians that you were the only one who had "the balls" to get things done. What did you mean?

CHISHOLM: People are not aware of the problems that black men caused me. Listen, I am a strong woman. I don't want to make any analogies, but Harriet Tubman and Sojourner Truth are my heroines. I am very much like them. I would say to the men: "Look, I know you all don't like me. You resent what I have done." They called me everything but a child of God. I don't make any bones about it. They were very jealous of a black woman who had such a multifaceted following. I had a following of women, whites, Hispanics. I was able to go beyond a base of blacks.

USA TODAY: How did you handle the double lash of racism and sexism? Did it break your heart?

CHISHOLM: No, it didn't break my heart, but it hurt. What hurt me was that some of these men attempted to destroy me politically. They badmouthed me in different ways. When I would go to conferences they would put me at the end of the stage because the cameras or reporters always came to me to get my opinions. The men resented this kind of attention so they tried shunting me aside.

USA TODAY: But you didn't make it easy.

CHISHOLM: My mouth could be heard 10 miles away. I had a knowledge of issues. Some of them said later: "We did not know what the hell to do with you. You just kept coming back." They tried to weaken me. Oh, they did everything, but I am strong. And that is supplemented by the confidence I have in myself. If I did not have that confidence I would have been destroyed a long time ago.

USA TODAY: How did you develop your sense of self-confidence?

CHISHOLM: I was born in this country, but I grew up in Barbados from the age of 2 to about 10. I grew up in a Quaker brethren home. The religion is very disciplined. When I was a little girl my grandmother — who was in her early 70s — would say: "Child you're black and you are going to be a woman and I don't think you can change either one of the two. But you are bright and you have a brain. Use it to show them you are coming through."

USA TODAY: Were you a leader as a child?

CHISHOLM: I was a little girl who would push older kids to sit down and watch me. My grandmother used to say to friends: "Look at little Shirley. She's got them under control."

USA TODAY: Did your strength also come from your early years with your family in the Caribbean?

CHISHOLM: In part. I also got my strength from a very strong Quaker religion. I got my strength from a grandmother who knew I had it and who kept telling me the world is filled with medio-

CHISHOLM PROFILE

Born: Nov. 30, 1924, in Brooklyn, N.Y.

Family: Widowed; no children.

Education: Bachelor of arts from Brooklyn College, New York City; master's from Columbia University, New York City.

On life: "When I was a little girl my grandmother — who was in her early 70s — would say: 'Child you're black and you are going to be a woman and I don't think you can change either one of the two. But you are bright and you have a brain. Use it to show them you are coming through.'"

Home: Williamsville, N.Y.

Role models: Sojourner Truth, Harriet Tubman and Eleanor Roosevelt.

MILESTONES

1964: Began serving four years as Democratic delegate to New York Assembly.

1968: First black woman elected to Congress.

1970: Autobiography, *Unbought and Unbossed,* published.

1971: Founding member of National Women's Political Caucus.

1972: First black person to run for the presidential nomination of a major political party.

1973: Her second book, *The Good Fight,* published.

1983: Retired from Congress; appointed to the Purington Chair at Mount Holyoke College, South Halley, Mass.

1984: Helped found National Political Congress for Black Women after both Republican and Democratic presidential candidates at the 1984 political conventions failed to interview black women as possible running mates.

1987: Keynote speaker for the National Women's Political Caucus; headed a summer institute at Fayetteville State University, Fayetteville, N.C.

cre individuals but excellence reaps rewards. She kept telling me that I had the ability to lead something some day. When you grow up in an atmosphere that is a testament to your ability or talents, it has to have an impact. It did.

USA TODAY: What should blacks do to gain political clout?

CHISHOLM: One of the biggest mistakes we have made politically as an ethnic group is that one party takes us for granted because they know we have no place else to go, according to their perception. The other party does not pay us any mind — benign neglect. If we had a certain amount of impact in both parties there would be more leverage of the power we could exercise at conventions. We could make gains.

USA TODAY: Other than Sojourner Truth and Harriet Tubman, who has inspired you and why?

CHISHOLM: Eleanor Roosevelt told me I was destined to lead. She met me at an oratorical contest in New York City where I won first prize. I was 15 years old. She had an impact on my life. She said: "You are black, but, young woman, there is something in you. Don't let your race or your sex hold you back, dear." I will never forget it. This humble, homely woman — but as she spoke there was something very beautiful from within.

USA TODAY: Are women who promote change taken seriously?

CHISHOLM: Every woman who is a catalyst for change in some way is laughed at and ridiculed. I knew I would be laughed at and ridiculed. But you can do it if you have faith in God and confidence in yourself. You can't accept defeat. Realize that defeat should never be a source of discouragement but a stimulus to keep plotting.

USA TODAY: How would you like to be remembered?

CHISHOLM: I don't want to be remembered necessarily as the first black woman to have made a bid for the presidency. Or even the first black woman elected to the U.S. Congress. I would rather be remembered as a daring, determined woman who happened to be black and was a catalyst for change in the 20th century.

CARDISS COLLINS

Though shy, she has stood out in Congress while fighting for a wide range of issues

COLLINS: 'There is something about success that has power of its own. All we have to do is understand how we got this far.'

IMPRESSIONS

On Dec. 8, 1972, a United Airlines Boeing 737 crashed near Chicago's Midway Airport, killing 45 people. U.S. Rep. George Collins was among them. Over the years I watched his widow, Cardiss, pick up the pieces of her life as a single parent and member of Congress. She has fought and won in politics long after the other black women in Congress — Barbara Jordan, Shirley Chisholm, Yvonne Braithwaite Burke — have retired. She has impressed and inspired me with her tremendous staying power.

— **Barbara Reynolds**

One of the few members of Congress to continue the push for comprehensive federal child care legislation, Cardiss Collins has been a champion for family life and the rights of women and blacks. She was elected in 1973 to fill the vacancy left by the death of her husband, Rep. George Collins. She has since forged her own path as an advocate for women's health rights, for Medicare reform, airline safety and environmental issues. An interview with Collins appeared on the USA TODAY Inquiry page July 19, 1984.

USA TODAY: How did you feel about running for your husband's seat in the House of Representatives after his death?

COLLINS: Initially I was in shock. But even after I began to recover from my husband's death, I was a little bit skeptical because of my son. He turned 13 two months before my husband was killed. It was his first year of high school. I was very concerned about him.

USA TODAY: Were there other concerns?

COLLINS: I was also concerned about making the adjustments in my lifestyle like the extensive travel and other responsibilities associated with serving in Congress. I had a talk with family members and then I decided that I would go for it.

USA TODAY: What were some of the obstacles to your running for office?

COLLINS: There really weren't any obstacles to my running. My husband had built such a good record with voters and people who made political decisions in Chicago. The Democrats — headed by Mayor Richard Daley — had a political machine and it slated me unanimously.

USA TODAY: How did your running affect your relationship with your son?

COLLINS: I was already working for the Illinois Department of Revenue, so it was not like I was a mother who was at home all the time. We were able to work it out very nicely because my mother was still in Chicago. She would come to my house every Monday morning and stay until I got home on Thursday night. That way she got to spoil him.

USA TODAY: Why didn't you take your son to Washington with you?

COLLINS: He felt that he would have to go through changes finding new friends and all that goes with being that age.

USA TODAY: Were there other sacrifices?

COLLINS: I didn't have the time that I needed to adjust to the loss of my husband. Grieving was deferred. But I most regret that I didn't get a chance to be with my son as much after his father's death and until he was 18 years old. I didn't know I was making a sacrifice. But when you go back over things you can see them much more clearly.

USA TODAY: During those trying years, who did you depend upon for comfort and strength?

COLLINS: My mom. I am an only child. We are still extremely close.

USA TODAY: Three other black women — Shirley Chisholm, Barbara Jordan and Yvonne Braithwaite Burke — have left Congress since you were elected. How does it feel to be the only black woman in Congress?

COLLINS: It's lonely. Shirley Chisholm retired. Yvonne had a child while she was a member of Congress and she wanted the child to be raised and educated in California where her husband lived. And Barbara Jordan, who was the greatest woman ever to serve in the body, decided that she wanted to go back to teaching. We definitely need more black women in Congress.

USA TODAY: How will that happen?

COLLINS: There are a great many women out there who will make fine members of Congress. They are raising issues important to all women, all people, but especially blacks. As members of the Congressional Black Caucus we have to encourage more qualified people to run. Black people have to support them if they run. And we have to make state party chiefs aware that more black women are needed.

USA TODAY: What do you feel you have been able to accomplish while a member of Congress?

COLLINS: If there is anything I can be proud of it is that because of Cardiss Collins, air travel is safer and some of the problems that existed in the transportation of toxic chemicals across our communities have been corrected. That pleases me immensely. But all of these accomplishments are just steps on the rock of success.

USA TODAY: For several years you seemed uneasy with your jump from accountant to politician. Is that uneasiness still there?

COLLINS: I have been shy all my life but I have learned to be a very effective behind-the-scenes worker. It is not always the one with the noise maker who is getting things done.

USA TODAY: **Do you think your shyness might be misunderstood?**

COLLINS: We all feel that way sometime. Most often we don't really understand other individuals. Everybody ought to know by now that my intentions are good, that I work very hard at what I do. If that isn't the way they see it, I regret that.

USA TODAY: **What major changes have you witnessed in Congress?**

COLLINS: I have seen many of the programs that we fought for in the '60s diminish tremendously. Under President Reagan I have seen many of the people-serving programs wiped out. A good example is the Community Services Administration, which was the only advocacy agency funded from the Johnson administration right through the Nixon and Carter administrations. But it has been absolutely dismantled under Reagan.

USA TODAY: **Who is affected by these actions?**

COLLINS: The poor, the elderly, the vulnerable, those who have the least are hurt. That bothers me a great deal because I know there are so many young people who would need help if their parents were dead. In the past, Social Security would assist them in going to college through age 22. The Reagan administration cut that completely. Now the government will only pay an annuity through high school, or at the end of age 17. This is just unfair to those children.

USA TODAY: **It has been 20 years since Dr. Martin Luther King Jr. died. How do you assess the state of the USA's black community since his death?**

COLLINS: So much was started during the civil rights movement that not even a hostile federal attitude can turn the clock back now. There are more than a million black students in college. They are getting law degrees, going to medical school in record numbers. Even reverse-discrimination suits have not stopped that. We are more mature now as a people. We can compete from the schoolrooms to the board rooms. There are so many role models in business that the mystique of starting one's own business has diminished. Many blacks are symbols of pride and excellence on Madison Avenue, on Wall Street. The ball is rolling. Momentum is build-

COLLINS PROFILE

Born: Sept. 24, 1931, in St. Louis.

Family: Widowed; a son, Kevin.

Education: Bachelor's degree from Northwestern University, Evanston, Ill.

On life: "I am a woman of simple goals. I don't have visions of grandeur. I simply want to be known as a helper. If I have helped somebody, if I have made somebody feel proud, if I have helped make people safe — that's enough. I would like to be remembered as a lady who made a contribution to the people of the U.S., and particularly black people."

Homes: Chicago and Washington, D.C.

Role model: Her mother, Rosia Mae Robertson.

MILESTONES

1972: Her husband, U.S. Rep. George Collins, killed in plane crash at Chicago.

1973: Won election to fill husband's congressional seat; Quality of Life award from National Welfare Rights Organization; Dr. Mary McLeod Bethune award.

1977: Named chairwoman of House subcommittee on Employment and Housing.

1978: Became first woman to chair the Congressional Black Caucus; first black and first woman to chair the Manpower and Housing subcommittee of the House Government Operations Committee; first black and first woman named Democratic whip-at-large in the House.

1982: Named member of Energy and Commerce committee; elected to Black Women's Hall of Fame.

1983: Named member of Government Activities and Transportation subcommittee.

1984: American Health and Beauty Aids award.

1986: *Dollars & Sense* magazine's Top 100 Black Business and Professional Women's Award.

ing. No one can pull the plug. There is something about success that has power of its own. All we have to do is understand how we got this far. We got here through struggle, unity and faith. That is how we must continue.

USA TODAY: What needs to change in black communities across the USA?

COLLINS: Attitudes. We must rid ourselves of the thought that someone owes us something. We must concentrate on what we can do and erase "can't," "won't" and "don't think so" from our vocabulary. When that happens it will be easier to grow as a community.

USA TODAY: After years of rule by Mayor Daley, Chicago elected a black mayor, Harold Washington. Did you consider his victory a sign that race relations were improving there?

COLLINS: Most definitely. In this time and age there should be no doors locked to anyone because of color or gender. It took the same requirements for me to get here as for anybody else who wanted to be in Congress. You have to be 25 years old, you have to be a resident of the state, and you have to be elected by as many as 500,000 people. The Constitution says there is no difference for blacks or whites, men or women. If there is a discrepancy in the way I am treated I would be the first one to say, "Well, hold on a minute now."

USA TODAY: How do you want to be remembered 10 years from now?

COLLINS: I am a woman of simple goals. I don't have visions of grandeur. I simply want to be known as a helper. If I have helped somebody, if I have made somebody feel proud, if I have helped make people safe — that's enough. I would like to be remembered as a lady who made a contribution to the people of the U.S., and particularly black people.

MARVA COLLINS

Her trailblazing teaching style gives students skills, self-confidence and spirit to be leaders

COLLINS: 'If people could make it in the darkness of slavery, there is no excuse for us in the light of today's alleged freedom.'

IMPRESSIONS

The West Side of Chicago always resembled an unwanted, dirty, disheveled stepchild that no one cared about. Nothing worked there. Education was no exception. That kind of thinking was exactly what was wrong, says super-teacher Marva Collins. The disillusionment of the surrounding community isn't allowed in her academy — Westside Prep School. I have watched her teach the nation that helping children know they are treasures and setting high expectations will make the difference in their lives. In my opinion, she would make a great U.S. secretary of education.

— **Barbara Reynolds**

A former public school teacher, Marva Collins decided to make a difference with her Westside Preparatory School, located in one of the poorest sections of Chicago. Her students, who range in age from 3 to 16, learn self-discipline, the value of hard work and self-esteem. She's frequently asked to consider franchising her methods or becoming a top education official in state or federal government, but she considers her charges too important to leave to traditional education methods. She also has trained thousands of teachers, principals and school administrators. An interview with Collins appeared on the USA TODAY Inquiry page March 7, 1983.

USA TODAY: Westside Preparatory School is in the middle of one of Chicago's poorest districts. Why did you start it?

COLLINS: The expectations of minority children are very, very low. It seems to be almost a hypocritical kind of situation. It is OK for them to be mediocre when they are young but all of a sudden when they get older they are stupid, they are inferior, they are welfare recipients. I believe our children did not have an opportunity to become citizens of the world, to compete in the marketplace for jobs.

USA TODAY: What is happening at the school?

COLLINS: We are creating children who will say to the world, "Either take my hand and come on with me, or I'm going anyway without you." We have children who do not have self-pity. We have children who do not have breakable wheels. We have children whose spirits can't be crushed. I have trained more than 2,300 teachers who reach about a million children.

USA TODAY: What drives your program?

COLLINS: I am determined to get people to understand that our children must be able to read, write, compute and think critically and analytically if we are to survive in the world.

USA TODAY: In 1983, your most famous Westside Prep student was 24-year-old Kevin Ross, a star college basketball player who went through 16 years of school without learning to read. How could that happen?

COLLINS: That's happening to millions of children. Kevin had enough sense to say, "I'm going to do something about it." People in my neighborhood do not read. There are about 30 million illiterate people in America. Kevin is just one of millions.

USA TODAY: Kevin progressed from a second-grade reading level to the 12th-grade level in about four months. How did he improve so fast?

COLLINS: I worked on vocabulary, starting with basic vowel sounds, comprehension and just constantly worked at it.

USA TODAY: How do you view public education?

COLLINS: Education is declining not only in public schools, but all over. We get children from very prestigious, very wealthy families that could send them to Switzerland or anywhere to school. Japan and Germany are having difficulties with their children in school.

USA TODAY: What is Marva Collins' method of instruction?

COLLINS: It is all about believing in yourself and not allowing people to break your spirit. It is about determination and belief in what you can do. You don't run around with a "poor black me, somebody is going to do it for me" attitude. Our creed is that society predicts but our students will determine. God is not some cosmic bellboy at their beck and call. We have to get rid of that zealous, religious fervor that believes God is going to take care of us. We teach children to think. We teach logic. We teach Latin. Marva Collins' way is the way children were taught in the 1920s. Children were taught elocution and taught that Shakespeare, Emerson and Thoreau were not too difficult for grade school students.

USA TODAY: Aren't you returning to basics?

COLLINS: We have to return to doing the things that built America. Go to the better stores, such as Saks, Lord & Taylor, and they almost look like K mart. There is a decline of merchandise and services. It's not just in schools. We were able to spell and be halfway literate in racist Alabama where I grew up. There was a time when public school children did learn to read. We aren't talking about being doctors, lawyers, chemists, scientists, but they were able to read the menu. They were able to read newspapers. I don't care how many excuses we make that might get us off the hook, it is not going to save us. We are talking about people now who can't complete an application.

USA TODAY: Why don't you support federal action such as tuition tax credits that might benefit private schools such as yours?

COLLINS: What makes us think that with government intervention all schools aren't going to return to being mediocre again? We keep putting Band-Aids on hemorrhages. I am not looking for benefits. I'll make my own way. I don't want anybody to do anything for me. Just get out of my way and I'll do it myself.

USA TODAY: Why don't you mass produce the Westside Prep concept so students all over the USA can benefit?

COLLINS: I have turned down $1 million to start 100 Marva Collins Inc. schools. I am not turning out Big Macs. At least Big Macs have quality control. How can I set up 100 Marva Collins schools and make sure children are learning? We would have the same illiteracy that we have now.

USA TODAY: It has been said that although you are teaching an appreciation of white literary artists, you are ignoring the works of black scholars.

COLLINS: That's not true. How do you segment knowledge? You certainly have to know about everything. It is so sad when people tell me they have not read Plato's *Republic*, because you have to if you are to understand white society.

USA TODAY: In recent years you have had your share of critics, including those who claimed you overstated test results. How do you respond?

COLLINS: What do I care about what people say? I bought the buildings housing our school. I pay the teachers here. I sponsor the children who can't pay. Society can continue to predict, but I shall continue to determine.

USA TODAY: Whites are also interested in sending their children to your school. Did you expect that to happen?

COLLINS: It is not unusual. If I can make a better mousetrap than my neighbor, the world will beat a path to my door. We have what the world needs.

USA TODAY: How do visitors react when they come to your classes?

COLLINS: It's intimidating to a lot of people. We have thousands of visitors per year, including superintendents, teachers and principals. Invariably, the first reaction is, "These children don't look and behave like poor children." How are poor children supposed to behave? Poverty has nothing to do with having class.

COLLINS PROFILE

Born: Aug. 31, 1936, in Monroeville, Ala.

Family: Married to Clarence Collins; three children, Cynthia Beth, Eric and Patrick.

Education: Bachelor of arts from Clark College, Atlanta.

On life: "There is no perfect situation. As a people, we need to stop looking for it. People see the icing on the cake. They don't see the pain or the problems of baking the cake. You don't plant a tree at night and pick the fruits in the morning, do you? . . . I am not a quitter. There have been some hard, hard times. I have cried, but I do it privately."

Home: Chicago.

Role models: Her parents, Alex and Bessie Nettles.

MILESTONES

1975: Founded Westside Preparatory School, Chicago.

1978: Named director of the Right to Read Foundation.

1979: Received Fred Hampton Image Award from Fred Hampton Foundation, and Watson Washburne Award from the Reading Reform Foundation.

1980: Named Educator of the Year by Phi Delta Kappa.

1981: Member of President's Commission on White House Fellowships; CBS aired *The Marva Collins Story*, a made-for-TV movie; received the American Public Service Award.

1982: Named Legendary Woman of the World by the city of Birmingham, Ala.

1985: Her projects received $500,000 donation from rock musician Prince.

1986: Received $10,000 donation from proceeds from a Prince concert.

1987: Announced plans to open a school in Compton, Calif., by September 1988.

USA TODAY: Where did you get your self-confidence?

COLLINS: From my parents. It came from being told: "Sit up straight. Walk straight. Look at me when I talk. Walk with your head high. Move with enthusiasm." My self-confidence came from things besides the three Rs. My parents told me every day that I was a bright child. I believe that our children can be more than what they are. Here when children do something wrong, we ask them: "Now why aren't you going to do that? Why aren't you going to make that noise?" And the child will respond, "Because I am too bright."

USA TODAY: What sustains you during the tough times?

COLLINS: Having a lot of faith, regardless of how bad times get. I always remember the parable about Jesus feeding the multitudes of 500 people with five loaves of bread and two fish. I told my staff during tough times that everything would be all right. And they would see that happen. I just never believed that it couldn't be done. I just have that belief and that faith in my people.

USA TODAY: Does every person have the components necessary for success?

COLLINS: In the beginning we all have. We have become acculturated somehow and we have lost it. I think as a people we would not have survived had we not had the strength to survive hard times. I have not forgotten that I am walking over bridges built by many people — Sojourner Truth and Harriet Tubman. If people could make it in the darkness of slavery, there is no excuse for us in the light of today's alleged freedom. There is no perfect situation. As a people, we need to stop looking for it. People see the icing on the cake. They don't see the pain or the problems of baking the cake. You don't plant a tree at night and pick the fruits in the morning, do you?

USA TODAY: When people look at Marva Collins they see a successful and extremely self-confident woman. What more is there?

COLLINS: I am not a quitter. There have been some hard, hard times. I have cried, but I do it privately.

BILL COSBY

Scorning TV's usual fare of sex and violence,
he showed that family love can draw, too

COSBY: 'First of all, I'm very good. Second, I deal with myself and my own likes and dislikes. . . . I don't play off of someone else's color.'

IMPRESSIONS

We met at Ben's Chili Bowl, an excellent chili-dog restaurant in Washington, D.C. Bill Cosby courted his wife, Camille, at Ben's during the lean days before his stardom. On the day he talked with me and other members of the press, he was just like one of the boys from his "Fat Albert" gang. He joked and warmed to his audience. We had heard he had an irascible temper when challenged, so we were content to listen to the golden guy of television hold court and hope to learn what he will do next with his Midas touch. The key? "Just do what you like and assume your taste is what the nation will like."

— **Barbara Reynolds**

An inveterate performer, Bill Cosby is a comedian, actor, writer, recording artist and businessman. He has challenged and changed the entertainment industry throughout his career. He learned early to pay attention to the little things that other people might not notice. He has risen from standup comic to television and film star. By teaming up with other black actors like Sidney Poitier, he was able to make movies about blacks without the violence and stereotypes. That was during a time when negative screen images of blacks were decried as a national problem. An interview with Cosby appeared on the USA TODAY *Inquiry page Sept. 30, 1985.*

USA TODAY: *The Cosby Show* **became TV's No. 1 show though it lacked the prescribed formula of sex and violence. How do you explain its success?**

COSBY: This show says something very, very important. People are starved to see the love of husband and wife. They're starved to see genuine respect children have for their parents and parents for their children. If you give people something that addresses their problems and their concerns behaviorally, it doesn't make any difference what color the people are. This is my gig, and this is what I worked very hard to do for the past 20-some years.

USA TODAY: **What impact has your show had on other situation comedies?**

COSBY: It's difficult to say because I don't think other producers and networks want to go up another level intellectually in subject matter. They just think: "Well, the family situation is back. Why don't we get a couple and then give them some children?" I don't think they really care about what *The Cosby Show* proved — that there are so many opportunities that can be played upon behaviorally. I'm really concerned.

USA TODAY: **Do you think other sitcoms have copied your show?**

COSBY: Too much is made of this because we are black Americans. You have to examine *Family Ties* or Bob Newhart's show. Look at them and think about the differences. They should be compared with the rest of television and not necessarily with our show. I've seen some of the shows you might have in mind, like *Charlie & Company,* where Flip Wilson played a civil servant. The char-

acters were nothing like mine. Flip was nothing like the character I play — Dr. Huxtable. And his family was nothing like the Huxtable family, so we ought to look for the differences that exist. I don't see them as copycats.

USA TODAY: **Is there any new show you're eager to get produced?**

COSBY: We hope to do some things with a new show that is now in development, the Lena Horne series. Lena will have a granddaughter who comes to live with her. The granddaughter has not finished college and does not want to. She just wants to be a star. She wants to be discovered. So her mother and father send her to live with her grandmother. And Lena Horne has agreed that she will not help this child unless the child wants to go to college. So what we have is the wise grandmother giving the philosophy to this little child, and it's a wonderful series.

USA TODAY: **What is your response to the criticism that your TV family, the Huxtables, is too affluent, too upbeat?**

COSBY: The overemphasis on some TV shows on feeling the blues keeps us from thinking of the positive potential that our children have and the positive potential the parents have. We also have been taught to disrespect those who are achieving — the lower economic groups have been taught to dislike the middle class groups, those who are going to college. But we have generations and generations of black families who have graduated from college, and they should be held up for all to see.

USA TODAY: **Does the criticism that your show is not typical of black family life bother you?**

COSBY: No. I don't know where racism comes from. I want white families to tell me what it is that some of them tell their children so that their children know not to dance with my daughter. I want to know what it is that makes a person realize that when a black person walks up, he or she is not supposed to have that job. I want to know what established that black Americans are inferior. I want to see two or three shows that tell me where racism comes from because if I show it and say it exists, people will say that's not true, you're making that up. So in the meantime, the Huxtables will give a great deal of positive behavioral insights to all Americans with a great deal of love.

USA TODAY: **Do you think you are getting this message across?**

COSBY: Someday, I will. One day when the Huxtables are played back by sensible people, it will register that the people in this black family were just human beings. And all this other stuff about juxtapositions based on color and sex is hogwash.

USA TODAY: Why do we never see poverty on your show?

COSBY: There are certain things that will work on television and certain things that won't work. Who wants to watch a series based on depressing situations? If I am depressed and poor, the last thing I want to watch is myself again at 8 p.m. I don't want to see another kid suffer or another mother and father who are fighting.

USA TODAY: But by avoiding it, are you avoiding reality?

COSBY: You can't say there was a reality about anybody's life on *Sanford & Son*. You can't say that *Alice* was real. Those were situations thought up by writers. There is nothing on television that is real; it is not meant to be real. As much as it was liked, *M*A*S*H* was not real. It had good acting, good scripts, but it wasn't real. People don't act like that in real life.

USA TODAY: Will your show open up opportunities for more black writers and directors?

COSBY: I don't know. We're doing fine with the ones we have. I don't hire for color and I don't fire for color, but we have some shows coming up that will make some definite moves with black writers and black directors doing major works. And we're going to make some major inroads with Asians and Native Americans.

USA TODAY: Do you agree with critics who say that TV's most prominent black child stars, Gary Coleman and Emmanuel Lewis, shouldn't have white adoptive parents?

COSBY: No. There's love there. We can look at the optimistic part. That's a very positive situation. What should bother you or me is that they probably put it together that way because they thought the public wouldn't be able to accept a white child with a black mother and father.

USA TODAY: When you look back on your past, what made the greatest impact?

COSBY: One thing was getting away from my parents. When I went into the Navy, I wasn't dealing with my parents. The Navy made me get up at 3 a.m. and stand and watch the clothesline, with no clothes on the line at all. When I found out how I hated that, I had to re-examine what I could be.

USA TODAY: Where did that lead?

COSBY PROFILE

Born: July 12, 1937, in Philadelphia.

Family: Married to Camille; five children, Erika, Erinn, Ennis, Ensa and Evin.

Education: Bachelor of arts from Temple University, Philadelphia; master's and Ph.D from the University of Massachusetts, Amherst.

On life: "The overemphasis on some TV shows on feeling the blues keeps us from thinking of the positive potential that our children have and the positive potential the parents have."

Home: New York City.

Role models: Buster Keaton and Orson Welles.

MILESTONES

1962: Began comedy career in Greenwich Village, New York City.

1964: Grammy for Best Comedy Album, *Bill Cosby Is A Very Funny Fellow ... Right?*

1965: Co-starred on *I Spy* with Robert Culp — one of the first dramatic television roles for a black actor that had nothing to do with race; Grammy for Best Comedy Album, *I Started Out As A Child.*

1966: Emmy for *I Spy;* Grammy for Best Comedy Album, *Why Is There Air?*

1967: Grammy for Best Comedy Album, *Revenge.*

1969: Emmy for *The Bill Cosby Special;* Grammy for Best Comedy Album for *To Russell, My Brother, Whom I Slept With.*

1974: Starred in film *Uptown Saturday Night.*

1975: Starred in movie *Let's Do It Again.*

1977: Starred in movie *Piece of the Action.*

1984: Launched *The Cosby Show* on TV.

1986: Book *Fatherhood* published.

1987: Began filming movie sequel to *I Spy;* starred in *Leonard, Part 6.*

COSBY: Until the time I joined the Navy, people told me that I was a very bright person, and that I should either be a lawyer or a doctor. I was really afraid to do these things because it meant work. So when I went into the Navy, I found myself being under people I knew I was much brighter than. At the end of about three weeks, I went to the base commander and I thanked him for what the Navy had done for me and told him I was now ready to go to college. So I changed from an underachiever to a point where I realized I had to get out and earn it.

USA TODAY: How do you explain your personal popularity, which ranges from movies to TV to commercials?

COSBY: First of all, I'm very good. Second, I deal with myself and my own likes and dislikes. And then I say this is the way I am, and then others say, "Well, yes, that's the way I am also." I've never really used street language for laughter. I've never really used black slang to draw laughter. I don't play off of someone else's color.

USA TODAY: So it doesn't bother you if people see you as a colorless Bill Cosby?

COSBY: You have to examine colors. What has to be examined is what is black — to say black is what? Is black a race of people who don't work? Is black a race of people who move into our neighborhood, and they shouldn't be there because we see their color first? In examining these things, the color doesn't disappear. When you have the Huxtables, what disappears is the baloney you've been taught about disliking these people. That disappears. I've read books, I've seen plays that said racism is wrong and showed people suffering, and it hasn't changed opinions one iota. So now we go into behavior. We allow people to enjoy this family, which doesn't demean itself, and good things begin to happen.

ANGELA DAVIS

Days on the run intensified her zeal to fight poverty, oppression, injustice

DAVIS: 'I consider myself a radical because I always want to try to understand what is at the root of our problems as black people.'

IMPRESSIONS

In Indianapolis, the capital of mainstream USA, Angela Davis and I sipped coffee at a downtown hotel restaurant and reminisced. After she was arrested in the late 1960s, hundreds of black women with Afros also were arrested on suspicion of being Davis. She was such a dangerous character in the eyes of the law that resembling her was cause for arrest. Because Davis is gentle, cerebral and professorial, I wonder what the fuss was about. Yet with her long dreadlocks and flashing eyes, you know she will never be content, comfortable and predictable as most of the rest of her generation has become.

— **Barbara Reynolds**

Known worldwide for her political activism, Angela Davis is committed to the elimination of suffering, poverty and oppression — particularly for blacks. Her vehicle has been the Communist Party since she was 24 years old. She was a student of political philosopher Herbert Marcuse while in college, and he considered her one of his best students. She is a writer, lecturer and college professor. She also is founder of the National Alliance Against Racist and Political Repression and a leader of the National Political Congress for Black Women and the National Black Women's Health Project. An interview with Davis appeared on the USA TODAY Inquiry page Aug. 21, 1986.

USA TODAY: What course do you expect the women's, black, and black women's movements to take in the future?

DAVIS: I think there needs to be a special emphasis on the needs and the aspirations of Afro-American women, both by the black movement and by the women's movement. We have made enormous contributions to the struggle for black liberation. We have made contributions to the women's movement as well. I think this is a period when it is so important to build bridges between people and movements if we are going to emerge from this era intact.

USA TODAY: Why?

DAVIS: Black women in ourselves embody so much. We embody a connection to the black movement. We embody a connection to the women's movement, to the working-class movement. Black women have played a role that unfortunately is also going unnoticed. This is a period when we need to become more overt in our participation.

USA TODAY: You are a member of the Communist Party. Would you have been a better role model if you had gone a different route?

DAVIS: It was precisely because of my membership in the Communist Party that I could even be considered a role model. If people did look up to me it was because of the substantiveness that I assumed with respect to my right to my beliefs and my ability to stand up and fight for those rights. Of course, as a communist, I don't ask people with whom I work and with whom I struggle to become communist

themselves unless they desire to do that. That's not a prerequisite for being involved in the struggle.

USA TODAY: Why are you a communist?

DAVIS: I joined the Communist Party because I discovered an organization of people committed to struggling for progressive change. I was looking for a multiracial organization that understood the relationship between fighting for the equality of black people and the overall struggle to emancipate the working class. It is the only organization that I encountered that understood the interconnectedness of our struggles. And I believe that the country should be controlled by those who produce its wealth.

USA TODAY: Does communism deliver that?

DAVIS: When we talk about communism, the first thing people say is the Soviet Union. The Soviet Union is a socialist country. It is still attempting to build its society. I am talking about the United States. I am talking about a struggle that is based on the history and the experiences of the multiracial working class in the United States of America.

USA TODAY: How do you evaluate your impact as a member of the Communist Party?

DAVIS: Some of us have to be willing to be the trailblazers. Some of us have to be willing to break the ground.

USA TODAY: But why the Communist Party?

DAVIS: In a sense, the communists have been trailblazers in this country. If you think back to the '30s when there was no unemployment insurance, no Social Security and no welfare system, members of the Communist Party first raised those demands. After awhile that demand became the demand of a mass movement. Many people today don't realize that the government in the '30s said unemployment insurance was a communist conspiracy.

USA TODAY: What are your current causes?

DAVIS: I decided in 1972, along with others, to build a movement to assist others who were victims of repression. A year after my acquittal on conspiracy, kidnapping and murder charges, we founded an organization called the National Alliance Against Racist and Political Repression. I chair the organization. I am committed to fighting against political repression. That's what framed me in the first place.

USA TODAY: You were a fugitive on the FBI's most-wanted list in connection with a breakout attempt at a California courtroom that left Jonathan Jackson and a judge dead. How do you characterize

that period of your life?

DAVIS: It was the most personally difficult time of my life. I was singled out as a symbol. Many black women were arrested at the time I was attempting to elude the FBI. That is an indication of the extent to which they used my case to intimidate and harass black women in particular. The message they wanted to convey to black women was: "If you become a political activist, if you associate yourself with the black movement, this is going to happen to you. You will end up where Angela Davis is."

USA TODAY: Were you afraid?

DAVIS: I was very much afraid. But at the same time, I recognized I couldn't allow fear to dictate my actions. I was young. There were times when I was underground that I thought I might not survive that day, that I might be shot down by who knows, the FBI or anyone else. But I realized that if I attempted to retreat in fear, I would certainly end up that way. The only way to provide the kind of defense that we all needed was to stand up and stand together with others and continue to fight.

USA TODAY: Where did you draw strength?

DAVIS: From the knowledge that there were others who were standing together for me. I would not have been able to sustain myself without their assistance during the time I was underground running from the FBI. I never knew when I woke up in the morning whether or not I was going to be alive when the sun went down. But I did know that there were people organizing on my behalf.

USA TODAY: You grew up in Birmingham, Ala., which was often called Bombing-ham because there was so much white-sponsored violence against blacks. Has it changed?

DAVIS: I do see a difference in Birmingham. When I go home today I can walk across the street without fear of being arrested. When I was a child the neighborhood across the street was a white zone. Legally, black people were not allowed to walk in that neighborhood. I see black people in places where we were not allowed before. I don't see the signs on the water fountains or on the restrooms. But I do see an incredible amount of unemployment. I see the steel mills have shut down. Black people received subsistence wages from those mills. There is homelessness in Birmingham. There are more and more people going to prison. In 1987, there were 88 people on death row in the state of Alabama. More than 50 are black.

USA TODAY: Why do you still identify with

the radical segment of society?

DAVIS: "Radical" means to grasp things by the root, to understand the essence of things. I consider myself a radical because I always want to try to understand what is at the root of our problems as black people. There are some black people, I imagine, who feel as if they can sever their ties to the majority of black people. The overwhelming majority of black people are suffering more than ever before. There may be a few who are visibly better, but as Dr. King said: "There are those who climb out of the swamp on the shoulders of their sisters and brothers. And when they get out of the swamp they forget the stench of the backwaters." I don't want to forget the stench of the backwaters.

USA TODAY: What was your family life like in Birmingham?

DAVIS: Even though some may have called my family middle class, they didn't make very much money. My mother is a teacher. My father was a businessman. My parents could not have paid for the education that I received. I had scholarships all the way through school. They couldn't have afforded to send four children to college. I knew that my opportunities were purely a result of the struggles of black people. I happen to be one of the few to make it through the door. I am not saying that there is anything wrong with material wealth. As a matter of fact, what I am fighting for is the extension of that comfort to all people.

USA TODAY: The 1960s represent a decade of great theater, poetry and activism. Do you miss it?

DAVIS: I don't miss the '60s and the '70s. I am not nostalgic because I see something much more exciting happening now. I think there is often the tendency to romanticize the '60s. Many people who participated have forgotten how difficult it was to organize. Those movements did not emerge spontaneously. There were dedicated organizers, most of whom never received any credit. They were not the spokespersons. And many of them were black women who did that unglamorous, very difficult work of organizing.

USA TODAY: What do you want people to remember about you?

DAVIS: I want it said that I left my footprints here, that I was able to assist in forging something that can be handed down to generations.

MERVYN DYMALLY

Knowing that education is a key to success, he pushes for better science, math training

DYMALLY: 'If I had my magic wand and I were addressing all blacks . . . I would say there is no substitute for hard work and education.'

IMPRESSIONS

Ideas so often fall on infertile soil unless they can be cultivated. U.S. Rep. Mervyn Dymally bemoaned the lack of clout that Africa and the Caribbean had on Capitol Hill and in the other U.S. power centers. Moreover, he felt that if the USA is to remain a world leader, it must have trained minds — including minorities — in science and technology. To cultivate his ideas, Dymally helped found TransAfrica, a lobby and education center that has been at the forefront of the Free South Africa Movement. He also has launched a new institute to promote the training of minorities in math and the sciences.

— **Barbara Reynolds**

Mervyn Dymally, trained as a teacher of mentally retarded children, was the first black man to serve as lieutenant governor of California. He served in the state Assembly and Senate before winning a seat in the U.S. House of Representatives, where he is chairman of the Congressional Black Caucus. Dymally has focused the caucus's efforts on educating black children. He has fought for human rights in South Africa. Born in Trinidad, he is an advocate for the Caribbean and for economic development for poor people in the USA. An interview with Dymally appeared on the USA TODAY Inquiry page Sept. 23, 1987.

USA TODAY: You were born in Trinidad, West Indies. Why does it seem that black immigrants become more successful than blacks who are native U.S. citizens?

DYMALLY: Every West Indian's ambition was to become a doctor or lawyer. When I go to high schools I tell students what children in the Caribbean would do if they only had the opportunities for free education and low-cost state college education. We lived under colonialism, and education became a passion. That was the only way you could move up in the world. But it was a caste system and it was very hard to move up.

USA TODAY: You came to the USA at age 19. What kind of life were you living in Trinidad?

DYMALLY: I came from a rural village. My wife once told a friend, "I never understood Merv until I went to his village." The village was made up of Chinese and Asians and Indians and blacks and a few whites — all kinds of religions and everybody marrying each other. We married into different races, blacks, Chinese and Indians. And the Catholics married Moslems. My father is a Moslem. My mother is a Catholic.

USA TODAY: Would anyone who knew you in those days have said you were destined to become a congressman?

DYMALLY: Oh, no. In my youth I was drifting into the happy life that was taking place — a lot of fun and festivities. I did that until my mother summoned me to straighten up and fly right. I had failed my senior exam in Trinidad. Over there they don't pass illiterates as we do here. So I ended up as a gofer in a small weekly trade union. I began reading about historically black colleges and I got a book about Booker T. Washington and I began to say to myself: "If he can walk across the county to get an education to succeed in very adverse times, then surely I can go to the United States and if nothing else, get an education."

USA TODAY: What did you do then?

DYMALLY: I began writing to a number of schools in the United States. The cheapest was Lincoln University in Jefferson City, Mo., so I came to this country and went there. I was the first foreign student to attend Lincoln, and I was unable to cope with the discrimination. I wandered around looking for that tree of opportunity I had read about. I wound up in California because the weather was comparable to Trinidad. I became an elementary school teacher for the mentally retarded.

USA TODAY: How did you become involved in politics?

DYMALLY: I met Bobby Kennedy and Gus Hawkins and got involved with the Young Democrats in California and was elected treasurer of the organization. Later I was the first black to be elected to the California Senate.

USA TODAY: What happened in the Senate?

DYMALLY: I was faced with a great deal of racism. I said to myself: "I don't have the capacity to deal with racism. It's my one soft spot. What do I do if I have to quit the Senate?" So I got my master's degree. When I became lieutenant governor I also had to get a doctorate degree because of this West Indian drive. It was a commitment to my village and to my family.

USA TODAY: You also have a commitment to black children. Why did you focus the Congressional Black Caucus on educating black children?

DYMALLY: Why not black children? Studies done in urban schools prove that where there is leadership and a commitment from both the administrator and the teacher, the schools succeed in the midst of poverty and unemployment. As black members of Congress, we have a responsibility to black children. If we don't speak up and do something no one else will.

USA TODAY: Why are black children faring so poorly when some other minorities are succeeding?

DYMALLY: The education system is in crisis. America is underachieving. We are behind Asia and Europe. Black children are behind in America. Blacks are suffering a 40 percent high school dropout rate and a decline in college enrollment.

USA TODAY: Why do whites fare better?

DYMALLY: They go to more affluent schools, and there is a deeper commitment. But white children in America are still behind the children of Europe and Asia.

USA TODAY: What legislative proposals is the Black Caucus pushing to improve education?

DYMALLY: We have passed legislation that attempts to put some incentives for success in the school system. In the past if a school failed, it got more money. If a school succeeded there was no incentive to repeat the success. Schools that do not succeed will be held accountable and the schools that succeed will be given incentives to continue.

USA TODAY: What other Black Caucus efforts have helped upgrade the nation's schools?

DYMALLY: We see our duty as answering the challenge America faces in education and training, with an emphasis on science and math. Rep. Augustus Hawkins and his committee have worked hard to save historically black colleges. We have written measures into the Higher Education Act to prevent other institutions from ripping off funds that were reserved for historically black colleges.

USA TODAY: In 1987 the Congressional Caucus on Science and Technology, which you chair, launched an institute to encourage minorities to study the sciences. How did that come about?

DYMALLY: Only a handful of people in the country received Ph.D.s in physics in 1987. I don't know if there were blacks included. Blacks are not going into postgraduate work. They go up to the master's level, if we can get them that far, and then they go into the private sector. So we don't have any teachers to train teachers to teach the children. It is a larger picture than just training for jobs or training to compete with the Japanese or the Germans or the Russians.

USA TODAY: Why don't more children in the USA choose science and technical careers?

DYMALLY: A study comparing Asian and American students provided some very startling results. American parents felt that their children must be very bright to go into science and technology. The Asians felt there must be an interest.

USA TODAY: What has been most frustrating in your political career?

DYMALLY: In my years in the California legis-

DYMALLY PROFILE

Born: May 12, 1926, in Cedros, Trinidad.

Family: Married to Alice M. Gueno Dymally; two children, Mark and Lynn.

Education: Bachelor of arts from California State University, Los Angeles; master's in government from California State University, Sacramento; Ph.D. in human behavior from the United States International University, San Diego.

On life: "In my youth I was drifting into the happy life . . . until my mother summoned me to straighten up and fly right. I had failed my senior exam in Trinidad. . . . So I ended up as a gofer in a small weekly trade union. . . . I got a book about Booker T. Washington and I began to say to myself: 'If he can walk across the county to get an education to succeed in very adverse times, then surely I can go to the United States and . . . get an education.' "

Homes: Los Angeles, Washington, D.C.

Role models: Augustus F. Hawkins, Hubert Humphrey, Adam Clayton Powell, Dr. Martin Luther King Jr., John F. Kennedy, Mahatma Gandhi.

MILESTONES

1956: Taught mentally retarded children in Los Angeles.

1962: Elected to the California Assembly.

1966: Elected to the California Senate.

1975: Elected lieutenant governor of California.

1980: Elected to the U.S. House of Representatives.

1981: Appointed to the U.S. House Foreign Affairs Committee.

1986: Elected chairman of the Congressional Black Caucus, Washington, D.C.

1987: First Annual Caribbean Convention Award from Virgin Islands Chamber of Commerce; appointed chairman of Census and Population subcommittee.

lature, as lieutenant governor and in the Congress, the Reagan years have been the most frustrating because of a failure to move forward in providing subsidized housing, in strengthening equal opportunity. The Department of Justice is not enforcing the Voting Rights Act in the South. Reagan handles the Congressional Black Caucus the same way the Brazilians handle race relations — by not mentioning it. He met with Mikhail Gorbachev but he has never responded to our request for a meeting to discuss a number of problems in America, such as housing, education and jobs.

USA TODAY: How has the Reagan administration progressed on civil rights?

DYMALLY: It has been at a standstill. He has withdrawn from America's poor, blacks and minorities. It is as if you retain a lawyer to defend you and he goes to court and opposes you. Our lawyer — the Justice Department — is going to the Supreme Court and opposing everything done to bring about a measure of equal rights in the '60s. Funding has been withheld. Reagan has made racism very respectable by not supporting affirmative action.

USA TODAY: Which state do you predict will elect a black person to the U.S. Senate?

DYMALLY: It'll probably happen in a progressive state like California.

USA TODAY: You have gotten ahead quickly in the USA. What's the secret?

DYMALLY: If I had my magic wand and I were addressing all blacks in America, I would say there is no substitute for hard work and education. Once I was going to school in the day and working at night. I was falling asleep and the foreman came to me and said, "Dymally, have you ever played baseball?" I said, "Yeah, not too much." He said, "Well you know about three strikes?" I said, "Yes, why?" He said: "You got two strikes. One more strike and you're gone." I said, "Thank you sir." I decided that day — Oct. 15, 1951 — that there's no messing around. On that day I became a self-driven man.

MARIAN WRIGHT EDELMAN

She works to move the whole nation to care for children as her family did

EDELMAN: 'It is time for every one of us to roll up our sleeves and put ourselves at the top of our commitment list.'

IMPRESSIONS

"Save the Children" was one of those slogans that seemed to spring out of the 1960s. But Marian Wright Edelman was still around when the rhetoric died. She made the slogan a reality through the Children's Defense Fund, which provides a voice for those too young and vulnerable to speak for themselves. She doesn't talk much or often about herself. I am grateful to have had the chance to see beyond her cause and meet this woman who knows how to use her time to keep the children ever in mind.

— **Barbara Reynolds**

I *n 1965, Marian Wright Edelman became the first black woman admitted to the Mississippi Bar. She had been active in the '60s civil rights movement in the South. She went to Yale Law School after learning there were few black lawyers in Mississippi. Her next frontier was the rights of children. Edelman comes from a family that built churches together and cared for foster children and the aged. She founded the Children's Defense Fund in 1973. An interview with Edelman appeared on the* USA TODAY *Inquiry page Nov. 18, 1982.*

USA TODAY: In the 1960s, Mississippi was a dangerous place for blacks. Why, of all places in the USA, would you choose that state in which to practice law?

EDELMAN: My first night in Mississippi was in 1961. I rode with the famed civil rights leader Medgar Evers to Greenwood and watched police with dogs attack defenseless, innocent people. Some were old and walked with canes. The night before I arrived, there had been shootings. You could bite the terror. I remember going to the courthouse where people were being arrested for trying to register to vote. I was pushed down the steps. All three black lawyers in the state were located 100 miles away. I determined from that second to be a lawyer in Mississippi. I also admired the grit of the people and wondered if I could be as good as them. I still keep an office there.

USA TODAY: You grew up in the South. What stands out when you look back on your childhood?

EDELMAN: My father, Arthur, a Baptist minister, started the first black old-age home in South Carolina. When segregation laws prevented blacks in Bennettsville, S.C., from entering public parks, my father opened a park behind the church. That taught me if you don't like the way the world is, you change it. In fact, you have an obligation to change it. My mother ran a foster home for children and a home for the aged. I learned from my parents that service is what life is all about.

USA TODAY: Were you poor?

EDELMAN: We never considered ourselves poor, although my father never made more than $3,000 a year. When he died he had holes in his shoes. We laugh about how if we ever asked him for money he said he didn't have any change. We thought he just had a big bill. When he died he had two kids in college and one in divinity school. I was 14. He died the week before the 1954 Brown vs. Board of Education landmark school desegregation ruling. Every morning he would say, "Maybe the ruling is going to be today."

USA TODAY: Did he give you any advice?

EDELMAN: The last thing he said to me before he died was, "Don't let anything get between you and your education."

USA TODAY: What values did your parents instill in you?

EDELMAN: A deep sense of faith, of the importance of service to others. That service is what you are put on this earth to do. A deep sense of self-discipline, of the importance of discipline and hard work and persistence. Those are the good old common-sense values that I would like to see many more kids have. We have gotten away from the basics and too much into style. We have forgotten what gives life meaning.

USA TODAY: People talk a lot about role models. How important are they?

EDELMAN: Through role models we see how to serve and how to change the things we don't like. That is what so many black kids today are lacking. They don't have those adult backers. They don't have those clear values or regular rituals. They don't have the strong support systems that we had from a variety of community people.

USA TODAY: Who were your role models?

EDELMAN: A slave woman named Sojourner Truth. She couldn't read or write but she never gave up talking or fighting against slavery or second-class treatment of women. Once a heckler told Sojourner that he cared no more for her anti-slavery talk "than for a flea bite." "Maybe not," was her answer, "but the Lord willing I'll keep scratching." That is how I feel. I also admired Harriet Tubman and Frederick Douglass. I greatly admire the ordinary people in Mississippi who had and have grit. They didn't have a lot of education but they had a lot of wisdom, determination and the courage to change things for their kids.

USA TODAY: Was Dr. Martin Luther King Jr. also one of your role models?

EDELMAN: He was. My first airplane ride was to Raleigh, N.C., with King for a founding meeting of the Student Non-Violent Coordinating Committee. I was impressed by his leadership. I was impressed even more by the fact that he was an adult and he was not afraid to speak about his uncertainties, his fears. He introduced me to the idea of taking one step even if you can't see the whole stairway when you start. Now I have a greater capacity to accept failure and move on.

USA TODAY: What inspired you to organize the Children's Defense Fund?

EDELMAN: It was a logical extension of my work in Mississippi. I had worked with the Head Start program there, and on a number of issues including school desegregation. As counsel to the child development group in Mississippi, I found myself spending a lot of time in Washington trying to lobby and protect the program from attack by Southern U.S. senators. I realized the poor didn't have a voice for themselves in Washington to protect their interests. There were no advocates for children. Over the years, I also learned the most important lesson of all — if you could put together a coalition based on self-interest as well as justice, that coalition could cut across race and class. In 1973 I began to focus on children full time.

USA TODAY: The Children's Defense Fund has grown into a $4 million national operation with 60 staff members, offices in Mississippi and Ohio and state projects in Minnesota and Texas. How difficult was it to reach that kind of growth?

EDELMAN: A lot of people helped me. Nobody does anything alone. The initial ability to survive in Washington came from a fellowship from the Field Foundation, which gave me a year to make the transition from Mississippi to Washington.

USA TODAY: Why do children need a special lobby? Aren't they covered by other interest groups?

EDELMAN: The children are the poorest Americans; poverty afflicts 13 million of them. This poverty and lack of economic stability for their families stem from unemployment and an eroding wage base. The kinds of job shifts in the economy from manufacturing to service jobs mean more and more people are working and trying to head families. Many are working in very low-paying jobs. They cannot lift their families out of poverty.

USA TODAY: Do you think we have failed this generation?

EDELMAN: The jury is still out. We face a fundamental threat to the black community's survival and leadership capacity. We have got to make every effort to recapture and strengthen our families to re-

EDELMAN PROFILE

Born: June 6, 1939, in Bennettsville, S.C.

Family: Married to Peter Edelman; three children, Joshua, Jonah and Ezra.

Education: Bachelor of arts in social sciences, Spelman College, Atlanta; law degree, Yale University, New Haven, Conn.

On life: "A deep sense of self-discipline, of the importance of discipline and hard work and persistence. Those are the . . . values that I would like to see many more kids have. We have gotten away from the basics . . . We have forgotten what gives life meaning."

Home: Washington, D.C.

Role models: Harriet Tubman, Frederick Douglass, Sojourner Truth and Dr. Martin Luther King Jr.

MILESTONES

1958: Merrill Scholar at the University of Paris in Geneva, Switzerland.

1963: Staff member with the NAACP Legal Defense Fund in New York City.

1964: Named director of Mississippi's NAACP Legal Defense Fund.

1965: First black woman admitted to Mississippi Bar.

1966: Named Outstanding Young Woman of America by the Aetna Foundation.

1968: Named director of Harvard University Center for Law and Education.

1973: Founded Children's Defense Fund.

1979: Named Professional of the Year by *Black Enterprise* magazine.

1980: Received Leadership Award from the National Women's Political Caucus.

1985: Awarded $228,000 MacArthur Foundation fellowship.

1987: Received Congressional Black Caucus Foundation's William L. Dawson Award; *Family in Peril: An Agenda for Social Change* published.

capture our young people. We are losing far too many to drugs, alcohol and tobacco addictions. There are more young men going off to prison each year than to college. We have got to play a strong part because if our generation lets the black family and black youth go, then essentially we will be labeled a failure. It is time for every one of us to roll up our sleeves and put ourselves at the top of our commitment list. Our forebears did what they had to do to survive through slavery and segregation and resegregation. We, with the proper leadership, can do the same. But it is late and we have got a hard road ahead of us.

USA TODAY: What can others do to help save the children?

EDELMAN: Join our efforts. We use volunteers in local communities to make people more aware of what is going on with children, to do local assessments on adolescent pregnancy. We need lots of hands and lots of voices and lots of people who write letters on behalf of kids.

USA TODAY: What are your organization's goals?

EDELMAN: We want to see that every child has health care, every mother has access to prenatal care, every mother and child has adequate nutrition before and after birth. We want to see that every child has strong basic skills, that young people delay parenting and pregnancy until they are out of school and there is a job at the other end. We want every young person to think they can be something. We know that they can — if we give them the opportunity.

USA TODAY: Where do you get your inspiration?

EDELMAN: I try to be a Christian.

USA TODAY: Your husband, Peter Edelman, a former aide to Robert F. Kennedy, is Jewish. Does that cause any family confusion about worship?

EDELMAN: We have three wonderful sons. We let our children know that we believe in God and that the things that unite us greatly exceed those things that divide us. It is that deep religious belief and respect for other people that I hope they will carry on.

WALTER FAUNTROY

After fighting for rights in the South,
he's intent on winning full rights for D.C.

FAUNTROY: 'All that I am . . . I owe not only to my mother and father and their love for their children, but also to the church.'

IMPRESSIONS

Sometimes when I see him making his rounds throughout the District of Columbia, he raises his thumb toward the sky. I nod knowingly. We both recall one of his greatest sermons: *It's Time to Get Up*. It's Walter Fauntroy's call for action for all seeking change. Dr. Martin Luther King Jr. would be proud of this disciple. Fauntroy has been a good shepherd on social and foreign issues, challenging others to action. He consistently pushes against great opposition and often overwhelming odds for his causes. As a true believer in King, he knows that no matter how great the odds, we do overcome.

— **Barbara Reynolds**

His cause is statehood for the District of Columbia, and Walter Fauntroy is perched to run for the Senate seat if New Columbia comes to be. A preacher, politician and civil rights activist, he is known to break into song at the end of a speech or a sermon. His favorite is The Impossible Dream. *He was the first in his family to attend college, and his church helped pay the cost of his education. He has served for 16 years as the District of Columbia's non-voting delegate to the U.S. House of Representatives. A column by Fauntroy appeared on the* USA TODAY *Opinion page June 9, 1987.*

USA TODAY: You are now pushing for voting rights for the District of Columbia. These issues aren't new to you. Why do you stay involved?

FAUNTROY: I was outraged when I learned that simply because of the color of my skin, I couldn't eat at a place called the Little Tavern Shop in Washington, D.C. That's where they sold nice hamburgers for 5 cents. I had to purchase my food and take it outside to eat it. And I learned that my brothers and sisters who were in the South had to ride in the back of buses and drink water from separate fountains. If I went South, I had to pack a bag lunch because they wouldn't feed me at a restaurant. I was outraged.

USA TODAY: What did you do?

FAUNTROY: When I completed my training for the Christian ministry in the 1950s, I hooked up with another minister who asked the question, "What is the good news that our people want to hear?" And we responded, "That the 'For Whites Only' signs would be coming down." So we went to the polls to translate what we believed in into public policy and practice.

USA TODAY: How difficult was it for blacks to express themselves through the political process?

FAUNTROY: I learned that our people in the South were not allowed to participate in traditional politics. They could not say to someone running for city council, "I'll vote for you if you promise to take the 'For Whites Only' signs down." They could not even vote without passing a literacy test at the polls.

USA TODAY: How did the poll test work?

FAUNTROY: They would ask whites, "Who was the first president?" They would say, "George Washington." And they would say, "You can vote." They would ask the blacks, "How many bubbles are in a bar of soap?" And whatever answer was given was incorrect.

USA TODAY: How did you meet Dr. Martin Luther King Jr.?

FAUNTROY: I met him while he was a student at Boston University and I was a student at Virginia Union University. He came through and spent the weekend with me. We talked about our outrage. We talked about the fact that as human beings in training for public service as ministers, we were subjected to that humiliation. And we were going to do something to change it. We were not going to take what our parents had been forced to take.

USA TODAY: What was your family like when you were growing up in Washington, D.C.?

FAUNTROY: We were a typical urban family, for blacks. I am one of seven children. Eight originally. One died in my mother's arms at nearly two years of age from a form of indigestion. My father worked for 44 years as a messenger in the patent office and as a clerk. With that meager income, he eked out a livelihood sufficient to raise us and to inspire one of us to go into the ministry.

USA TODAY: Were you active in the church when you were growing up?

FAUNTROY: Oh, without question. All that I am and all that I hope to be I owe not only to my mother and father and their love for their children, but also to the church. I am the pastor of the church of my childhood, New Bethel Baptist Church. The members sold fried chicken and chitterlings to send me to college. They did it because they knew I wanted to go into the ministry.

USA TODAY: Is there a major obstacle that you had to overcome to achieve your goals?

FAUNTROY: The same that every black child has to overcome: The stigma of inferiority that can condition us to think that because we are black, because we are poor, because we come from the inner city, because our parents are not educated, we are not equal to others and we cannot achieve. I kept telling myself what they taught me in the church school: "I'm somebody. I'm a child of the King. And given the opportunity, I am able to excel in anything I do." I believed that if I was given the opportunity to go to school, I'd do well. And I said the same thing about running for Congress.

USA TODAY: How can this philosophy be used

to help poor and disadvantaged black children who seem to have no hopes for their future?

FAUNTROY: This kind of knowledge in the heads of some of these motherless and fatherless children may awaken them to say, "I may be a bastard child but I can be somebody."

USA TODAY: You have lobbied for the District of Columbia to become the 51st state. What has hampered the success of the statehood movement?

FAUNTROY: The narrow self-interest of some in the House and Senate. For example, there are legislators who have a rural interest and obviously they say: "Look, there will be two urban senators. They will be voting against me. So I am not going to allow them to have what I have." That's a narrow self-interest. And quite frankly there are those who have a racist orientation. They don't want those colored people represented.

USA TODAY: There are many who would agree that the District of Columbia should be able to vote for its own congressional representatives, but it doesn't need to be a full-fledged state. Do you agree?

FAUNTROY: I was born and grew up in this city. We pay more per capita in federal taxes than the residents of 49 of the 50 states. More of our young people were killed in the Vietnam War, per capita, than were killed in 47 of the 50 states. And they all died defending a democracy that district residents do not fully share.

USA TODAY: How would New Columbia, the 51st state, work?

FAUNTROY: It's not going to be much different from the District of Columbia of today. We already have an elected government that performs state functions. What we will be doing is electing a governor instead of a mayor. And instead of a 13-member city council, we'll elect a 25-member house of delegates. The federal Washington, D.C., the seat of federal government, will remain the same. The federal service area would include all the monuments, the White House, the Capitol and all federal agencies. That will be Washington, D.C. People will still fly in to National Airport in Virginia, come to Washington, D.C., and visit the museums and monuments and the Capitol and the White House.

USA TODAY: What would statehood provide?

FAUNTROY: In many areas we will be equal to other citizens. We will have full representation in the U.S. House of Representatives and the Senate. We will have budget autonomy. We are the only ju-

FAUNTROY PROFILE

Born: Feb. 6, 1933, in Washington, D.C.

Family: Married to Dorothy Fauntroy; a son, Marvin Keith.

Education: Bachelor of arts from Virginia Union University, Richmond, Va.; bachelor of divinity from Yale University, New Haven, Conn.

On life: "(The major obstacle I overcame was) the stigma of inferiority that can condition us to think that because we are black, because we are poor, because we come from the inner city, because our parents are not educated, we are not equal to others and we cannot achieve. I kept telling myself what they taught me in the church school: 'I'm somebody. I'm a child of the King.' "

Home: Washington, D.C.

Role model: Dr. Martin Luther King Jr.

MILESTONES

1959: Named pastor of New Bethel Baptist Church, Washington.

1963: D.C. coordinator for the March on Washington for Jobs and Freedom.

1965: Coordinator of the Selma-to-Montgomery march.

1967: Appointed vice chairman of the D.C. City Council.

1972: Elected to U.S. House of Representatives as non-voting delegate for the District of Columbia.

1973: Congress passes Home Rule Charter he designed, giving District of Columbia residents the right to elect their own mayor and city council.

1982: Elected chairman of the Congressional Black Caucus.

1985: Co-founder of the Free South Africa Movement; organizer and strategist for Jesse Jackson's presidential campaign.

1987: Served on House Select Committee on Narcotics Abuse and Control.

risdiction in the country that has to submit its budget to the Congress for approval of local matters. And we will have control of our court system.

USA TODAY: Why has there been so much opposition?

FAUNTROY: The opposition is simply from four sources. We call it the four "toos." The District of Columbia and its residents are too urban, too progressive, too democratic, and for some people, too black.

USA TODAY: What role do you expect to play once statehood happens?

FAUNTROY: If I am around when statehood comes, I will probably seek the Senate seat. I hope to be there trying to declare good news to the poor.

USA TODAY: You have said you have the hardest job of any member of Congress. Why?

FAUNTROY: I represent more tax-paying Americans than any member of the House of Representatives. And they all have ready access to me. On top of that, I don't have a vote. So I have to respond to more and am given less with which to respond. That's why I think we're going to have this change soon.

USA TODAY: You were elected to Congress in 1971. Why are you never opposed?

FAUNTROY: When I was first elected we could not elect our own mayor and city council. But I organized our people. I crossed the country in congressional districts, particularly across the South, to defeat some of our enemies against home rule. Eventually we got a bill passed that enabled us to elect our own mayor and city council, to do our own budgeting and tax matters. I continue to be elected because people believe that if I keep on working as I have been, I'm going to get all those other things that we are denied.

USA TODAY: Where do you want to be 10 years from now?

FAUNTROY: I have never done that kind of planning. But I plan to work for the best, hope for the best and take what comes. I might not be here 10 years from now. But I am going to die serving the Lord and trying to do the things that have enabled me to make some contributions to black life and culture.

KIM FIELDS

With values in place, she leaped from Harlem to glitter of Hollywood

FIELDS: 'Young people don't seem to care about other young people. Otherwise, people in school wouldn't say, "Man, take this drug." '

IMPRESSIONS

Kim Fields is easy to talk with. She isn't enamored of the Hollywood life. She's just a sweet kid who happens to be an actress. It is her mom, Chip Fields — an actress in her own right — who helps her stay that way. The Fields are born-again Christians and the church plays an important role in their lives. When out socially with Kim and her mom there is no drinking, smoking or swearing. There are no limousines taking them to the supermarket. Kim's greatest worry seems to be whether fans and friends love her for her role on *The Facts of Life* or for herself. The answer: a lot of both.

Kim Fields' days in the spotlight started with a Mrs. Butterworth's commercial and led to a successful run as one of four major characters on the television sitcom, The Facts of Life. *The series has kept her busy throughout her teen years, but she has not allowed the glamour of Hollywood — or its pressures — to take her away from her goals. She plans to produce and direct movies and television shows when she completes college. Her biggest fan and greatest asset is her mother, actress Chip Fields, who co-starred in the movie* Blue Collar *with Richard Pryor and starred in the Broadway play* Don't Get God Started. *Fields was interviewed for the* USA TODAY *Inquiry page on Sept. 14, 1987.*

USA TODAY: You have been acting about 12 years. What was it like growing up on TV?

FIELDS: It was very difficult. Your life is basically an open book. Crucial stages that really nobody but your mom and dad should be privy to are shared with millions of people all over the world.

USA TODAY: Like what?

FIELDS: Your first couple of dates, your first boyfriend, or crushes, the awkward or ugly stage that girls go through of baby fat and braces. Those are things that are real private, that not every girl wants to go through on national television. Of course, the overall belief is that you would prefer that because of the money, the education, the celebrity status and the other advantages. But there are some disadvantages. There are the normal pressures of the teen years, such as making good grades, being elected to the student government, making the cheerleading squad or getting to go out with the captain of the football team. Add to that the pressures that come with the demands of the job, like keeping weight off.

USA TODAY: What's the chemistry on your TV show *The Facts of Life*? Why does it work?

FIELDS: The chemistry among us four girls is something that no one really has been able to explain. But it comes from us growing up with each other and liking each other right off the bat. We are four extremely different characters, both on and off the show. We are not a threat to each other. We enjoy what we do. We enjoy being with each other and really making the show work.

USA TODAY: How did you get started?

FIELDS: My mom, Chip Fields, studied in New York and took me to acting classes with her because she couldn't afford a baby sitter. Eventually the company that my mom was with started a company for kids and we did small shows. When I was six, we moved to Los Angeles and I got a commercial for Mrs. Butterworth's syrup. That was my first job. And that's where it all started.

USA TODAY: Is it true that you actually had to hitchhike to make that commercial?

FIELDS: Yes. When we moved to California we didn't have much money or a car so we took the bus to the audition. As soon as we got back home, we got a telephone call that we needed to come back because the tape was messed up. At that hour buses had stopped running. So we hitchhiked. A nice man saw a little girl and her mom standing on the street corner and gave us a ride to the studio. He also brought us back.

USA TODAY: Was your mother your coach?

FIELDS: Yes, and as a coach she taught me a lot. I mostly observed her and learned a lot. I still do that today. I admire my mother a lot as an actress and have a tremendous amount of respect for her, for what she does.

USA TODAY: You were born in Harlem. Do you remember anything about living there?

FIELDS: Oh, yes. Harlem is the definition of a ghetto. I remember the people and the unhappiness in their eyes and the poverty of my neighbors and my community. But my mother made every effort to make sure that I was always happy. I remember the roaches and sleeping in the basement. I am so glad that we moved to Los Angeles. But the move was more like an adventure than anything else. I thought we were going to come back.

USA TODAY: Teen-agers have such problems coping. In Hollywood, pressures must be greater. How do you deal with pressures of work and family?

FIELDS: The bottom line is having a strong family life and a strong group of friends who support you and are there for you with your highs and your lows. But even before that is prayer and knowing the Lord, going to church, talking to my pastor, listening to the message, praying, listening to gospel music. These are things that really set me at peace and at rest with myself.

USA TODAY: How were your strong religious feelings formed?

FIELDS: My mother and I were doing a benefit musical dealing with the issues of young people for a church. We were asked to go to different churches to promote the show. One of the churches we attended moved me in a way that nobody could ever understand. There were many people who were coming forth and testifying about how they felt when they found the Lord. I was 14 and it had a profound effect on me.

USA TODAY: **Many people think of you as your television character, Tootie. How do you deal with people wanting Tootie as a friend rather than Kim?**

FIELDS: I am a very private person. I am very shy. I am more of an observer. I deal with those people who only care about Kim as Tootie or Kim as the celebrity with caution. I can recognize them immediately. And I pray about it and say: "Well, Lord does this person really want to be around me for me? If that's not the case, then take him or her out of my life." Now, if I can feel right away we could have a very good friendship going, then I am very open with that person.

USA TODAY: **Have you ever felt that you have been discriminated against?**

FIELDS: In my career, yes and no. On my show, no, because I and the other three girls on the show are treated equally. My character has never been stereotyped. Tootie is not a hooker. She's not an unwed teen mother. She doesn't use slang or carry a ghetto blaster or wear 12 earrings. And because of that, she has been able to cross over into every kind of audience in the world: black, white, Mexican, Chicano, Italian, German. Tootie is known and liked all over the world.

USA TODAY: **How have you been discriminated against in your career?**

FIELDS: As an actress and as a young black woman, we are discriminated against because you don't see us in movies or in many commercials or in the theater. Many people cannot imagine us in roles other than being pregnant, being slapped around or being a hooker. That's why I commend Robert Townsend for making *The Hollywood Shuffle*. He made a major statement that black actors and actresses have felt for a long time.

USA TODAY: **Do you see any similarities between yourself and Tootie?**

FIELDS: There are times when Tootie is a lot more immature or babyish than Kim is. And then there are times when she's a little bit more on the

FIELDS PROFILE

Born: May 12, 1969, in New York City.

Family: Single. Mother, Chip Fields; stepfather, Barry Hankerson.

Education: Majoring in telecommunications at Pepperdine University in Los Angeles.

On life: "Harlem is the definition of a ghetto. I remember the people and the unhappiness in their eyes and the poverty of my neighbors and my community. But my mother made every effort to make sure that I was always happy. I remember the roaches and sleeping in the basement. I am so glad that we moved to Los Angeles. But the move was more like an adventure than anything else. I thought we were going to come back."

Home: Los Angeles.

Role model: Her mother, Chip Fields.

MILESTONES

1974: Appeared as a walk-on in an episode of the children's TV program *Sesame Street.*

1976: First role in a Mrs. Butterworth's syrup commercial.

1978: Cast as Tootie on TV series, *The Facts of Life;* testified before the U.S. House of Representatives on behalf of the Youth Rescue Celebrity Peer Council.

1980: Guest appearance, *Mork and Mindy.*

1981: Guest appearance, *Good Times.*

1982: Served as March of Dimes Walk-America ambassador for three years.

1984: Released her first record, *Dear Michael,* a love letter to superstar Michael Jackson; youngest-ever campaign chairperson for the Brotherhood Crusade, an organization that provides funds to a variety of non-profit agencies in Los Angeles.

1987: Hosted Disneyland special with Tony Randall and one-hour TV special on teen pregnancy.

same level. We are alike because we are in the same year of college and we enjoy being around the girls.

USA TODAY: You have acted in themes dealing with drug abuse, drunken driving, suicide and even child abuse. Have those roles given you any insight into why people do these things?

FIELDS: It's a number of things. A feeling of being unloved or unaccepted by their parents or friends, peer pressure, poor self-images and feelings of inadequacy. Many people who don't have a strong support system of family and friends and who don't have God in their lives absolutely crumble when faced with problems. They turn to drugs, alcohol, suicide or just lose their minds.

USA TODAY: What should your generation do to help the disadvantaged?

FIELDS: In my generation everybody is so wrapped up in themselves they don't realize that's only taking them 500 steps backward. We need to start caring about each other. Young people don't seem to care about other young people. Otherwise, people in school wouldn't say, "Man, take this drug." But, of course, you have to care about yourself first. However, we are scared to death there's going to be a nuclear bomb, but we are not scared together.

USA TODAY: So you're a college student now?

FIELDS: I'm at Pepperdine University and I'm having a ball. I'm making excellent grades. My first semester I made a 3.65 grade point average. I'm a telecommunications major. I plan to produce and direct, maybe even write after graduation.

USA TODAY: What do you want to be doing 10 years from now?

FIELDS: I would like to be performing in any of four avenues: acting on stage, in films, on television and singing and dancing. Hopefully, in 10 years I would have covered all four of those avenues and been quite successful. Rather than covering them all at once and being pretty good or OK, I want to be fantastic in every way.

JOHN HOPE FRANKLIN

His studies make history come alive and help us understand each other

FRANKLIN: 'I certainly don't suffer under any illusion that everything is hunky-dory and we can all lie down in peace.'

IMPRESSIONS

He rates as one of the USA's greatest historians and a man who helped bring a very special black woman to life. She was Ida B. Wells, the gun-toting turn-of-the-century journalist who faced down Southern terrorists and campaigned against lynching. John Hope Franklin stepped in to help Wells' daughter, the late Alfreda Duster, get her mother's life story published. No one else had tried to help during the 30 years she lobbied. Before Duster died, she gave me an autographed copy and compared me to her mother. I cherish Franklin for making it all possible for me, the nation and the world.

— **Barbara Reynolds**

An internationally respected black historian, John Hope Franklin is the author of such classics as From Slavery to Freedom, *the epic historical work on blacks in the USA. An accomplished orator and writer, he has testified before Congress and was among the voices raised against the Reagan administration's nomination of Judge Robert Bork to the U.S. Supreme Court. He is committed to urging young men and women to study history to unlock the mysteries of the struggles and strengths of their ancestors and as a guide for what lies ahead. An interview with Franklin appeared on the* USA TODAY *Inquiry page Feb. 4, 1987.*

USA TODAY: In the early 1900s, your father became one of the first blacks licensed to practice law in Oklahoma. Was life any different for you than for other blacks of the era?

FRANKLIN: It had no bearing on how we were treated. My father, for example, became so frustrated trying to make it in the white world where judges refused to let him represent his clients and ordered him out of the courtroom, that he took his family to an all-black village. They would not let him practice. He simply said, "This is not a world I want to have anything to do with."

USA TODAY: Where did your father take you?

FRANKLIN: He took my mother, my sisters and my brother to Rentiesville, Okla., which was a little black village. That's where I was born. My father did not want us to grow up facing all these terrible people. There were relatively few ways a professional could make a living there. We stayed anyway. My father became postmaster, justice of the peace, notary public and about 16 other little things. But none of them really made a living. He finally went to Tulsa to practice law and came home on weekends. My mother taught at the local school.

USA TODAY: When were you first exposed to racism?

FRANKLIN: When I was 7 years old, we took a train trip. The train was loaded with people, so we just sat down in the white-only section. The conductor told us we had to move. My mother refused because we were going only six miles. The conductor stopped the train and put us out in the woods. That was a searing experience a 7-year-old lad would never, never forget.

USA TODAY: When you reached adulthood, had conditions for blacks improved?

FRANKLIN: Not much. Blacks did not even win that much after fighting in World War II.

USA TODAY: What do you mean?

FRANKLIN: In 1945 I was traveling from Greensboro to Durham, N.C., by train during the closing months of the war. The blacks aboard were crowded in a half coach while about five whites rode in a full coach. I suggested to the conductor that we exchange with them so we could all sit down. He told us those whites were German prisoners of war and they could not be moved. Those prisoners were watching us, laughing as we stood and stumbled because we didn't have anywhere to sit.

USA TODAY: You've described the stings of racism. Can you say that racism is gone now?

FRANKLIN: What do you mean it's gone? How can it be gone when a white English girl living in New York City tells me that I cannot visit her because her landlady said that if any black person comes into the building she is going out when that black person goes out. That happened in 1987. I don't mean that we haven't had changes, because we have. But I certainly don't suffer under any illusion that everything is hunky-dory and we can all lie down in peace.

USA TODAY: How far would you say blacks have come?

FRANKLIN: We have come a long way. Now maybe I don't have to go in the back door. Or maybe I can get something to eat somewhere. Black people should never forget that whites were not only committed to slavery, they were committed to the degradation of those black persons who were not slaves. Racism is deep, very deep.

USA TODAY: What is the importance of black history?

FRANKLIN: It's important first for blacks to know there are men and women among them who are of sterling character and extraordinary abilities and accomplishments. These people have stood the test of time. They have been measured by the most stringent, exacting standards that can be imposed. And whites, who have been too long subjected to stereotypical conceptions of blacks, also need the education that black history will give them.

USA TODAY: Is Black History Month enough to counteract the stereotypes?

FRANKLIN: No. People spend 11 months wallowing in the distorted and inaccurate stereotypes of blacks. They need 12 months of education to understand that blacks are human beings and as much a part of this country as anybody. Indeed, more than most Americans. After all, blacks have been here more than 300 years. This country is what it is because of the blood, sweat, toil and tears of blacks. And to deny them their rights is unconscionable.

USA TODAY: How are most black school children introduced to their history?

FRANKLIN: Almost invariably, elementary school children are introduced to blacks in American history through slavery. I have no problem with that. Slavery is a fact of life. White Americans — particularly those who fancy themselves as preservers of the great tradition of liberty and freedom — must be reminded that they are as guilty as almost anybody of kicking people down and holding them down. White people need to be reminded of that. Black people need to be reminded also that slavery is a part of their history.

USA TODAY: Why do blacks need to be reminded of the historical importance of slavery?

FRANKLIN: They have their own holocaust. And they need to know it. They need to understand it. If they don't, they won't understand who they are and where they are in 1988 or in the year 2000.

USA TODAY: What are the important lessons of history that blacks must know to progress?

FRANKLIN: We first have to be absolutely alert and aware that racism is very deeply entrenched and very, very virulent. We have to keep our eyes on the prize. Those of us who have the resources and who are articulate, those of us who know what the problem is or can see it must continue to analyze it.

USA TODAY: What do you mean "keep our eyes on the prize?" What prize, total equality?

FRANKLIN: In a sense. I am not interested in the political situation in the Persian Gulf until we can solve problems in this country. I am not interested in mining the harbors of Nicaragua while leaving unattended the economic and social problems in our own country. I just am not. I don't care how it sounds and looks. We simply have to take care of home first.

USA TODAY: What other lessons are beacons of black progress?

FRANKLIN: Blacks must be uncompromising

FRANKLIN PROFILE

Born: Jan. 2, 1915, in Rentiesville, Okla.

Family: Married to Aurelia Whittington Franklin; a son, John Whittington Franklin.

Education: Bachelor of arts from Fisk University, Nashville, Tenn.; Ph.D. from Harvard University, Cambridge, Mass.

On life: "We first have to be absolutely alert and aware that racism is very deeply entrenched and very, very virulent. We have to keep our eyes on the prize."

Home: Durham, N.C.

Role model: "I never list heroes or role models."

MILESTONES

1943: Professor of history at North Carolina College for four years; *The Free Negro in North Carolina* published.

1947: Professor of history at Howard University, Washington, D.C.; *From Slavery to Freedom: A History of American Negroes* published; appointed to the board of directors of Illinois Bell.

1950: Guggenheim Fellow.

1956: Appointed professor of history and chairman of the Department of History at City University's Brooklyn College in New York City.

1960: Taught at Australian National University, Canberra, as distinguished American Fulbright professor.

1963: Appointed professor of American history at the University of Chicago, authored *The Emancipation Proclamation.*

1976: *Racial Equality in America* and *A Southern Odyssey: Travelers in Antebellum North* published.

1982: Appointed James B. Duke professor of history, Duke University, Durham, N.C.

1987: Testified against the nomination of Judge Robert Bork to the U.S. Supreme Court; *From Slavery to Freedom: A History of American Negroes* reissued.

in their willingness, in their determination to reject racism as un-American. They must hold white America to its professions of a belief in equality through legislation and the courts if necessary. We can do that only if judges and legislators are the kind that will listen to reason. We must function in the electoral process and turn out of office the people who have no sense of what our problems are and elect to office people who have some commitment to equality.

USA TODAY: What are your thoughts on those who are caught up in crime, alcohol and drug abuse?

FRANKLIN: Those poor people have been driven to that by social, economic and political circumstances over which they had no control. But we've got to speak for them, act for them and work for them. We don't do that by waving the flag and shouting about vengeance toward the Iranian government or some other foreign power.

USA TODAY: Is racism the biggest foe?

FRANKLIN: I don't know. I do know that this nation could have a policy that could do something for dependent children, for single parents that could modify our welfare program in such a way as to stimulate pride. Instead, the government is undercutting advances we have made. They talk about welfare queens and other things that mean nothing. They leave the people who need help alone, unconsoled, unaided and irreformable. Those people need somebody who has the resources to help them move up.

USA TODAY: What do Jesse Jackson's presidential bids say for the USA?

FRANKLIN: It is a great experience for this country. This country needs the experience of having an able, attractive, articulate, black candidate. This country needs to mow down the stereotypes and notions about blacks. They can't imagine the Negro talking about problems other than civil rights. And when he is able to talk about foreign policy in the Middle East or in the Far East or in South Africa or in Europe or on financial or fiscal policies in the United States, import, export, immigration — they need to hear this.

MARY HATWOOD FUTRELL

Reforms to help 'at-risk' children
top her agenda for USA's teachers

FUTRELL: 'Without adequate resources we cannot maintain existing programs and provide high-quality services to the children.'

IMPRESSIONS

Flying south, we were braced along the sides of a plane that was so small it resembled a tube of toothpaste. Fear aside, Mary Hatwood Futrell didn't miss the chance to brief me on how the National Education Association was improving the nation's schools. She's committed to improving schools. She came from an impoverished, segregated school system. And she remembers that her teachers knocked down some of the barriers that society and circumstances had imposed on her life. What makes her special? She still has that burning desire to give back. What does she give? Herself.

— **Barbara Reynolds**

As president of the National Education Association, Mary Hatwood Futrell has reform at the top of her agenda for the nation's teachers. She's a strong advocate for students and teachers and is committed to improving the chances of minority students and the disadvantaged. She established Operation Rescue to cut the enormous number of student dropouts across the USA. The program earmarks $1 from each NEA member's yearly dues. She hopes to reach these young people before it is too late. Interviews with Futrell appeared on USA TODAY Inquiry pages May 8, 1984, and July 14, 1987.

USA TODAY: You are one of the nation's most recognizable teachers. What impact did teachers have on you as a child?

FUTRELL: My teachers reinforced what I was taught at home: that nothing — not poverty, race, sex nor peer pressure — would ever be enough of an excuse for my not achieving in school. My teachers held high expectations, both academically and behaviorally. They opened whole new worlds for me — the worlds of Shakespeare and Chaucer and Socrates, the worlds of math, science, history and business. As I look back, I think the only time they ever failed was when they tried to teach me to sing. They were, after all, human. Later these teachers not only helped me get grants to attend college, but raised money through local churches to help finance my education.

USA TODAY: As a teacher and while president of the National Education Association, have you ever been tempted to quit?

FUTRELL: I know of no more moving expression of the inspiration that comes with knowing how critical our work is than a poem by Ivan Fitzwater in a volume that is titled *Teachers Make a Difference*. By now I have memorized those words: "I am a teacher. What I do and say are being absorbed by young minds who will echo these images across the ages. My lessons will be immortal, affecting people yet unborn, people I will never see or know. The future of the world is in my classroom today, a future with the potential for good or bad. The pliable minds of tomorrow's leaders will be molded either artistically or grotesquely by what I do . . . I must be vigilant every day lest I lose one fragile opportunity to improve tomorrow."

USA TODAY: You grew up in Altavista, Va. How would you describe your childhood?

FUTRELL: My family was very poor. My mother, a widow with two young daughters, had to raise her children alone on the salary she earned working as a maid and short-order cook for $15 a week. But what I remember most is that she never let adversity in any way dilute the emphasis she placed on education. Neither my mother nor my teachers were ever easy on me. They both set high standards. I also grew up in a segregated community and we had separate schools. They were unequal schools because many of the programs and services in the white schools were not available in the black schools. But I was fortunate in that I grew up in a caring family and had teachers who said the only limits that you will have will be those you impose on yourself.

USA TODAY: Why did you become a teacher?

FUTRELL: I wanted to emulate those who had had a tremendous influence on me. I wanted the opportunity to return something to the society that had given so much to me.

USA TODAY: You became president of the NEA in 1983, the same year that the *A Nation at Risk* report warned of a rising tide of mediocrity in the nation's education. How do you rate the reforms since then?

FUTRELL: We are now stripping away the outer garments and looking at the tough issues: How are we going to address the at-risk children? How are we going to raise standards for not only the profession but also the children who are coming out of schools? How are we going to do a much better job of educating young people? What we're beginning to face now are the hard decisions about where do we get the resources, where do we get the time, where do we get the support, how do we involve teachers in that decision-making process? Unless we answer those hard questions, we will have a very superficial reform movement.

USA TODAY: One reform the NEA accepted was competency testing for new teachers. Many have failed the tests. What can be done to help?

FUTRELL: We're trying to encourage school districts to form partnerships with colleges and universities to make sure that we teach students what they will need to know to meet the requirements to get into college, to graduate from college, and to get into a profession. As we look at those standards — especially those relating to minority students —

we're finding that many minority students are not enrolled in academic programs. If they are to be more successful they must have the proper educational background.

USA TODAY: Are local school systems equipped to deal with the reforms needed?

FUTRELL: Unfortunately, too many states and localities — and I marvel at what they have done so far — have not been able to make up the difference in funding following federal education cutbacks. They have their own budgetary problems. They are having to divert funds to offset the cuts made by the administration.

USA TODAY: Does the NEA believe the federal government should increase education funding?

FUTRELL: We are told to do more and to help children achieve at higher levels. We need support. Without adequate resources we cannot maintain existing programs and provide high-quality services to the children. It will be very difficult to implement education reforms that have passed not only at the national level but at the state and local levels as well. No national effort to keep both high standards and students in school can succeed fully without the ongoing help of the federal government.

USA TODAY: How does the NEA feel about AIDS education in the classroom?

FUTRELL: We believe sex education courses should be made available in all schools to give young people appropriate information so they can decide whether to become sexually active. They need to know the pitfalls. Hopefully some will be encouraged to abstain so they will not get pregnant or get AIDS. We're also working with the U.S. surgeon general to develop guidelines for the schools.

USA TODAY: Would the NEA advocate condom use or other contraceptives for students?

FUTRELL: I am sure that part of what we will advocate is abstinence and then sex education designed for the appropriate age level. We also have indicated that we will advocate and support communities pursuing the concept of clinics in the schools. The communities will have to decide whether those clinics will distribute any birth control devices. That will not be a decision made by us.

USA TODAY: Some educators are calling for children to start school as 4-year-olds. What is your opinion?

FUTRELL: I have called for NEA members to be much more aggressive in pursuing the develop-

FUTRELL PROFILE

Born: May 24, 1940, in Altavista, Va.

Family: Married to Donald Futrell.

Education: Bachelor of arts from Virginia State University, Petersburg; master's from George Washington University, Washington, D.C.

On life: "My teachers reinforced what I was taught at home: that nothing — not poverty, race, sex nor peer pressure — would ever be enough of an excuse for my not achieving in school."

Home: Lorton, Va.

Role models: Her mother, Josephine Austin; Dr. Martin Luther King Jr. and John F. Kennedy.

MILESTONES

1963: Began teaching career at all-black Parker-Gray High School, Alexandria, Va.

1967: Organized a minority caucus within the Virginia Education Association.

1973: Elected president of the Education Association of Alexandria, Va.

1976: Elected president of the Virginia Education Association.

1978: Re-elected president of the Virginia Education Association.

1980: Elected secretary-treasurer of the National Education Association for a two-year term.

1983: Elected president of the National Education Association for a two-year term.

1984: Received American Black Achievement Award.

1985: Elected to a second two-year term as NEA president.

1986: Named one of USA's top 100 Black Business and Professional Women by *Dollars & Sense* magazine.

1987: Re-elected NEA president.

ment of programs for 4-year-olds. This would help the children have better skills and attitudes so when they enter kindergarten and first grade they will start with a stronger foundation. They will have a much higher level of self-confidence and self-esteem as they enter the regular school program.

USA TODAY: Does starting school so early rob children of their childhood?

FUTRELL: Studies show that young people who participate in preschool programs tend to be much more successful academically than students who do not. These programs should be open to all parents who wish to enroll their children whether they are disadvantaged children or not. But they should primarily focus on disadvantaged children to give them a better opportunity of being successful in their academic pursuits.

USA TODAY: Why are so many students dropping out and what does that mean for the rest of us?

FUTRELL: Our dropout crisis reflects problems that have been festering in our society's core for far too long. Poverty, adolescent pregnancy and substance abuse are only some of the factors that drive children out of school. In the end, they earn less than high school graduates and that translates into lower tax revenues and economic productivity. We pay more than $75 billion a year in unemployment, welfare and other costs. Even our democratic system of government is in jeopardy. Dropouts mean a less-educated electorate.

USA TODAY: What can we do to overcome the dropout problem?

FUTRELL: We can develop innovative community partnerships to grapple with the causes. We can develop special support programs to provide tutorial and remedial assistance to students at risk of dropping out. We can invest in our nation's future.

NIKKI GIOVANNI

In the '60s her poems 'photographed' life; now they 'paint' life's richer images

GIOVANNI: 'We made a change in the world. Black Americans owe it to ourselves to say, "Congratulations, well done!"'

IMPRESSIONS

When my first nephew was born, I convinced my sister to name him Giovanni. In the 1960s, Nikki Giovanni's poem, *Ego-Tripping,* became such a hit that the hand-clapping beat and gutsy lyrics stuck in my heart. I was certain Giovanni was a name of an African prince, certain that Nikki had assumed that name during the decade when name-changing was common for those of African descent. Everyone looked the other way when my grandmother said, "That's an Italian name." After Nikki and I became friends, I asked about her African name. "African? That's my family name. It's Italian."

— **Barbara Reynolds**

Nikki Giovanni began her career as a writer and poet during the 1960s when poetry was a staple of the civil rights and youth movements. She has written books and has lectured to packed audiences throughout the USA and abroad. In 1971 she had a gold record with a gospel album featuring one of her poems. She teaches creative writing and literature at Virginia Polytechnic Institute in Blacksburg. An interview with Giovanni appeared on the USA TODAY *Inquiry page Sept. 19, 1985.*

USA TODAY: In the 1960s you were one of the pre-eminent figures in black literary circles. What were you trying to accomplish?

GIOVANNI: I was trying to say what I thought. I was more a photographer. I am more a painter now.

USA TODAY: What do you mean "a painter?"

GIOVANNI: As a photographer I was trying to capture the moment because we as a people did not have a voice. And during that period we didn't have that many people to explain what we were feeling and the rightness of that desire. In the '80s we really are a capable people. Now I don't have the obligation to speak for anyone. There is a multitude of voices out there and there should be. Painters get to paint what they see, what they believe, as distinguished from a photographer, who can only photograph what is there.

USA TODAY: Weren't you vitriolic in the 1960s?

GIOVANNI: That's a big word. I am alive with change, new ideas and creativity. But, vitriolic I won't accept. I think I must have been quite charming. I was looking over an *Ebony* article about me that came out in 1971. The title was *I am Black, Female and Polite.* I was always polite. I was not angry. I wanted change but you can't make change without the people who have to live with change.

USA TODAY: You did a gospel album in 1971 that featured a gutsy, hand-clapping poem called *Ego-Tripping.* Where did that idea come from?

GIOVANNI: *Ego-Tripping* was really written for a little girl. I almost hate to say that because little boys like it. I really got tired of hearing all of the little girls' games, such as *Little Sally Walker.* You

get so sick of that crap. And they were always turning to the east and to the west. It was tiresome.

USA TODAY: How successful was the album?

GIOVANNI: It went gold. But I did not know enough about the record industry to protect myself. I got about $500. And then I sued, and I won. I am just not fond of the record industry. It is a difficult industry for me and I have been burned. I cannot stand aggravation. Rather than be aggravated, I have avoided it.

USA TODAY: How do you evaluate black progress now that we are in the 1980s?

GIOVANNI: We have done damn well. I remember going downtown in Knoxville, Tenn., and not being able to get a glass of water. If you remember things like that, then you know we've come a long way. Then there was a big amusement park that we got to go to only once a year. To this day I hate amusement parks.

USA TODAY: How did those events affect your family?

GIOVANNI: I tried not to put a lot of my hatred onto my son. I hope that I have been successful. And I hope that his generation does not have to live with our bad memories. We as blacks want to live in the past to some degree. And I have said that in my book, *Sacred Cows and Other Edibles.* I don't think we want to recognize that something did happen. We made a change in America. And we made a change in the world. Black Americans owe it to ourselves to say, "Congratulations, well done!"

USA TODAY: What should be the focus of the USA's black community in the future?

GIOVANNI: The question is: Where do you place the demands? For example, teen-age pregnancy. We don't place demands on the boys. A lot of us are concerned but we pretend it is all right because there was a sexual revolution going on. But they are children. They should not be a part of any revolution, sexual or otherwise. I see the kids in what we would call predominantly white colleges. Many are not doing well. I think it is because they thought there was paradise out there. But it is just an opportunity to do better.

USA TODAY: Where are other opportunities?

GIOVANNI: It pains me when I look at the drug scandals from some of our athletes. It pains me that we can put a young man in a position to make a couple of million dollars and he has to snort cocaine and get arrested. That's appalling. Or he cannot read or write. And then you are saying: "What do you think we sent you to college for — to play in the pros? No we didn't. We sent you to college to be educated." And this is how we made it possible: We opened up a lot of doors. A lot of people thought it was magic. But there is no magic.

USA TODAY: You seem concerned about the future of the black family. Why did you choose to have a child and not marry the father?

GIOVANNI: People would say to me I shouldn't have done it because I was a role model. Well, I was 26 and making about $50,000 a year. I could afford to have a child and not marry. If people aren't willing to look at the whole picture, they have no right to imitate.

USA TODAY: Are you comfortable in your 40s?

GIOVANNI: I recommend it. It's like being in a cave. You have been in the cave and you have gone through the mold. And somebody says we are ready for you now. It is a total blossoming. I really like it. Your kids graduate. Thomas, my son, and I went to Paris when he was 18. It's been great fun getting to know him as a young man. We are having a ball. It is a whole new perspective on life.

USA TODAY: Who is your audience?

GIOVANNI: I think that 99 percent of the time I am fortunate that my audience is limited but intelligent. I have not had a best seller. Most of the people who were reading me still like what I am doing because they were going through the same changes. They had their children when I did. They had termites when I did. You know, the normal stuff. And that's a part of it.

USA TODAY: You suggest that you are just Nikki Ordinary. Are you being too modest?

GIOVANNI: I am ordinary. It is just that I am bright. That's probably the only difference. Mentally, I am an Edwin Moses. Probably anybody that practiced the way that he could, could run as fast. But others won't practice that way. I am an integrated personality.

USA TODAY: What do you mean?

GIOVANNI: I can take on anybody or any subject on any given day. On any given day you have a lot of things to do. You have to feed somebody, your child, your husband, your mother, whoever. You are cooking. You are cleaning. You are also looking out and you are seeing the world. Me? I feel something is missing because I didn't get to my birds today. I didn't get out to put my water in my

GIOVANNI PROFILE

Born: June 7, 1943, in Knoxville, Tenn.; name originally was Yolande Cornelia Giovanni Jr.

Family: Single; a son, Thomas Watson Giovanni.

Education: Bachelor of arts from Fisk University, Nashville, Tenn.

On life: "We have done damn well. I remember going downtown in Knoxville, Tenn., and not being able to get a glass of water. If you remember things like that, then you know we've come a long way. Then there was a big amusement park that we got to go to only once a year. To this day I hate amusement parks."

Home: Cincinnati.

Role models: Her mother, Yolande Giovanni; her grandmother, Louvenia Watson; past president of Delta Sigma Theta sorority, Lillian Benbow; Robert Kennedy.

MILESTONES

1968: Wrote the book *Black Feeling, Black Talk.*

1969: Named one of 10 Most Admired Black Women by *Amsterdam Daily News,* New York City.

1970: Founded Niktom, Ltd. publisher.

1971: Recorded her poetry *Truth Is On Its Way;* wrote the book *Spin A Soft Black Song.*

1972: Received Woman of the Year — Youth Leadership Award from *Ladies Home Journal;* life membership scroll of the National Council of Negro Women.

1973: Nominated for a National Book Award for *Gemini.*

1983: Published *Those Who Ride the Night Winds;* YWCA Woman of the Year.

1986: Co-chair of the Literary Arts Festival, State of Tennessee Homecoming.

1987: *Sacred Cows and Other Edibles* published.

bird bath until about 5 a.m. That's a part of what I do because I enjoy my birds. I miss that if I don't do it. But there are things going on in this world.

USA TODAY: What issues do you care about?

GIOVANNI: I am concerned about illiteracy. I am concerned about hunger, about people not being able to feed themselves. I am not so interested in how do we ship grain out. I am interested in how we make a system that people can plant and know that the crops will be there.

USA TODAY: What else do you care about?

GIOVANNI: I love space a lot. I really like the fact that this generation accepts it. I am very happy that we now have a black female astronaut. I have bitched about it. I have written the White House. I wanted to be an astronaut. They said they didn't want me because I smoke. We need a smoker in space. We need somebody ordinary. We need a smoker just to find out if you can inhale in weightlessness. But I am glad to see that with Dr. Mae Jemison, we are going to get a black female up there.

USA TODAY: Why did you become a poet?

GIOVANNI: I don't think I have any other identifiable skills. If you wait you will find what you are good at. Waiting is like prayer. It's action. You prepare and prepare and prepare. Then you see where you are. Writing is a marvelous profession.

USA TODAY: You made a few enemies in 1985 because of erroneous reports that you had performed in South Africa. How did you make it through that difficult period?

GIOVANNI: I did finally talk to the principles involved. And they were saying, "Oh, it was a mistake." And I asked them to please admit it publicly because it is a mistake that hurts. I had a career in excess of 20 years, and I had never been hurt before. I picked myself up and went back and talked to people and explained what had happened. My friends came through. My family — my mother, sister, son and friends — always come through.

USA TODAY: What do you think about life?

GIOVANNI: Life is fun. I recommend laughter. And I say this to the kids too. You cannot assume that the Earth is going to come to a stop. You must assume that we are not going to have a nuclear war. Why? Because you don't want to be disappointed 30 years later when you find the Earth is still here and you are still alive. You must assume love.

DICK GREGORY

He uses fasting to focus attention
on human and political issues worldwide

GREGORY: 'Once you see the beauty of the black struggle from within, it's hard not to be totally committed.'

IMPRESSIONS

There is nothing on earth to compare with Dick Gregory. A free spirit, he makes his own rules, fitting comfortably into the roles of athlete, comedian, social critic, international jet-setter, guru, naturalist, entrepreneur and practical joker. I have written about him as he prayed and fasted in Tehran for U.S. hostages. I have accompanied him into famine-wrenched Ethiopia. Along with his wife, Lil, I followed him to the beaches of the Bahamas, to New York, Philadelphia and parts of New England. His radar is tuned to a sense of right that keeps him moving from issue to issue, continent to continent.

— **Barbara Reynolds**

From comedy to civil rights to nutrition, Dick Gregory has become a master of many things. He is the founder and chairman of Correction Connection Inc., which produces and sells products to help people end their addictions. The father of 10 children, he moved his family from Chicago to Plymouth, Mass., in 1973 to give them "clean air and the experience of nature." A civil and human rights activist, he has fasted for causes and met with world leaders to press the need for a commitment to world peace and human rights. He has received more than 100 awards for his work in civil and human rights. Interviews with Gregory appeared on USA TODAY Inquiry pages Oct. 22, 1984, and May 18, 1987.*

USA TODAY: Your company produces not only a weight-loss product but, more recently, a product to control substance abuse. Why are you treating drug abuse as a nutritional issue?

GREGORY: People who abuse drugs in any form — nicotine, caffeine, alcohol or drugs — usually have a need for vitamin A or vitamin B, which are destroyed in the body by drugs. You have to put those vitamins back before you can deal with the cravings. We are using the Correction Connection in various jail and drug-abuse programs. And like the Bahamian Diet, we can't produce it fast enough. Both products are selling out.

USA TODAY: Back to weight loss. Why are so many people obese?

GREGORY: Because they're not getting the right nutrients when they sit down at the dinner table. If the body has the proper nutrients, it tends to have fewer cravings for food. When you get thirsty, that is your body saying you need liquid in the body. Once you drink liquid the craving leaves. With a good physical fitness program your whole system functions better. You digest your food better. The metabolism works better.

USA TODAY: Are you saying we overeat because our body malfunctions?

GREGORY: Yes. One thing that puts on a lot of weight is drinking cold drinks while eating. Your stomach digests your food at a temperature of 121 degrees-plus, just like an incubator. So if I'm eating and I'm drinking iced tea or a cold glass of water, I lower the temperature of the stomach and that stops the process of digestion.

USA TODAY: Aren't you a poor salesman for nutrition since you don't always look healthy?

GREGORY: I don't think that has anything to do with it. I've never seen anybody who is heavily into whiskey who looks healthy. And that is a billion-dollar industry. Go beyond what I look like. I don't look my age. I'm 55 years old. I ran from New York to Los Angeles, averaging nearly 50 miles a day for 71 days. The whole world watched when I came off of a 70-day fast and walked and ran that 100 miles from New Orleans to Baton Rouge.

USA TODAY: You have almost starved to death several times while fasting to protest social problems. Why do you choose fasting?

GREGORY: One thing I have always been able to do is reach up to a higher level. Fasting does that. But I do not assume that everybody should reach that level.

USA TODAY: What does fasting accomplish?

GREGORY: Fasting cleanses the body. It helps me because I can take the visibility that God has permitted me and focus that on the social problem. And I don't have to go through a guilt trip about not using this talent to give back to the community.

USA TODAY: Why do you have such a strong commitment to social change?

GREGORY: We understood from the beginning that the civil rights movement was bigger than me, bigger than my wife, Lillian, and bigger than our children. This movement is so big that there is no way we could worry about what might happen to me. Instead we have to worry about what impact we can have. Once you see the beauty of the black struggle from within, it's hard not to be totally committed.

USA TODAY: Is it true you have donated about $13 million to social-action groups?

GREGORY: When I signed the Bahamian Diet contract, one of the promises I put in the contract was that we would be able to give $1 million apiece to about 15 organizations in this country that I feel have worked to make not just this country, but the world, a better place. What we would do is give them $100,000 a year for 10 years.

USA TODAY: Which organizations received these donations?

GREGORY: The Southern Christian Leadership Conference, Mrs. Martin Luther King Jr.'s foundation, the NAACP, Ralph Nader's group, the Salvation Army, the Red Cross, the United Negro College Fund, the National Council for Negro Women, the Jesse Owens Foundation, the National Urban League, the Rosa Parks foundation, Father Clements' foundation in Chicago to adopt black children and Amnesty International.

USA TODAY: Over the years people have said, "Dick Gregory is crazy." Does that bother you?

GREGORY: What bothers me is that when Dick Gregory was smoking four packs of cigarettes and drinking a fifth of Scotch a day, weighed 300 pounds and hadn't exercised in 15 years, nobody said I was crazy. Nobody worried about my health! Now I'm one of the healthiest human beings on the planet and people question my health — my mental attitude. If I ever came close to being crazy it was when I was in those nightclubs abusing my body.

USA TODAY: You often say growing up black in the USA means cigarettes, soda pop, candy bars, dope, beer and whiskey. What do you mean?

GREGORY: It is no accident that when I was coming up anytime a black wanted to borrow some money to open up a cleaners, to open up a legitimate business, they told him he couldn't borrow it. But he could borrow money to open up a nightclub or a liquor store. The money is there when it is for shucking and jiving. But when it is for serious business it is not available.

USA TODAY: Your family was on welfare from 1932 to 1950. How do you remember that time?

GREGORY: My mother was dead at 42. She worked herself to death. My father died when he was in his 60s. He was a chef, a cook. He and mom were never together that much. He worked on the railroad. She loved him and whenever he came home, she was happy to see him. She never knew when he was going to come home. Every day she was ready for him to walk in the house. There were some times he wouldn't come home for three or four years. So we never really knew our father other than through our mother.

USA TODAY: What was your mother like?

GREGORY: She was the type of woman who smiled all the time. When she did, it was like the sun was in her mouth. It was an honor to know her, let alone be her child. She loved her children. There were four boys and three girls.

USA TODAY: How did you discover that humor was your forte?

GREGORY PROFILE

Born: Oct. 12, 1932, in St. Louis.

Family: Married to Lillian Gregory; 10 children, Michelle, Lynne, Paula, Pamela, Stephanie, Gregory, Christian, Ayanna, Missy and Yohance.

Education: Attended Southern Illinois University, Carbondale.

On life: "One thing I have always been able to do is reach up to a higher level."

Home: Plymouth, Mass.

Role models: His mother, Lucille Gregory; his wife, Lillian Gregory; Dr. Martin Luther King Jr. and Malcolm X.

MILESTONES

1961: Opened as a comedian at Chicago's Playboy Club.

1962: *From the Back of the Bus* published.

1964: *Nigger: An Autobiography* published.

1965: *What's Happening* published.

1967: Fasted 40 days in protest against the Vietnam War.

1968: Received 200,000 votes as a write-in presidential candidate.

1971: *No More Lies: The Myth and Reality of American History* published.

1973: *Dick Gregory's Natural Diet for Folks Who Eat: Cookin' With Mother Nature* published.

1974: *Dick Gregory's Bible Tales* published.

1978: Co-wrote with Mark Lane *Code Name Zorro: The Murder of Dr. Martin Luther King, Jr.*

1980: Fasted more than four months in Iran during hostage crisis; met with Ayatollah Khomeini.

1984: Developed the Bahamian Diet.

1987: Founded Correction Connection Inc. to produce and market the Bahamian Diet and other nutrition products.

GREGORY: I knew from my early school days when the dudes would stand on the corner and talk about one another's mama. If you were rapping strong and everybody was laughing with you, the whole crowd was on your side. So I would lay up at home and practice.

USA TODAY: During the 1960s you criticized the government. How were you treated?

GREGORY: They spied on me 24 hours a day. They brought new agents in and lied to them and told them I was a threat to national security. But they always knew what I was talking about because I don't keep any secrets. The minute I find out anything I tell it.

USA TODAY: You never seem to be afraid. Are you just a pro at disguising fear?

GREGORY: I am a pro at being serious about my God. If my God can't keep some slimy filth off me — like the FBI, the CIA or the Mafia — I'll be the first one to say I'm praying to the wrong thing. I know my God can protect me. That's not debatable. I call him the Universal God Consciousness.

USA TODAY: What do you mean by that?

GREGORY: That same universal force that works in the whole universe, where there is no Jesus, where there is nothing but Buddha and where there is nobody but Allah. The God who I pray to is as universal as the moon is universal.

USA TODAY: You and Lillian have 10 children. How would you describe your relationship?

GREGORY: Let me describe her first. If God came back to this planet today I could recognize God because He would have to look and act like her. And if He didn't then I'd know it wasn't God.

USA TODAY: Fighting for so many causes keeps you away from home. How do you feel about being away from your children?

GREGORY: Let me answer it this way. I'm your husband. We have five children. The war breaks out in Vietnam. They draft me. I get blown away. What about my responsibilities to my children? What about all the fathers that march off to war, that get blown away? Nobody asks them, "What about your children?" At least the choice to be away from home, to be dedicated to the civil rights movement is a choice I made. I can change it anytime.

ROSEY GRIER

He bounced back after hitting bottom; kids benefit from what he has learned

GRIER: 'I tried to show the kids that I loved them. . . . They just wanted something to do and they wanted someone to care about them.'

IMPRESSIONS

A towering bear of a man met me with out-stretched arms at the door of his youth community center in Los Angeles. Since Rosey Grier announced his switch to the Republican way, he has received more than his share of criticism. But the more Grier and I talked and prayed together that time in Los Angeles, the more I was convinced he is a committed man with an abiding faith in God. And although he has taken an atypical political road, his self-help programs, his belief in God and his ability to share his love set him apart.

— **Barbara Reynolds**

A college and professional football star, Rosey Grier now is making his goal-line stands against the problems facing youth. After college football at Penn State, he played professionally with the New York Giants and Los Angeles Rams. He became part of presidential hopeful Robert Kennedy's inner circle. He disarmed Kennedy's assassin. Grier founded "Are You Committed?" in South Central Los Angeles, a program to help disadvantaged teens. He also has worked through Giant Step, a project affiliated with the Kennedy Foundation, to help needy children and senior citizens in the Los Angeles area. A stage, television and movie performer, he writes and performs Christian songs for young people of all religions. An interview with Grier appeared on the USA TODAY *Inquiry page Dec. 26, 1986.*

USA TODAY: You have gained prominence as an athlete, an actor and a singer. Why then did you become depressed and contemplate suicide in the 1970s?

GRIER: I had married one time and was divorced. I got married another time and got divorced. My life was not working. I had all the trappings that are supposed to mean you are successful, but I still was the little kid that I was in the cotton fields and peanut fields back in Georgia.

USA TODAY: How did you pull yourself out of that stage of your life?

GRIER: I searched. Why am I alive? Where did I come from? How am I going to get there? Why am I here? Just to pay bills? I mean life has to be more than that. I didn't want people holding my hands. I felt every time a woman held my hand, it was like she wanted to own me. I didn't want that.

USA TODAY: What's wrong with a woman depending on you?

GRIER: I want her to be strong. Sure, hold my arm. But don't hold it as if without it you're going to fall down. You ain't going to fall. So, I went out to South Central Los Angeles to work with the gang kids because they needed help. That's when I found out they needed much more than what I was trying to give them. And one day it just seemed like I had been out there too long.

USA TODAY: How did you know you had reached the breaking point?

GRIER: I was shaking when I came home one day. I couldn't stop crying. It seemed like my world again had crumbled almost like when Bobby Kennedy was killed. I thought about how I had lost my dad. I was just crying and I didn't know where to turn. I had no friend to turn to. I had no one to call who would understand where I was at. I was lonely. I was tired of running around from one woman to the next. I was tired of trying to go out grinning, trying to be at all the "in" places, trying to find another movie part. It was just like the end. I understood why people kill themselves. I thought about it myself.

USA TODAY: What else were you thinking?

GRIER: I was depressed and I thought the whole world was going to blow up. And then I went down to buy some gas. Twenty-eight dollars filled my tank up. It used to be four or five dollars. I saw they were converting the apartments into condos around me. I had no place I could stand without it costing money. And I didn't have enough money. I had no job despite all my skills and talents.

USA TODAY: How did you break through?

GRIER: A man came to my house and told me about the Bible. At 45 years old I had never read the Bible. I had read the dictionary one summer and never read the Bible. He told me I ought to study the Bible. An airline stewardess told me about a man who was teaching the Bible on television. And I began to watch Fred Price on Sunday.

USA TODAY: Did you go to his church?

GRIER: My son and I ended up at the church one Sunday and for the first time in my life I heard the Gospel of Jesus Christ preached. At the end of the service the minister asked if anyone wanted to know Jesus as "your Lord and Savior." I raised my hand, and then I went through a personal battle. I was crying and then something inside me broke. And my son, Rosey, raised his hand and he was crying. And both of us decided we would know God. It was the most wonderful experience. One day my son asked me to take his mom to church. To my amazement, when we called she said she would go. Her life was changed just like mine and my boy's. Then I began to look at her. I couldn't before because of my guilt from running around with so many women. She looked wonderful. Eventually God helped me get my wife back.

USA TODAY: How is your marriage now?

GRIER: It works. We have been back together for about six to seven years. Now, when my wife and I have arguments or discussions that are not pleasant to either one of us, we sit down and just talk about it and work it out.

USA TODAY: You have a big building in Los Angeles housing a youth program called Are You Committed? How did this program come about?

GRIER: In 1973 I started working in the inner city with the kids. I wanted to show kids that whatever they could think of, we could probably do — if we were willing to pay the price. I began to work with these kids. I bailed them out of jail. I visited the prisons. I tried to show the kids that I loved them. I wanted the kids that no one wanted. The bad kids particularly. They used to tell me down at the mayor's office: "Don't bring those bad kids down here. You keep them over there." I said OK, but we have to get jobs. I began to see that these kids were not bad kids. They just wanted something to do and they wanted someone to care about them.

USA TODAY: How did you reach them?

GRIER: I began telling them: "You're precious. You're valuable. You're unique. You're one of a kind. There's no one else in the world like you. Think about that for a second. The question is how do we take that uniqueness and develop it so we can sustain ourselves and help others? The answer is we must learn about love, which is wanting the very best for you at all times."

USA TODAY: Many people have given up on kids — and adults — in areas like South Central Los Angeles. What keeps you involved?

GRIER: When I look at the inner city I see an incredible opportunity. I see all these people. Some are broken down on the highway of life, needing a push. The motor needs to be tuned up and the battery needs to be recharged. In the process, I found I couldn't do anything without God. Then I began to see what the kids were missing. They needed the love, power and wisdom of God.

USA TODAY: You didn't have many advantages when you were a boy in Georgia.

GRIER: I remember eating salt and pepper sandwiches. We lived strictly on what was in the peanut fields. But we did have corn bread and we ate a lot of gravy and a little chicken. We made our own clothes. We didn't wear shoes.

USA TODAY: Once you broke into sports you found a ladder up. Were there any bad experiences?

GRIER: Initially, whites didn't want any blacks on the football teams. But Jackie Robinson did a lot

GRIER PROFILE

Born: July 14, 1932, in Cuthbert, Ga.

Family: Divorced twice, now married to Margie Grier; two children, Cheryl Tubbs and Rosey Kennedy Grier.

Education: Bachelor of science from Penn State University, University Park.

On life: "I had married one time and was divorced. I got married another time and got divorced. My life was not working. I had all the trappings that are supposed to mean you are successful, but I still was the little kid that I was in the cotton fields and peanut fields back in Georgia."

Home: Los Angeles.

Role models: Robert Kennedy and Jackie Robinson.

MILESTONES

1955: Started pro football career with the New York Giants and was an All-Pro defensive tackle.

1957: Started two years of service in the Army.

1963: Traded to the Los Angeles Rams, where he played through 1968 and was a member of the "Fearsome Foursome."

1966: Began acting career on stage, in motion pictures and television.

1968: Disarmed Sirhan Sirhan, who assassinated Robert Kennedy while he was campaigning for the Democratic nomination for president.

1973: Started working with youths in South Central Los Angeles.

1979: Became a born-again Christian.

1983: Launched Are You Committed?, a Los Angeles community program to help disadvantaged youth.

1984: Speaker at the Republican National Convention.

1986: *Rosey: The Gentle Giant*, an autobiography, published.

in changing attitudes. In college there were a lot of bowl games. I was told, "You probably deserve to play in some of these post-season games, but they're only going to have one black and this is reserved for a running back. Not a defensive lineman." So I wasn't invited to play in any of those college-sponsored games. I was very hurt. Then I was picked to play in the All-Star Game, which is the biggest one you would want to be in. So I felt pretty good.

USA TODAY: How did you become involved with Robert Kennedy?

GRIER: They invited a whole group of celebrities to a fund-raiser for kids from the inner city around Washington, D.C. I went and met Bobby. The Kennedys really took me in. They were all very supportive of one another and I really gravitated to that. Bobby took me under his wing. When he ran for the presidency I called him and told him I wanted to help.

USA TODAY: On June 5, 1968, Kennedy was shot in a Los Angeles hotel during his campaign for the Democratic Party's nomination for president. How did you disarm the assassin, Sirhan Sirhan?

GRIER: Ethel Kennedy was beside me. I could see over the crowd. Bobby was not far ahead of us. I was trying to catch up. Then the shots rang out. Ethel went down and I went down for a second. And then I jumped up and took off. I saw Sirhan and went for his leg because no one had control of him. George Plimpton had Sirhan's gun hand and was grappling for the gun, but it was pointed right at Plimpton's face. I took my hand, covered the gun and put my thumb under the trigger so it couldn't go off in Plimpton's face. I just wrenched it out of Sirhan's hand and put it in my pocket. It was an awful time. It was a shattered dream.

USA TODAY: But now you're a staunch supporter of Ronald Reagan. Why?

GRIER: It's not about Ronald Reagan or Bobby Kennedy. It's about who I am and what life is about. I made a decision about Christ in my life. And I began to see the need for him to be involved in the life of this nation. God is on the right side. Prayer is needed in this country. When I went to Washington, D.C., to try to win the right for children to pray in school, the people I prayed with were the Jack Kemps and the Ronald Reagans. We were on the same team about prayer. The ones I had supported all those years were on the other side. That was a sign for me to change. And I did.

ALEX HALEY

After helping many to find their roots, he's immersed in new book adventures

HALEY: 'I tell younger writers that indeed it is devastating to be rejected. You feel like the bottom dropped out of your world.'

IMPRESSIONS

In 1976 Alex Haley and I sat together, jointly feted during an authors' party. As I forked fresh salmon on china plates, I told Haley about the days in the 1950s when I accompanied my mother, Mae Stewart, to Bexley — a rich suburb of Columbus, Ohio. She worked in Bexley as a maid earning $8 a day plus car fare. The unwritten law banned blacks from living in the area. It was in that area that we were now being toasted. Together we marveled at the leaps our lives had taken. And Haley told me about his upcoming book, *Roots*. Years later at his Tennessee country estate, we again shared stories.

— **Barbara Reynolds**

His fame and fortune were made with the saga of his family portrayed for the world in Roots. *He began his writing career while in the Coast Guard and free-lanced articles for national publications before his tale of a black family was published. He enjoys writing and researching stories about people, and plans to complete a biography of Madam C.J. Walker, a black woman who became the center of one of the nation's largest black businesses. He also plans to complete a book on the life of the people of Appalachia. An interview with Haley appeared on the* USA TODAY *Inquiry page June 27, 1984.*

USA TODAY: *Roots* made a lot of people cry. Did you cry while writing it?

HALEY: Yes. As my writing and research led me to the point where Kunta Kinte is going to be captured I became so immersed in my writing that I talked to him. We would walk around together. And I'll tell you the truth. I cried like a baby.

USA TODAY: What was going on?

HALEY: I just couldn't let him get captured. This was my Kunta. This was like my little brother. So I had Kunta take his little brother for a walk. And that walk shouldn't be in the book. It makes that section too long. But I did it just to hold back from letting Kunta get captured. I remember writing and all of a sudden everything went blank. That's a convenient thing when you are so distressed that you can't deal with it anymore. So you let everything go blank.

USA TODAY: What did you do then?

HALEY: I just couldn't seem to write the capture and let him get into the slave ship and cross the ocean. Then I knew I had to get myself both physically and emotionally closer to what Kunta experienced. So I went to Monrovia, Liberia. After awhile I got word there was a cargo ship going out. It had the perfect name — The African Star.

USA TODAY: What happened aboard ship?

HALEY: Every evening after our dinner I would slip down in the hole. It would be early dark. I would take off my clothing down to my underwear and lie on my back on a plank and fantasize that I was Kunta. By the third night I had a terrible cold. I was feeling miserable. It seemed what I was doing was so foolish. Here I was trying to simulate Kunta in a wooden, stinking, filthy slave ship hole and I am on a big, stately steel ship. That third night I felt so badly about my ridiculousness I could not make myself go down in that hole. Instead, after dinner, I followed the rail of the ship.

USA TODAY: What were you thinking?

HALEY: I stood there looking out into the water in the fog. It seemed like all the troubles in the world came down on me. I owed everybody I could think of. I had borrowed to make this trip. Everybody I knew that knew anything about the book was telling me I was silly. They said it would never amount to anything. I had talked to a number of black scholars. Almost every one of them asked me why in the world would I want to dig up slavery again. "Write about civil rights. Write about anything else." It seemed almost everybody I knew was against the book. I was tired, beaten down. I didn't think much of myself. It looked like I was just hanging on to something worthless. And in that spirit a thought appeared in my head: "There is a way to get out of all of this mess right now. No problem."

USA TODAY: Jumping overboard?

HALEY: Yes. It came to me all I had to do was step through that rail and drop into the sea. I want to stress that there was no sense of fear, no great sense of drama. It was just a feeling that jumping would take care of it. And it was right at that point — standing there on the fantail of that ship — that I had the most uncanny experience.

USA TODAY: What happened?

HALEY: I began to hear conversation behind me. They were saying things like: "No, you must go ahead. You must do it. No, it's all right. You must continue." There were my grandmother and Miss Kizzy, who I never dreamed I'd see or hear. There was Chicken George. And they were all speaking to me. I remember when it broke through to me what I was hearing. It was like a tug of war all of a sudden.

USA TODAY: Did the urge to jump go away?

HALEY: No, the urge was too great. The sea was right down there. All I had to do was step out and boom, I'm in it. I had never had an experience like that before. I remember pulling my hands away from that rail as if they were numb. I remember turning quickly and getting on my hands and knees, and scuttering like a crab across the hatch. I wanted to stay in the center of the ship. I didn't want to get near the rails on either side because the temptation was so great. I cried dry. It was almost like a purging. I cried until there were no more tears.

USA TODAY: How did you recover?

HALEY: I went back down in the hole about midnight and took off my clothes. I laid on my back on the plank and for the first time I was kind of calm. I had a long yellow tablet and a pencil. And I would just lie there on my back. I tried to picture Kunta lying there and what he would be going through. I wrote in the dark. I had my yellow pad with a lot of large scrawling on it. That's how I started to write that chapter.

USA TODAY: How did Africa receive *Roots*?

HALEY: I heard in South Africa that *Roots* was shown through the U.S. Consulate. It wasn't just standing room for the showing; it was people standing on each other's heads to see it. I also was asked to give permission for the first half of *Roots* to be printed in a volume of children's simplified French for the teacher's association of West Africa, which extends from the Ivory Coast to Senegal. They were not interested in the U.S. side of *Roots*, just the African side. They said the translation would provide African students with a better sense of their heritage and culture than any of the books they were studying. That was very moving.

USA TODAY: What advice do you have for young writers?

HALEY: I tell younger writers that indeed it is devastating to be rejected. You feel like the bottom dropped out of your world. But, there is something that I've come to know now that the top editors in the top publications come to my farm and enjoy weekends. Every publisher is looking just as desperately for that next exciting new writer. Editors and publishers are making it on the strength of the writers they develop.

USA TODAY: Did racism handicap you?

HALEY: The first stories I sold had nothing to do with blackness. I wrote about sea rescues, animals. Because I was in the service, I couldn't be out interviewing about racial matters. I had to deal with what I could do on the ship, then get ashore and rush to a library.

USA TODAY: What should others, particularly blacks, do to make more progress as writers?

HALEY: We've got to be less accepting of "second-rateness." At least 60 percent of our problems are our own problems. Problems that we can solve. I know that 15 sociologists or other kinds of people

HALEY PROFILE

Born: Aug. 11, 1921, in Ithaca, N.Y.

Family: Divorced; three children, Lydia, William, Cynthia.

Education: Elizabeth City Teachers College, Elizabeth City, N.C.

On life: "We've got to be less accepting of 'second-rateness.' At least 60 percent of our problems are our own problems. Problems that we can solve. I know that 15 sociologists or other kinds of people would jump to attack my saying so. But I just never accepted that I couldn't do and couldn't be."

Homes: Norris, Tenn., and Knoxville, Tenn.

Role models: His grandfather, Will Palmer; his father, Simon Haley.

MILESTONES

1939: Began service in the Coast Guard, where he started his writing career.

1959: Retired as chief journalist after a 20-year career in the Coast Guard.

1962: Initiated the "Playboy Interviews" feature for *Playboy* magazine.

1964: Began research on his book that would become *Roots: The Saga of an American Family*.

1965: *The Autobiography of Malcolm X* published; he was editor.

1972: Founder and president of Kinte Corporation, Los Angeles.

1976: *Roots: The Saga of an American Family* published.

1977: Special citations for *Roots* from the National Book Award Committee and the Pulitzer Prize Committee.

1977: *Roots*, the miniseries, appeared on television to critical acclaim.

1987: Went to sea aboard the SS Columbus-Wellington to write his book on black beauty care and business leader, Madam C.J. Walker.

would jump to attack my saying so. But I just never accepted that I couldn't do and couldn't be. Maybe it has a lot to do with my being a writer. People had told me they wouldn't hire me but I soon figured out that writing was something I could do myself.

USA TODAY: You wrote *Roots* and now you are writing a book about Madam C.J. Walker, one of the nation's earliest black business owners, aboard a ship. Why do you do your writing on ships?

HALEY: A cargo ship carries freight and a maximum of 12 passengers. And they are very quiet and lonely and low-keyed. Most of the people who go are people who want to eat or play cards or be calm. The ship goes to the most glamorous places on earth. And they unload their cargo and take on more and go on to the next. There is no whipped cream and orchestra and dancing. For me it is exquisite isolation. No phone, no this, that and the other. If you have to contact somebody, you could do it by telex. It's fantastic. I average literally 14 to 16 hours of work every day.

USA TODAY: You are also writing a book about Appalachia. How did that come about?

HALEY: The general image of the people there is the cartoon, *Snuffy Smith*. That is not a true picture. These are culturally rich, marvelous people. They live with what they can do with their hands. They distrust that which is store bought. Deals are made to this day with a handshake. And I was very attracted to that. They are holding on more than most of us do to yesteryear. Mostly white, they are really marvelous people.

USA TODAY: You have a home on 128 acres in Norris, Tenn., a stone mansion and two condominiums in Knoxville and other property. How much did you make on *Roots* and its spinoffs?

HALEY: I really have no idea. The best answer I have is millions. I don't know. I don't have all that many millions now. And then next year I might have more or I might have less. I'm really not so carried away with money as a lot of others are. I take the view that if I have enough to do what I want to do, I am not really awfully concerned about building up the number of millions.

DOROTHY HEIGHT

Dream of a career in social work sparked 5 decades of service to women, family life

HEIGHT: 'Black women . . . have carried a major role since slavery in holding the family together. We simply can't give up now.'

IMPRESSIONS

It's difficult to attend any major gathering in the USA or abroad where the issues of women or blacks are being debated, and not see Dorothy Height. Even when her health failed, she never stopped advocating. She never stops pressing others to do the right thing. She has spent decades stirring ideas, setting the agenda and brainstorming solutions. Though she is in her 70s, it's hard for me to keep up with this dynamo. She is young at heart and more active mentally than most who are one-third her age. I look to her for tips on the true meaning of leadership and determination.

— **Barbara Reynolds**

An advocate of self-help, Dorothy Height has been active in the National Council of Negro Women since 1937. She was a close associate of its late founder, Mary McLeod Bethune, whom she met in 1937. Known for her oratorical skills and her dedication to the preservation of the black family, Height frequently repeats the sentiment of Frederick Douglass when she says, "If one is suffering then one must agitate. You have to speak up." As president of the National Council of Negro Women, she leads 4 million women who have placed the survival of the black child and black health at the top of their agenda. An interview with Height appeared on the USA TODAY *Inquiry page Sept. 25, 1986.*

USA TODAY: The National Council of Negro Women sponsors a Black Family Reunion that draws thousands to celebrations in a number of cities, including the nation's capital. Why did you organize this celebration?

HEIGHT: In the face of many negative projections about the black family, we felt it was time to build upon the strengths. We are a people with a past, a present, a future. We have a heritage, a strong cultural base, a strong religious base. We need to use those strengths to face our problems.

USA TODAY: Is there anything positive to be said about mothers raising children alone?

HEIGHT: Almost 50 percent of black families are headed by women. We do not confuse the unwanted children of teen-age mothers with those of women who, for a number of reasons, may be heading families. A family is not automatically wrong because it is headed by a woman. It all depends upon the resources the woman has. Most black women earn women's wages and are working in jobs that are not protected. There are black women who have excelled in every field, but poverty is a major factor affecting families headed by women. Many families have demonstrated strengths because of the strength in many of the women.

USA TODAY: Why are so many black men unable or unwilling to support their families?

HEIGHT: There are many who are supporting their families. We never hear about that. Also, there are so many black men who are incarcerated, are on drugs or alcohol. That reduces the number of men.

High unemployment means many men do not feel they are in positions to take the responsibility they need to take. We tend to focus on women, but the reality is we have to look at what is happening to men and to women.

USA TODAY: You are often referred to as the Grand Dame of Civil Rights. How did you get involved?

HEIGHT: I have been involved in civil rights all of my life. But from 1937 when I became active in the National Council of Negro Women with Mary McLeod Bethune, I found myself getting more deeply involved.

USA TODAY: Bethune, the founder of Bethune-Cookman college and a confidante to Eleanor Roosevelt, inspired many. What was she like?

HEIGHT: She was a person who had a great concern for people. I learned a lot from her. She was brought to Washington by President Roosevelt to assist him as his national affairs adviser with the National Youth Administration. As a result, she saw the importance of organized power and she organized the National Council of Negro Women.

USA TODAY: Can you give an example of what those days were like?

HEIGHT: When Mrs. Bethune held council conventions, Mrs. Roosevelt always gave a party. Mrs. Bethune found that people came in time to go to the White House tea but they didn't come to the convention. So Mrs. Bethune told me that our convention registration fee would be $5. I told her you can't charge people to go to the White House. She said, "We'll just tell them to pay the registration fee." And she was right because many of them came in time to go to the tea and she got the $5.

USA TODAY: How did she relate to others?

HEIGHT: She never said mean things. She never got embroiled in it, never responded to it. Once she told a group of women: "If you see my petticoat hanging, come and tell me. Don't talk about it and tell it to everybody else. Tell me because I'm the only one who can do anything about it."

USA TODAY: What is Bethune's legacy?

HEIGHT: Her legacy is a message to us all. She said, "I leave you hope and love and faith and racial pride and the challenge of working together and a respect for the use of power, the responsibility to our young people." She spent her life opening doors and trying to see how she could prepare her people to go inside.

USA TODAY: What has been your greatest challenge?

HEIGHT: The challenge has been for me to help realize the significance of her message. The significance of what she was trying to say to women about working together. She was saying, "It is so much easier to be competitive than it is to be cooperative." The philosophy of the National Council of Negro Women has been to leave no one behind. I have been trying to help us all see that we have to take more responsibility for each other and work together. We have to improve life, not just for those who have the most skills and those who know how to manipulate the system. But also for and with those who often have so much to give, but never get the opportunity.

USA TODAY: The Black Family Reunion reaffirms deeply rooted values. What was your own family life like?

HEIGHT: I am the older of two children born to parents who were both widowed twice before I was born. I came late in their lives. Mine was a close-knit family. My mother was a nurse. My father was a building and painting contractor. During the height of the Depression, we lived in a small town in Pennsylvania. All things centered around the church and family life.

USA TODAY: You have been working with the black community for more than 50 years. What is different about the black family today?

HEIGHT: Years ago we had a sense of kinship that wasn't always related to blood ties. This had come with us from our African history. Many people talk of tribalism in a negative sense. What they do not understand is the way African people grouped together and had a sense of caring for each other, of responsibility for each other. When I was growing up people who really had no blood relationship felt free to stop you if they saw you going astray. There was also much more emphasis on values through the church and other organizations. With so much crime and drugs in society many people are almost afraid to speak to young people about their behavior. Young people want to be challenged. And many adult leaders have to be willing to give messages that are not popular.

USA TODAY: What organizational hurdles have you had to overcome?

HEIGHT: People are accustomed to their own primary group, their own sorority, lodge church or club. When you say, "let's come together," every-

HEIGHT PROFILE

Born: March 19, 1911, in Richmond, Va.

Family: Single.

Education: Master's from New York University, New York City; advanced studies at Columbia University, New York City, and at New York School of Social Work.

On life: "I have been trying to help us all see that we have to take more responsibility for each other and work together."

Home: New York City.

Role model: Mary McLeod Bethune.

MILESTONES

1937: Traveled to Oxford, England, under the auspices of the United Christian Youth movement; met Mary McLeod Bethune.

1938: YWCA representative to the World Conference of Christian Youth in Amsterdam, Holland.

1944: YWCA national board staff; developed interracial, ecumenical programs.

1947: Began unprecedented nine-year term as Delta Sigma Theta Inc. president.

1952: Visiting professor, Delhi School of Social Work, University of Delhi, India.

1954: Elected president of National Council of Negro Women.

1961: Appointed to the President's Commission on Status of Women.

1965: Developed and became first director of the Center for Racial Justice.

1973: Named to American Revolution Bicentennial Commission.

1975: Participated in International Women's Year Conference in Mexico City.

1977: Keynote speaker at the national convention of the Black Women's Federation of South Africa in Johannesburg.

1983: Leadership Award from the National Conference of Black Mayors.

1987: NAACP Key of Life Award.

one wonders what's in it for them. So we now talk about coalition. The black leadership family seeks ways to work together. It's not perfect but it's a sign of our maturity and growth and our recognition that we keep talking about "we and they." But it's really "us and we."

USA TODAY: What difficulties do you find in being a woman leader surrounded by male leaders?

HEIGHT: Black male leadership is no less chauvanistic than white male leadership. Often it isn't recognized that black women make tremendous contributions that go unnoticed because they are always in the shadow. That often has deterred some of our younger women from trying to achieve. For example, in 1963, although I was a part of the civil rights leadership, the male leadership did not see the importance of having female participation in the March on Washington. The only woman's voice you heard was Mahalia Jackson's — beautiful as she was. Those same males would have resented it if she had asked to speak and not sing. Twenty years later a woman, Coretta King, initiated the 20th anniversary celebration. The men accepted it and came along.

USA TODAY: Why aren't the concerns of black women addressed by civil rights or women's groups?

HEIGHT: We suffer the double handicap of race and sex. Some things happen to black women because we are black. Many other things happen to us because we are women. As long as women earn less than men and we are women, we earn what women earn. So long as blacks earn less than whites and we are black, we earn less than what people of different races earn. And within our group, black women earn less than black men. We're at the bottom. Yet black women are the backbone of every institution in our community and have carried a major role since slavery in holding the family together. We simply can't give up now.

USA TODAY: What is your legacy to the USA?

HEIGHT: All of my life I have been so enriched by what so many people have done and have inspired me to do. I just hope that I leave a little of something that has helped me have a real appreciation of what it means to be black and a woman.

JENNIFER HOLLIDAY

Spiritual upbringing and strong family guide her commitment to the arts

HOLLIDAY: 'I've become a young woman on the road. I've learned a lot, but I missed being a teen-ager.'

IMPRESSIONS

The last thing I would say about Jennifer Holliday is that she acts her age. She seems much older, wiser than a woman in her 20s. She exudes confidence as she sits regally in a Washington hotel suite with her Pekingese, her constant traveling companion. The phone rings. She directs her financial advisers while checking her wardrobe for that night's show, all while concentrating on the questions I pose. Questions about such heady topics as reincarnation, music, faith and family. Onstage she brings young and old to their feet as her songs touch many hearts, minds and souls.

— **Barbara Reynolds**

Jennifer Holliday's star rose in the Broadway show Dreamgirls. *Her Tony-winning performance sparked comparisons with Ethel Merman, Barbra Streisand, Maria Callas, Billie Holiday and Judy Garland. She has starred in other productions, including* Sing Mahalia Sing. *Her promising solo singing career has sparked nationwide tours and albums. An interview with Holliday appeared on the* USA TODAY *Inquiry page Jan. 9, 1986.*

USA TODAY: Many people say your performances remind them of Billie Holiday or Judy Garland. Why do those comparisons come to mind?

HOLLIDAY: I always tell people that I have been here before. People from down home in Houston say I have "mother wit" — meaning that somebody walks with me and helps me have these feelings and pass them on. When I say I've been here before — the reincarnated type of thing — maybe some singer from the 1920s was on the road and died tragically in an accident and now this is her chance to come back and complete her career.

USA TODAY: Do you consider yourself more mature than others your age?

HOLLIDAY: I'm far more mature. I grew up in a Southern atmosphere and you're just taught different things down there with your grandmothers and your aunts. It's a different kind of respect. I was the oldest in the family — there were three — and my mother worked very hard. I wanted to be able to help her, and so I just matured and really aged a little earlier.

USA TODAY: Did you receive formal voice training?

HOLLIDAY: No. It was a gift from God.

USA TODAY: When did you begin your career?

HOLLIDAY: I started singing at 17½. I wish I had started at 21. I would have had a chance to be a teen-ager and turn into a young lady. I've had my 18th birthday on the road, my 21st birthday on the road. I've become a young woman on the road. I've learned a lot, but I missed being a teen-ager. No guy ever carried my books to the dorm.

USA TODAY: What was your childhood like?

HOLLIDAY: My mother was a schoolteacher, and we lived in a very nice black neighborhood that was filled with teachers, lawyers and other professionals. My mother worked very hard to keep us in that neighborhood. We really couldn't afford to stay there without a father, but she kept us there and provided us a good home. We had seven newspaper routes and sold water cans and bottles. I worked at Denny's. We all worked.

USA TODAY: What is important to you?

HOLLIDAY: The things that are important to me now were important to me before. They include family and strength. That's because we were raised very spiritually. That spiritual strength has allowed me to be so strong and rise above everything. Show business is an up-and-down career. And when I'm down, I'm going to be fine because the things that are most important are still going to be there — my family and my friends.

USA TODAY: Why are you called a spiritual gambler?

HOLLIDAY: Because I walk out and do things on faith. I know I'm going to be OK. And that's not because I think I'm so great. That's just because I have a deep spiritual belief that can move mountains. It is something you've got to practice every day. If you're going to trust and believe in God, then that's what you've got to do.

USA TODAY: Do you get depressed?

HOLLIDAY: Oh yeah! If I can't go home for Christmas or if I miss a friend or if my dog gets sick, I get depressed. And I let it happen. If I feel pain, I want to feel pain. If I am sad, I like to be sad because when I am happy you'll know it. I do not like to pretend. I'm very truthful and very honest.

USA TODAY: From where do you draw your strength?

HOLLIDAY: A lot of blacks, including me, really draw strength from getting involved in our communities. The church really has been a strong backbone for blacks for many years. We go to the church and we pray a lot. And we have a lot of faith. In many cases, we are trying so much harder to prove something to ourselves. Not to anybody else. We are trying to prove that we can accomplish things, set different goals and achieve them without turning back after failures.

USA TODAY: Failure and hurt lead some people to alcohol or drugs. What do you do with hurt?

HOLLIDAY: I figure out why I am hurt and if my hurt is justified. I try to find out if I knew I was going to be hurt, if it was a total surprise, if it was planned or unintentional. Then I just kind of go inside myself. When I finish inside, I try to deal from the outside. I will pray about it and try to be logical about what is happening to me. I make myself remember that when things happen to me the rest of the world keeps going on like everything is fine.

USA TODAY: How did you avoid alcohol and drugs?

HOLLIDAY: By not indulging in anything. No alcohol. No cigarettes. I won't even drink coffee. I like to be in control of my life.

USA TODAY: You have 250 pairs of shoes. Does shopping help you handle depression?

HOLLIDAY: No. I just accumulated them over the years. I am also into clothes. But I buy the shoes first. One hundred of those 250 I probably have never worn. I like to look at them. It has nothing to do with having the money to buy them.

USA TODAY: Where did you get your resolve?

HOLLIDAY: I was never a follower. I was always a leader. My mother depended on each of us because she needed us. There was really no time to be a teen-ager and have fun and be ridiculous. We had just about everything that everybody else had because we worked for it. We didn't have two parents in the house. It wasn't like my father offered to buy me a car for graduation. I had to say, "I want a car" and then save for a year. But I got it.

USA TODAY: Do you consider yourself stronger than most people?

HOLLIDAY: I am not an outwardly emotional person, but I can't handle every blow that falls. Some people take drugs because they are very, very weak and they cannot deal with reality. A lot of people who sing are chain smokers. I just don't want to smoke because I don't want to get addicted to it. When I have a nervous time I will just be nervous. And I will get over it.

USA TODAY: How do you assess the progress of blacks in the USA?

HOLLIDAY: We have definitely progressed. I don't get discouraged much about the progress. I get more frustrated about what we do not understand and what we do not realize. We don't understand or realize that it is important to vote. Many of us have gotten lax. We just don't deal with inequity toward others. We think that if we just do our jobs and achieve our own successes, those other people will make it on their own. I get concerned about that. We are not a community as much as we should be.

HOLLIDAY PROFILE

Born: Oct. 19, 1960, in Riverside, Texas.

Family: Single.

Education: High School of Engineering Professionals, Houston.

On life: "The things that are important to me now were important to me before. They include family and strength. That's because we were raised very spiritually. That spiritual strength has allowed me to be so strong and rise above everything. Show business is an up-and-down career. And when I'm down, I'm going to be fine because the things that are most important are still going to be there — my family and my friends."

Home: Houston.

Role models: Barbara Jordan and Barbra Streisand.

MILESTONES

1971: Joined the choir at Gethsemane Baptist Church in Houston as a soloist when she was in the fifth grade.

1974: Hired by Pleasant Grove Missionary Baptist Church, the largest black Baptist church in Houston, to sing solos on the church's televised weekly service.

1978: Left home at 17 to audition and eventually perform with the touring company of *Don't Bother Me, I Can't Cope.*

1979: Opened in touring company production of *Your Arms Too Short To Box With God.*

1980: Made debut on Broadway in *Your Arms Too Short To Box With God;* signed recording contract with Geffen Records for album to include songs she wrote.

1981: Opened on Broadway in *Dreamgirls.*

1982: Tony award for *Dreamgirls.*

1983: Moved to Los Angeles for *Dreamgirls* opening; released her first album, *Feel My Soul.*

1986: Starred in *Sing Mahalia Sing.*

USA TODAY: What do you want to be doing 10 years from now?

HOLLIDAY: I would like to be a producer and have a production company that's working and discovering talent. I probably will own a lot of companies. But one of my main goals is focusing on how I can be of some help to the black community. That's very important to me.

USA TODAY: What would you say to encourage others to push for success?

HOLLIDAY: You can do it. I can do it. We can do it. Whatever we want to accomplish can be done. Black people need to care more, to pay closer attention to politics and economics. Shed a little light on the things we can do to help ourselves, to protect our families. Otherwise a lot of our traditions and heritage — the things that are ours alone — will be gone.

LENA HORNE

She has gently touched 3 generations through a life filled with pain, passion

HORNE: 'I realized there were white and black people who could understand things the same way. Then I lost a lot of hostility.'

IMPRESSIONS

All my life I had known of Lena Horne. Finally, backstage at the Warner Theatre in Washington, D.C., I was face to face with a legend. Middle-aged groupies — people who follow her from performance to performance — waited in the wings while we talked. I had believed those stories about her having tasted the cream of Hollywood while other black actresses scuffled for skim milk. What I hadn't known: how lonely and unhappy she had been. While we talked, she offered a glimpse of her pain. I remember thinking as she talked: "Lena, it wasn't just you. We live that pain in some ways today."

— **Barbara Reynolds**

In the 1930s, Lena Horne performed at the Cotton Club in New York. She later joined Charlie Barnett and took to the road with his orchestra. In the 1940s, she became the first black woman to sign a long-term contract with a major film studio, leading to roles in such movies as Cabin in the Sky *and* Stormy Weather. *She was blacklisted during the McCarthy era because of her friendship with Paul Robeson and her interest in the African Freedom movement. In the 1950s, she fought for the right of blacks to attend her performances. An interview with Horne appeared on the* USA TODAY *Inquiry page May 27, 1983.*

USA TODAY: Many fans view you as a legend, almost a cult figure. Why?

HORNE: A great deal of it has to do with curiosity. They want to see that an old woman can live, work and be entertaining. This is a very wonderful part of my life. I can't think of a time when black people have identified with me more. In the years I was singing in expensive nightclubs, many of them couldn't afford it. I was performing there when segregation kept blacks out.

USA TODAY: Why do you have such a huge following among young people?

HORNE: I guess there is a whole new generation that saw *The Wiz* and this strange character named Lena Horne they had heard their mothers and grandmothers talk about. Now, young people wait outside the theater at night. I don't know if everybody is just star struck because I'm supposed to be an old movie star. I never thought I'd have this kind of attention. I've been around long enough to collect three generations.

USA TODAY: Writers have portrayed you as bitter because you didn't achieve more success as a Hollywood actress. Is that true?

HORNE: If I had been grieving about a movie career since the '40s, I should have had my head examined. It amuses me now. It didn't in 1942 or 1946 because half the time when I could have worked, I was being punished for refusing to do a show for MGM called *St. Louis Woman.* Black groups were protesting blacks not being allowed in audiences and the lack of proper roles. I was used as a wedge in the protest. For that they didn't let me

work. I was put on layoff. I didn't begin to enjoy my career until I was about 50.

USA TODAY: You were the first black woman to sign with a major Hollywood studio. What was the image of blacks in films then?

HORNE: Most images were projected by Rochester, Bill Robinson, Lincoln Perry who was Stepin Fetchit, natives in *Tarzan* and maids like Louise Beavers and Hattie McDaniel — the best friend I had in Hollywood. There was no serious, thoughtful or even glamorous role until the 1960s.

USA TODAY: How much have things changed over the decades for black actors and actresses?

HORNE: For a while it seemed more blacks would get jobs. It never happened. It is rough to even do anything about it because it is just as bad now for whites.

USA TODAY: There was a time when you were resented by your own race. Why did that happen?

HORNE: Promoters were telling people that to make it you had to be like Lena. Blacks resented it and I resented it. It increased the isolation between us. I was isolated anyway because I was working in white clubs and my own people didn't know me. Billie Holiday and Hattie McDaniel told me, "You have two babies and you have to pay your rent, so sing anything they ask."

USA TODAY: What was Miss McDaniel like?

HORNE: I loved Miss McDaniel. Her house was gorgeous. She was the most elegant woman I have ever met, and she told me: "This is my house and this is the way I am. When I go to the studio, I put the handkerchief around my head. I wear two hats because with the money I have made I have supported my family and bought everything I wanted. And that is what you must do."

USA TODAY: Sometimes your career was like the title of one of your favorite songs, *Stormy Weather.*

HORNE: I was sorry the roles weren't more varied. I also got teed off when I was entertaining the troops because they put the black soldiers in the mess hall behind the POWs. I was always getting angry. My grandmother had been a suffragette and a social worker. Oddly enough, I didn't realize what a loner I was making myself until I struck a guy in a Hollywood restaurant who had called me a dirty name. I got so much mail from black people who said, "We love it." But I wasn't trying to be a folk boxer. I was just making it through the day.

USA TODAY: Why did you become involved in the civil rights movement?

HORNE: In the 1960s it was because I had a terrible revulsion. I had to quit work. I couldn't bear to sing one more glamorous song. I was unhappy because I had been in a show called *Jamaica* and it was one of the first in a long time for a black or mixed show. This was in the 1950s. Two years later, I ran into five or six of the kids that had been in the show and they were still unemployed. I suddenly realized that all of this about being the exemplary black and the one behaving so that she could make it better for other people was a crock. I just said the hell with all of this. I can't sing these songs. I couldn't stand what I was doing anymore. I stopped and I traveled with the National Council of Negro Women and worked seriously for my sorority, Delta Sigma Theta.

USA TODAY: How did you overcome all that bitterness and anger?

HORNE: I had been, for many years, very prejudiced and I had tired myself out by trying not to be. I realized there were white and black people who could understand things the same way. Then I lost a lot of hostility. Not toward the movies or anything like that, but just toward life. And when I found myself alone after my husband, father and son died in the same year, I knew I had had the worst happen to me. Where else was I going to go, but just open up and be free? So I came out vocally, being more free.

USA TODAY: Do young people in your audience understand your history?

HORNE: They come and they understand that I am talking about surviving, about intensely living. I try to be compassionate. I used to be very cold. It is good to know because the one thing I find that I miss in the young generation is that fire about something. When you are cold you miss passion in your life. I went for years just like ice. I was killing myself. It also kept me from loving back. I didn't want to love anybody, and I didn't like people. I never cried, never did any of the things that would make me open myself. When you don't like people, it affects you worse.

USA TODAY: Did this coldness affect your children?

HORNE: Yes. My daughter told me once that I was her best friend, but she didn't think I loved her.

USA TODAY: How was your own childhood?

HORNE: When my mother left me when I was

HORNE PROFILE

Born: June 30, 1917, in Brooklyn, N.Y.

Family: Widowed; son, Teddy Jones, died in 1970; daughter, Gail Lumet Buckley.

Education: Attended Girls High School, Brooklyn, N.Y; left school at 16 to help her mother financially.

On life: "I used to be very cold. . . . When you are cold you miss passion in your life. I went for years just like ice."

Homes: Santa Barbara, Calif., and Washington, D.C.

Role models: Paul Robeson and Walter White.

MILESTONES

1934: Began career as a dancer at Harlem's Cotton Club.

1942: Appeared in *Panama Hattie*, her first film role.

1943: Played in films *Cabin In the Sky* and *Stormy Weather*.

1957: Star of *Jamaica* on Broadway.

1959: Grammy for *Porgy and Bess*.

1962: Grammy for *Lena Lovely and Alive*.

1970: Three of the people closest to her died of illnesses: her second husband, Lennie Hayton; her father, Edwin F. "Teddy" Horne; and her son, Teddy Jones.

1978: Portrayed the good witch in the movie *The Wiz*.

1981: *Lena Horne: The Lady and Her Music* opened on Broadway, became the longest-running, one-woman show ever; won special Tony award and Grammy for album.

1984: *Lena: A Personal and Professional Biography of Lena Horne* published.

1985: Kennedy Center Honors Award for Lifetime Achievement.

1986: Daughter, Gail Lumet Buckley, published *The Hornes, an American Family*.

three, I would just see my grandmother once in awhile. I didn't think anybody wanted me. I thought that I was a blot on the earth. Every time I was left with a family that was good to me; many times they were so poor they didn't know where the next meal was coming from, but they shared with me. If I let myself like them, my mother or somebody would come and take me away.

USA TODAY: As someone who was married to a white man, do you think society is finally ready for intermarriage?

HORNE: I don't know if many people have grown used to that. There are still some families who are going to intermarry with other families who have the same amount of money. It doesn't have to do with color when it is all boiled down. It is money, position.

USA TODAY: What are your thoughts on marriage now?

HORNE: I wouldn't get married if you paid me. I am too set in my ways. I am happy. I go with somebody if I like them. It is very difficult to be married, very difficult. I had one great marriage.

USA TODAY: What happens between you and your audience?

HORNE: Sometimes when the audience works with me, I'll get into it and we'll do our own thing. Then I am free and I can't contain myself. I am glad that before I die I knew that kind of freedom with the audience.

JOHN H. JOHNSON

Mother's sacrifices, discipline set foundation for building of his publishing empire

JOHNSON: 'Failure is a word that I simply don't accept. As long as you don't accept it, you're not failing.'

IMPRESSIONS

In my house when I was growing up, right next to *Life* and *Look* magazines, there were two publications — *Ebony* and *Jet* — where I could see people who were black like me. Not long after I graduated from Ohio State University, *Ebony* was my first stop as I reached for my dream of becoming a first-rate journalist. The owner, John H. Johnson, was as creative as he was fastidious. I remember him standing on the stairs greeting tardy staffers. His Johnson Publishing was the only building in Chicago's Loop owned by a black man. I remember him as a giant.

— **Barbara Reynolds**

With a fortune estimated at $138.9 million by Forbes magazine, John H. Johnson is one of the USA's top entrepreneurs. He owns the USA's No. 1 black business, Johnson Publishing Co. He's editor and publisher of Ebony, Ebony Jr. and Jet magazines, president of radio stations WJPC, Chicago; WLOU, Louisville, Ky.; and WLNR, Lansing, Ill. He also is president of Fashion Fair Cosmetics and chairman of Supreme Life Insurance Co. An interview with Johnson appeared on the USA TODAY Inquiry page April 16, 1986.

USA TODAY: Though born in poverty, you have built a publishing empire and have been listed by Forbes as one of the 400 richest people in the USA. What's the key to your success?

JOHNSON: In a word, my mother. She gave me a strong faith and belief in myself. Although she never went beyond the third grade, she believed passionately in education. She believed that if you worked hard there was always the chance that you could succeed. She was also aware that you could work hard and not succeed. But, she said you'll never know unless you try. My mother made many sacrifices for me to get an education. She left the deep South and came to Chicago. She even let me mortgage her furniture to start my business. It took $500. I always felt that I couldn't let her down.

USA TODAY: In the 1940s you were a college student working at Supreme Life Insurance, a prominent black firm. Is that when you saw your opportunity to move into publishing?

JOHNSON: Fortunately, in 1942 I was editing in-house magazines for their agents and employees. The president of the company gave me a job giving him a digest or briefing each week on what was happening in our community. He was impressed with what I was doing. I would be in a social situation and I would say, "You know, I just read such-and-such a publication," and people would reply: "Gee, that sounds interesting. How can I get that?" I knew about Reader's Digest so the thought occurred to me to put out a Negro digest.

USA TODAY: In Chicago you saw enterprising blacks succeeding and that motivated you. How important are role models for youth?

JOHNSON: They are very important. When I lived in Arkansas City, Ark., the only man in that city I saw wearing a suit was the minister. Most of the people wore work clothes. Occasionally they dressed up on Sunday. Initially I wanted to become a minister. I couldn't imagine doing anything beyond that until I came to Chicago.

USA TODAY: Zenith was among the many companies that denied you advertising. How did you turn around that situation?

JOHNSON: I have always felt that you had to find ways to do things. And, it's better to get smart than to get mad. I try not to get so insulted that I will not take advantage of an opportunity to persuade people to change their minds. I wrote the president of Zenith and asked if I could see him about advertising. He wrote back and said he didn't handle advertising. I was told he handled "policy." I wrote back and asked if I could see him about his policy toward advertising. He said: "I cannot help but believe you still want to try to get an ad. I can assure you that if you bring up the subject I will ask you to leave my office."

USA TODAY: How did you handle that?

JOHNSON: I found myself with this appointment to talk to him about the one thing he wouldn't let me talk about. I looked him up in Who's Who and found he was interested in exploring and he knew Matthew Henson, a black man who had been with Robert E. Peary when he went to the North Pole. I found that Matthew Henson had written a book and was living in New York. I visited Henson.

USA TODAY: How did the Henson visit help?

JOHNSON: By the time I had my appointment at Zenith I had something else to talk to the president about. During my visit, the president said: "You know, I am acquainted with Matthew Henson. Do you know him?" I said: "Of course. And it just happens that I have a copy of his book that he autographed to you." He was very pleased and said, "Well young man, if you had any kind of magazine about black folks, you'd have something about Matt." I said, "Well, it just so happens we have." As he thumbed through my magazine and saw the story about Henson, he said he didn't see any reason why Zenith should not advertise. It's all a matter of developing rapport with people.

USA TODAY: You often have found ingenious ways to get around racist attempts to obstruct you. I've heard, for example, that once you disguised yourself as a janitor to buy a building. Is that true?

JOHNSON: I had tried to get an appointment to

see about buying an office building. When I identified myself as president of the Negro Digest Publishing Co., I could just feel the tension in the owner's voice. He was not going to see a black man. That experience convinced me to later change the name to Johnson Publishing. I simply went to a white lawyer friend and asked him to inquire about the building and just say that he was inquiring for some publishing company out East. Of course, the building was immediately available. I dressed in work clothes and went along with the white lawyer. That's how I got my first look at the building that became our first headquarters. After we bought and renovated the building, it became a show place. I invited the guy who wouldn't sell it to me. He was almost in tears as he apologized.

USA TODAY: Is it true that you virtually never take no for an answer?

JOHNSON: Failure is a word that I simply don't accept. As long as you don't accept it, you're not failing. Even if you're not succeeding, you're not failing.

USA TODAY: How did you convince department stores to carry a line of cosmetics for blacks?

JOHNSON: None of the stores wanted to carry the line. So I did the same thing I had done years and years ago. I found out who could introduce me to the CEO of Marshall Field's stores, which was noted for its liberalism toward blacks. I joined a number of organizations Marshall Field was in. I got to know him well. I sought his advice on how I could deal with this problem. Eventually I was able to sell him on getting me into the store. We are in major stores around the world now.

USA TODAY: Is that from the John Johnson textbook of good salesmanship?

JOHNSON: If you can sell, you can succeed. You have to forget what your objectives are. You can think only in terms of what the other person would like to have. I have young people coming in to me for jobs telling me they want jobs in order to get more experience. Now why should I give them a job for them to get more experience? Why shouldn't they come to me and tell me they want a job because they can help sell more magazines? Now that I will listen to!

USA TODAY: Have you ever made a sales pitch along racial lines?

JOHNSON: I never say, "Help me because I'm black." I never say, "Help me because it's the right thing to do." I say, "Let me help you make more

JOHNSON PROFILE

Born: Jan. 18, 1918, in Arkansas City, Ark.

Family: Married to Eunice Rivers Walker; two children, John Harold Jr., who died in 1981 of sickle cell anemia, and Linda Johnson Rice.

Education: Attended University of Chicago, Northwestern University, Chicago.

On life: "It's better to get smart than to get mad. I try not to get so insulted that I will not take advantage of an opportunity to persuade people to change their minds."

Home: Chicago.

Role models: His mother, Gertrude Johnson; Frederick Douglass, Booker T. Washington, Dr. Martin Luther King Jr.

MILESTONES

1942: Launched *Negro Digest.*

1945: Launched *Ebony* magazine, the flagship of Johnson Publishing.

1951: Founded *Jet;* accompanied Vice President Richard Nixon to Russia and Poland.

1960: Purchased WGRT — later changed to WJPC — his first radio station and Chicago's first black-owned station.

1961: Appointed by President John Kennedy as special ambassador to independence ceremonies for the Ivory Coast in Africa; launched book publishing division.

1970: Appointed by President Nixon to the president's commission for observance of the United Nations' 25th anniversary.

1972: Named Publisher of the Year by Magazine Publishers Association.

1984: Johnson Publishing Company topped *Black Enterprise* magazine's 100 leading black firms in the USA.

1985: Launched *EM,* a fashion and lifestyle magazine for men.

1987: Named *Black Enterprise* magazine's businessman of the decade.

money."

USA TODAY: What is the formula for *Ebony* magazine, the flagship of your corporation?

JOHNSON: We try to inform, educate, inspire and entertain. We look for achievement. Every time a black person has a breakthrough, every time a black person succeeds against the odds, we rush it into a story. We ask, "How did you do it?" We pass that along to our readers. I'm sure they pass it on. *Ebony* has been the largest-circulating black magazine for more than 40 years. That's not an accident.

USA TODAY: Why are there so few black businesses?

JOHNSON: The best brains in the black race went into fields other than business in the past. They went into medicine; we have great black doctors. They went into law, teaching, preaching. But the same kind of talent has not gone into business. We are going to see a difference in the next decade.

USA TODAY: Is your daughter, Linda Johnson Rice, whom you named president and CEO last year, an example of that difference?

JOHNSON: Yes. She is interested in business. She has a degree in journalism and in business and she's working here every day participating in decisions. I am absolutely confident that she is capable of running this company.

USA TODAY: How do you want to be remembered?

JOHNSON: The real John H. Johnson sets his own goals, works to satisfy himself, tries very hard to be fair with the people he deals with. He doesn't like to lose. He believes if he really works hard at most things, he can win. I want to be remembered as someone who gave hope when hope was needed, who gave direction when direction was needed and who set an example when an example was needed.

BISHOP LEONTINE KELLY

Methodist leader smashed barriers to give blacks, women bigger role in the church

KELLY: 'We were reared to believe a single failure was one that we could not afford. . . . I hope we can regain that urgency.'

IMPRESSIONS

At first blush, Bishop Leontine Kelly seems much like a Sunday school teacher. But a close look shows she is more: a leader, organizer, nurturer, scholar. In Atlanta, where she received the Southern Christian Leadership Conference Drum Major for Justice Award, she preached up a storm, surprising many who thought Methodists were quieter than Baptists. But her sermons are not just bombasts. They are intellectually powerful. She's quick to take on anyone who dares quote Apostle Paul's chastisement of women as a reason to keep them out of the pulpit: "Paul didn't call me, Jesus did."

— **Barbara Reynolds**

A maverick in her church, Bishop Leontine Kelly is the first black woman and second woman to be elected bishop in the United Methodist Church. She considers preaching an "amazing journey" and takes every opportunity to use her skills in the pulpit as well as in the office. Her rise within the United Methodist Church occurred while she was bringing up four children as a single parent. An interview with Kelly appeared on the USA TODAY *Inquiry page April 5, 1985.*

USA TODAY: As a bishop in the United Methodist Church, what do you do?

KELLY: I am the chief administrative officer and spiritual leader of more than 100,000 United Methodists in Northern California and Nevada. We elect bishops in jurisdictions. My area goes from Bakersfield (Calif.) almost to Los Angeles, up to the Oregon border and across Nevada. I appoint the pastors for the 437 churches in my area, or conference. I have seven district superintendents who advise me and serve as members of my cabinet.

USA TODAY: Are there other black women bishops in your denomination?

KELLY: I was the second woman elected to the episcopacy in our denomination, but the first black person. It was an amazing experience.

USA TODAY: What has been the most difficult part of your journey?

KELLY: The hardest was the failure of my marriage. That was very hard for me and my children, who are close to their father. Divorce was devastating but I had to keep moving forward because of my children. Also, because of my children there was a need for a rebirth in me. In the midst of failure I had to develop my own faith system. What I grew up with was not enough.

USA TODAY: How did you develop that faith system?

KELLY: I disciplined myself through prayer, meditation and Bible study long before I went to the seminary. I had to trust and say, "If my faith is real, then I have to trust it." The joy of my life as a young child came from the faith of my mother and father, faith that my black forebears gave their children. The same faith that knew a day would come when slaves would be free. Faith that education was a way of helping the whole race.

USA TODAY: Was your divorce a barrier to becoming a bishop?

KELLY: One of my friends told me I shouldn't become a bishop because I was divorced. I really struggled with that before I entered the ministry. The questions about my being divorced were raised by people who obviously had a problem with it. Eventually I felt God called me as I was.

USA TODAY: Were there other barriers?

KELLY: Some people who were dear friends felt it was foolish for a black woman to consider running hundreds of churches.

USA TODAY: You were pastor of the Asbury church in Richmond, Va., for seven years. Did that help you on your road to becoming a bishop?

KELLY: We ran an urban program that helped the seniors and enriched the education of the young people. Both programs were highly successful. I was very active in the community as a minister's wife and teacher for 10 years. I was on the Richmond school board. And I was active in the clergywomen's movement across the country. It was women from this group that asked me to become a candidate for bishop.

USA TODAY: How difficult was it to get the nomination?

KELLY: I was a member of the Southeastern jurisdiction. When the women in the Southeast asked me to be their candidate for the episcopacy in 1984, we knew there was no way that the South was going to elect a black woman bishop. The women went to work. All across the church, clergywomen were saying if I couldn't be elected from the South, then I would be elected from another part of the country. There was a deliberate movement to keep me from being elected, even from being eligible to run.

USA TODAY: Why couldn't you enter the episcopacy through the traditional routes?

KELLY: You enter the episcopacy in three ways: as a president of a seminary or a Methodist college, as a district superintendent or as a general officer in the church. There wasn't a woman in any of those areas because they had to be appointed. So we knew there had to be a new way of doing things. We had to make that happen.

USA TODAY: How did you feel during the fight?

KELLY: Sometimes I felt like giving up, but in my heart I knew I would be nominated if the Lord intended it. And if it wasn't the will of the Lord, I didn't need it. I was also part of a powerful group of clergywomen who met and prayed. One young minister came up to us and said, "The clergywomen are not very politically astute, but they have great theology." We said, "We will stand on our theology, rather than political astuteness."

USA TODAY: So you were nominated from outside your jurisdiction?

KELLY: In 1984 I had suffered a great loss. I was returning from my mother's funeral in Cincinnati when I got a call from the clergywomen in California. They didn't believe a black woman could be elected from the Southeast; they wanted to know if I would mind if they nominated me. I went up to my room and prayed about it and said, "Well, this is really serious." And sure enough, that conference voted to nominate me.

USA TODAY: Were members of other ethnic groups nominated at the same time?

KELLY: A Japanese and a Hispanic were also nominated. One of the delegates asked if I could justify a ballot without a single Caucasian on it. I said, "Sure I can justify that because I've been voting on ballots with nothing but Caucasians on them most of my life."

USA TODAY: When were you elected?

KELLY: I was elected in July 1984 and was consecrated the next day as a bishop. It was a beautiful ceremony. The three bishops were consecrated in Boise, Idaho. My daughter Angela was there. The first consecration was in Spanish. It was very powerful. I was elected next. Somebody began to sing *We Shall Overcome.* When I finished speaking, people sang *Amazing Grace.* Young people stood up in the balcony. You are talking about 1,000 people. I looked up there and there were Hispanics, Native Americans, blacks and Caucasians. They began singing *We Are A Rainbow Ready to Shine.* The place was on fire.

USA TODAY: Were you crying at that point?

KELLY: Of course. Everybody was crying. And a young black woman started singing *When You Give the Best of Your Service, He'll Understand And Say Well Done,* which was my father's favorite.

USA TODAY: What is the significance of your election?

KELLY: It was the first for a black woman in the

KELLY PROFILE

Born: March 5, 1920, in Washington, D.C.

Family: Divorced and widowed; four children, Angela Current, Gloster Current Jr., John David Kelly and Pamela Kelly.

Education: Bachelor of arts from Virginia Union University, Richmond; master of divinity from Union Theological Seminary, Richmond, Va.

On life: "Divorce was devastating but I had to keep moving forward because of my children. Also, because of my children there was a need for a rebirth in me. In the midst of failure I had to develop my own faith system. ... I disciplined myself through prayer, meditation and Bible study long before I went to the seminary."

Home: San Francisco.

Role models: Her mother, Ila Turpeau; Mary McLeod Bethune.

MILESTONES

1969: Succeeded her late husband, James D. Kelly, as lay speaker at the Galilee United Methodist Church, Edwardsville, Va., serving until 1975.

1976: Pastor of Asbury United Methodist Church, Richmond, Va., serving until 1983; ordained an elder and full member of the Virginia Conference of the United Methodist Church.

1981: Grass-roots Leadership Award from the Virginia unit of the Southern Christian Leadership Conference.

1983: Member of the national staff of the United Methodist Church, based in Nashville, Tenn.

1984: Elected to the episcopacy in Boise, Idaho; appointed resident bishop of the United Methodist Church for the San Francisco Bay Area in September.

1986: Recognized by *Ebony* magazine for contributions to religion.

1987: Southern Christian Leadership Conference Drum Major for Justice Award.

history of Christiandom in a major denomination, as far as we know. When the news of my ordination hit, there was dancing in the street.

USA TODAY: Do you still face much sexism in the ministry?

KELLY: Yes. As one man said to me, "You are doing a great job, but you just shouldn't be doing it." But Apostle Paul said in the New Testament that in Jesus Christ there was neither slave nor free, Greeks nor Jews, male nor female. All are one in Jesus Christ.

USA TODAY: If women were equal in the eyes of God, why didn't Jesus pick any as disciples?

KELLY: Women were not called to be disciples. That is true. But Jesus revealed who he was to a woman — the woman at the well. Women were the first to witness the resurrection of Jesus. And then Jesus sat and talked with women, which was contrary to the mores of the day. He was the same with the Gentiles. He gave universalism to the whole understanding of the Gospel, as did Paul later.

USA TODAY: You work with young people. What can be done to counter negative influences that they face?

KELLY: We have got to begin with adults. There was a time when black professionals had a commitment to community. You were always pulling people up. Now, to be professional does not mean that. I am talking about a feeling of relationship between people. That sense of relationship that enables them to work together for the common good of all. Individual skills, individual abilities are developed, but they are developed for the good of all rather than just for self-attainment. We were forced to do that in a segregated society.

USA TODAY: You are talking about a different set of values we once had. Are they lost?

KELLY: We grew up in a generation where people were concerned about what you were going to be, not just your name, because the race needed you. We were reared to believe a single failure was one that we could not afford. We could not afford people on street corners. We could not afford to lose young people. Our educational institutions were based on this. I hope we can regain that urgency.

CORETTA SCOTT KING

She's making her own strong impact while keeping her husband's dream alive

KING: 'Martin had the kind of love that reached out to people. They responded in kind — not only in this nation but around the world.'

IMPRESSIONS

I met her on assignment. I was writing a magazine cover story for the *Chicago Tribune.* In the years that followed, Coretta Scott King became my teacher, mentor and friend. Once we spent Thanksgiving together at her parents' home in Marion, Ala. She shared with me her dream of a center for social change long before it became a reality in Atlanta. She taught me more about moral leadership and about working with the spirit of God than most because she did it not with words, but by example. The longer I know her the more I understand the possibilities for my own life.

— **Barbara Reynolds**

She stood with her husband through the 1960s protests and worked for his dream after he was felled by an assassin's bullet in 1968. Coretta Scott King continued as a single parent, rearing four children. She built The Martin Luther King Jr. Center for Nonviolent Social Change, taking up two blocks along Auburn Avenue in Atlanta, and has worked for other programs to continue King's legacy of justice, peace and brotherhood. In the 20 years since Dr. King's death, his widow has emerged as a leader in her own right and a powerful force in the worldwide movement for equality. She was also a leader in the move to commemorate Dr. King's life with a federal holiday. Interviews with her appeared on USA TODAY *Inquiry pages Jan. 14, 1983, Oct. 9, 1984, and Jan. 15, 1986.*

USA TODAY: When you hear Dr. King's famed "I Have A Dream" speech played today, what do you recall about your husband and the era in which he lived?

KING: That he was lifting people above the reality. When he spoke about his dream in 1963, it was nowhere near the reality. People had to go back to their segregated communities. It was a kind of philosophical statement of where we needed to be in the spiritual sense. At that moment it was happening because we were right there together with black and white people at the Lincoln Memorial. If it could work right there and we could experience what it felt like, then the next step was, "Why can't we have it?"

USA TODAY: Are you satisfied with the course civil rights has taken since your husband's death?

KING: I can't say I'm totally satisfied. But we have made great strides. In 1963 we had a totally segregated society. The next year we had the desegregation of public accommodations. One year later we had the Voting Rights Act. We had our first two black mayors elected in 1967 — Carl Stokes in Cleveland and Richard Hatcher in Gary, Ind. Since that time we have elected many black public officials at different levels. There are very few major cities left that don't have black mayors.

USA TODAY: Is the dream unfulfilled?

KING: In the achievement of economic justice we still have a mighty long way to go. We have

hardly begun. In 1978 Congress passed legislation called the Humphrey-Hawkins Full Employment and Balanced Growth Act. It said every person has a right to a meaningful job with decent pay and working conditions. It was the first time there was a major policy statement on economic rights.

USA TODAY: How has the dream come alive in your family?

KING: There is one small incident I can give. When Yolanda was a child I had to tell her why she couldn't go to the Fun Town amusement park. It took me awhile to do it because every day this jingle would come on television and they were singing, "Fun Town." Yolanda and Marty would say, "Oh, Mommy take us to Fun Town!" And I would say, "Well, we'll go one day."

USA TODAY: What did you finally tell her?

KING: I had to sit her down and explain that the people who built Fun Town, unfortunately, were not nice people. They liked some people, but they didn't like black people. So they decided they wanted to make it just for white people. But one day they would be able to go because what their daddy was doing now was working to make it possible. I told them, "One day in the not-too-distant future, we're going to be able to go."

USA TODAY: Did your children ever go?

KING: They did! When the Civil Rights bill passed in 1964, we went to Fun Town, all of us together. And it was really great. A white lady ran up and said, "Is that your daughter?" The Fun Town story had been written about in *Ebony* magazine and this lady must have been reading it. I said, "Yes." And she said, "Well, good," and walked away. She didn't say anything else. My children saw the change come about. I guess it helped a great deal. I couldn't tell them all the ugliness about it. Most parents try to protect their kids. Thank goodness, I had something very positive to say about Martin's involvement. It helped them accept the fact that although he loved them, he had to be away so much.

USA TODAY: Despite tragedy after tragedy, your children have never been in trouble and all show strong leadership skills. As a single parent, how were you able to do so well?

KING: We tried to demonstrate in our lives the values that our children would embrace and learn to respect. And children do learn by example. I feel they understood the life their father lived and they have understood the life I have lived. I wanted them to become their best selves and understand that they had to give back something.

USA TODAY: Have your children encouraged you to remarry?

KING: It would be nice sometimes to have companionship, but it's not a serious problem. The children have thought about that. I think in a sense they felt my work took me away from the possibility of developing a personal life. As I grew older they learned to appreciate that.

USA TODAY: None of your children has married. Is being a King larger than life for them?

KING: I'm sure there are always expectations that people have for children of people who are in the limelight. They're aware of this and it is something they have carried well. I don't know how much of an impediment it has been to their getting married. The older children have had a normal interest in getting married. But most of them aren't ready yet.

USA TODAY: What is the most important aspect of the life of Dr. King?

KING: Martin had the kind of love that reached out to people. They responded in kind — not only in this nation but around the world. Love is such a powerful force. It's there for everyone to embrace — that kind of unconditional love for all of humankind. That is the kind of love that impels people to go into the community and try to change conditions for others, to take risks for what they believe in.

USA TODAY: How do we learn to love?

KING: The ability to love is a gift from God. God is love. Martin's love was an unconditional love. He didn't prejudge people. Most of us have a tendency to make judgments about other people. We prejudge before we even give people an opportunity to express themselves. We develop an attitude or opinion. That often becomes a prejudice.

USA TODAY: So love is not a passive concept?

KING: No. It is the most important ingredient of many non-violent crusades. When people carry this "love force" in their own lives and express it to others, it has a transforming effect. It becomes a force for bringing things together, for unifying. It is that kind of force that can help people do what they really want to do but can't manage to do otherwise.

USA TODAY: Can that concept be used to deal with today's problems?

KING: Love directs you — out of compassion

KING PROFILE

Born: April 27, 1927, in Marion, Ala.

Family: Widowed; four children, Yolanda D., Martin Luther III, Dexter S., Bernice A.

Education: Bachelor of arts from Antioch College, Yellow Springs, Ohio; postgraduate studies at the New England Conservatory of Music, Boston.

On life: "It's important to involve your children so they feel a part of what you're doing."

Home: Atlanta.

Role models: Eleanor Roosevelt, Paul Robeson, Mary McLeod Bethune and Mahatma Gandhi.

MILESTONES

1948: Concert debut as a vocalist in Springfield, Ohio.

1953: Married Dr. Martin Luther King Jr.

1959: Toured Europe and Asia with Dr. King.

1962: Delegate to Women's Strike for Peace at 17-nation disarmament conference in Geneva, Switzerland.

1964: Performed more than 30 "freedom concerts" of lectures, poetry and songs illustrating the civil rights movement.

1968: Dr. King killed.

1969: *My Life With Martin Luther King, Jr.* published; founded The Martin Luther King Center for Nonviolent Social Change, Atlanta.

1978: Worked for passage of the Humphrey-Hawkins Full Employment and Balanced Growth Act.

1982: Opened Freedom Hall Complex of The Martin Luther King Jr. center.

1983: Bill making the third Monday in January the national King holiday is signed.

1987: Filed suit against Boston University to recover papers Dr. King donated to the school before his death.

and the need to translate problems into solutions for such issues as the homeless, nuclear war and social justice. Love is transforming not only for the victim but also for the oppressor.

USA TODAY: Since 1968 many have been working to honor Dr. King with a national holiday. How should the USA observe the King holiday?

KING: I don't have any problems with the fireworks and the picnics. But I do have problems if it is limited to that. It should be a serious day when we think about the meaning of Martin Luther King Jr.'s life and engage in non-violent action.

USA TODAY: Does it bother you that a few cities and states don't observe the holiday?

KING: I expect many people who oppose it will begin embracing it. When the Civil Rights Act was passed, when segregation became illegal in public accommodations, a lot of people went along and accepted it. They respected the law. Pretty soon they'll forget they once opposed it.

USA TODAY: Is it a black holiday?

KING: It is not promoted as a black holiday. We promote it as a holiday for people of all races and religions and color. It should be an all-American holiday and it should be celebrated as such. I would be disappointed if it turned out to be a black holiday. He was all-inclusive. As some people have said here in the South, "He freed more white people than he did black people." I suspect that's true.

USA TODAY: You are saying that the movement cuts across racial, economic and sexual lines?

KING: The large numbers of poor whites in this country don't have an advocate for their cause; therefore, the general public does not know that they exist. They are part of the invisible poor. My husband aided them, too, because legislation enacted for minorities affects poor whites as well. It's important to note that the whole women's rights movement gained respectability and momentum after the civil rights movement had been successful.

USA TODAY: What is most important to you?

KING: My four children. I've always told my staff that if the president of the United States is talking to me, I want to be interrupted if any of my kids call me. Never keep them away from me. It's important to involve your children so they feel a part of what you're doing. They grew up in the movement. It was a way of life for them. I told them they didn't have to be like anybody but themselves — their own best selves.

MARTIN LUTHER KING SR.

His life symbolized love and forgiveness though hatred killed his wife and son

KING: 'Those of us who want peace . . . who want to share . . . have not been able to get our message across as well as the other side.'

IMPRESSIONS

"No one can make me stoop low enough to hate." That was Martin Luther King Sr., father of one of the world's greatest human rights and civil rights activists. Daddy King. I can still see him rise to his full height and rock with conviction as he said those words in that preacher's tremolo. His conviction, his song of life, took on special meaning because he was a man whose wife and son were claimed by men who hated. When others turned to bitterness, Daddy King reached for the Bible and responded with love. I remember him fondly and wonder how many of us can follow his example.

— **Barbara Reynolds**

He was the father of one of the world's greatest leaders, but Martin Luther King Sr. was a civil rights activist in his own right. He led a march through the streets of downtown Atlanta in 1936 to fight for voting rights at a time when such public protests were not popular and were very dangerous. Pastor of Ebenezer Baptist church in Atlanta for more than 40 years, his last interview with Barbara Reynolds was done in January 1984, about 10 months before his death. Interviews with King appeared on USA TODAY Inquiry pages Nov. 24, 1982, and Jan. 16, 1984.

USA TODAY: In 1986 the nation will begin celebrating the birthday of your son, Martin Luther King Jr., as a national holiday. How do you feel about that?

KING: I think it is tremendous. We are grateful as a family. We all worked hard for the Martin Luther King Jr. birthday bill. The young folks marched in the streets of Washington for it and we are now all looking forward to that day when it really is a reality.

USA TODAY Do you think all states will recognize the holiday?

KING: No matter what they say, every state is not going to fall into line.

USA TODAY: How will you convince the states to adopt a King holiday?

KING: We may have to take a few to court and spend a lot of money forcing them to do right. We also have to sell the idea to the general public. Don't forget there still are some people in America who don't know who Martin Luther King Jr. was — or who George Washington was, for that matter. So we have to educate people to help us.

USA TODAY: How do you think the USA should celebrate your son's birthday?

KING: I hope there won't be firecrackers like on the 4th of July. I hope there won't be a lot of drinking like on New Year's Eve and I hope it won't turn into the worship of materialism like on Christmas.

USA TODAY: Why?

KING: Dr. King was a church person, a religious man. So I hope people won't drink and carouse.

USA TODAY: What sort of commemoration would you like to see?

KING: I hope that the schools and churches will study the life of Dr. King and study his methods of non-violence. On that date, maybe we will pause and think about peace, love and brotherhood and how to create a society where those things are more important than war, hate and violence.

USA TODAY: How will you observe his birthday?

KING: I will be very much in prayer. I hope the nation will do likewise, praying for peace on earth, and studying the philosophy of non-violence.

USA TODAY: How would you grade President Reagan on civil rights?

KING: He would definitely flunk. I strongly wonder if he cares about the little man. I am afraid he is not concerned about the least of these. And there are more of them than there are of the rich.

USA TODAY: Do you have any examples?

KING: Remember when he said he grew up not knowing about segregation? Where had the man been? He came up in the heyday of segregation in this country. In fact, he was a part of that era.

USA TODAY: What specific objections do you have to his civil rights policies?

KING: He has tried to pack the Civil Rights Commission with people who are against affirmative action as a means of enforcing civil rights. He wanted to use taxpayers' money to support institutions that refused to admit blacks. The Justice Department seems to spend more time fighting so-called reverse discrimination than it does discrimination against blacks, women and other minorities. The whole ball game has changed since President Carter left the White House.

USA TODAY: Your son dreamed of an egalitarian nation where all have an equal opportunity to succeed. How is that dream faring?

KING: We thank God for the progress we've made, but this is still very much a racist society. We have a lot to do to totally rid the nation of racism. The current administration could turn the clock back on civil rights if we aren't careful.

USA TODAY: What is the best method for changing society?

KING: We should never get too tired or too sophisticated to march. That kind of response never goes out of style. And we should vote. Right now that is a powerful weapon in the hands of black America. When we vote our strength, we are demonstrating power. When we change the occupants in political office, from the statehouses to the White House, then we will be living up to the promise of the 1965 Voting Rights Act.

USA TODAY: If your son were alive, what would he be doing?

KING: He would be preaching and practicing the message of love. I'm afraid the teachers of hate have gotten their message across much better than the teachers of love. Those of us who want peace, not war, who want to share, not take, have not been able to get our message across as well as the other side. So if Dr. King were here today, his message, his life would tip the scale on the side of justice and right.

USA TODAY: Is it realistic to talk about love in a world preoccupied with strength and force?

KING: Look at Martin's life. He didn't have bombs and bullets. He was a student and practitioner of non-violence, a disciple of Gandhi. Gandhi used the same tactics to change India as Martin did to change America. And the world will never be the same because they lived. There are more powerful weapons in the universe than bombs. These are the principles that we teach at the King Center here in Atlanta. We believe that non-violence is today's answer to a violent world.

USA TODAY: Many have said that the civil rights movement died when your son was assassinated. Do you agree?

KING: No. That's because they don't understand what my son was about. My son was a powerful instrument for good, for social change, for love.

USA TODAY: What is your dream for the future?

KING: I just hope that the older people, with direction and vision, will help inspire the young to continue working for change. And I hope that the goal of abolishing racism is never forgotten. I, for one, will never stop. I will continue preaching about the power of love.

USA TODAY: What concerns you about children today?

KING: Some are misled, misguided, far less tutored and read than they should be. We're not teaching them what we used to call home training, respect for adults and each other, manners, good behavior. Their heads are filled up on sex and vio-

KING PROFILE

Born: Dec. 19, 1899, in Stockbridge, Ga.

Died: Nov. 11, 1984, in Atlanta of a heart attack.

Family: Married to Alberta, who was shot and killed in 1974; three children, Christine Farris, Rev. A.D. King, drowned in 1969, and Dr. Martin Luther King Jr., assassinated in 1968.

Education: Bachelor of arts from Morehouse College, Atlanta.

On life: "We thank God for the progress we've made, but this is still very much a racist society. We have a lot to do to totally rid the nation of racism. . . . We should never get too tired or too sophisticated to march. That kind of response never goes out of style. And we should vote. Right now that is a powerful weapon in the hands of black America."

Role model: Benjamin Mays.

MILESTONES

1931: Became pastor of Ebenezer Baptist Church, Atlanta; served there for 44 years.

1936: Led several hundred to city hall in Atlanta in a voting rights march.

1968: Dr. King killed.

1969: His son, Rev. A.D. King, drowns in family swimming pool in Atlanta.

1972: Named Clergyman of the Year by the Georgia Region of the National Conference of Christians and Jews.

1974: His wife, Alberta W. King, killed by gunfire as she sat at the church piano during Sunday morning service.

1976: Delivered invocation at the Democratic National Convention.

1979: Delivered a eulogy at the funeral of former Vice President Nelson A. Rockefeller.

1980: Delivered invocation at the Democratic National Convention.

lence from the TV and the movies and the music. You see, the parents should be living closer together, sharing more with the children and with their neighbors and their fellow man. This is a daily matter. A daily example of living for their children to see. And they should be teaching their children how to pray, and praying with them, too.

USA TODAY: Your son was assassinated in 1968. In 1974, a gunman murdered your wife while she was playing the piano in church. Did the murders leave you bitter?

KING: I refuse to be bitter. This is not the end of it. I thank God that He let me live long enough to know that the end is not here. The Lord always leaves you something to be grateful about. Look at all my grandchildren. And look at Martin Luther King III, a fine young man. My name is still living.

USA TODAY: What do you feel toward those responsible for your son's and wife's deaths?

KING: I will never stoop low enough to hate. Never. I don't feel bitterness in my heart against anybody. I forgave them. There is no time for hate, no reason for hate either. You cannot stoop any lower than hate. I don't let hate penetrate my heart.

USA TODAY: Did you ever doubt your faith, doubt the existence of God?

KING: Oh, no, no. I am a deep believer in God. I was before; I still am. I couldn't have made it but for that. And I don't accept that my loved ones are dead. My son will never die. He's just not here as such. I don't believe in death and dying.

MARTIN LUTHER KING III

Family unity has helped him strengthen
the civil rights foundation laid by his father

KING: 'Daddy was, in my mind, such a loving and caring person. I didn't understand why anybody would dislike him enough to kill him.'

IMPRESSIONS

Fighting back tears one day in the basement of his Atlanta home, Martin Luther King III talked about his father, about the twin bikes father and 10-year-old son had received for Christmas 1967. The bikes they never got to ride together because of an assassin's bullet the following April. He told me he missed his daddy, Dr. Martin Luther King Jr. I worried that the weight of the tragedy would one day break his heart. But his father once said that a leader had to have both tender heart and tough mind. As the son of the great civil rights leader grows older, he shows both.

— **Barbara Reynolds**

He says he would like to be a U.S. senator one day, and Martin Luther King III has begun a career in politics as a Fulton County, Ga., commissioner. Along with two sisters and a brother, he watched his mother pick up the pieces and hold his family together after the death of his father. Her positive images and the powerful memory of his father, Dr. Martin Luther King Jr., shaped his dedication to God and the rights of all people. King says he does not live in the shadow of his father, but he says his father lives in his memory each day. An interview with King appeared on the USA TODAY *Inquiry page Aug. 24, 1983.*

USA TODAY: You were elected to the Fulton County, Ga., Commission in 1987. How deep is your commitment to politics?

KING: I plan to serve as long as I can make a contribution and as long as the people in our community want me to be involved in the political arena. This is one way to contribute to the community that nourished my growth and development.

USA TODAY: What do you believe is the value of black involvement in politics?

KING: In the 1960s many of us could not be in the political arena. It would take years to accomplish things that today might only take four votes. For example, the county commission can adopt legislation and sign bills into law at the stroke of a pen and help create opportunities for people. The political process is one that allows you to really help massive numbers of people.

USA TODAY: Was politics an area in which your father thought blacks could make great gains?

KING: This is one of the major avenues. But we have only begun to scratch the surface nationally. We have mayors, but we have no governors and no U.S. senators. The real thrust has got to be economic development.

USA TODAY: Can government help?

KING: It certainly can. One key example here in Atlanta is Herman Russell, one of the largest black contractors in the country. He was doing well when Maynard Jackson became mayor. But Russell really began to do much better when Jackson initiated an affirmative action contract-compliance program.

USA TODAY: How do you explain the fact that new immigrants are becoming more successful at running businesses in black areas than blacks?

KING: We are programmed against ourselves. Granddaddy used to say that we had to "unlearn" that which has been learned. The point he was making was that some of us have been conditioned to believe that anything sold to us by other people will be better than what blacks would sell.

USA TODAY: You were only 10 when your father was assassinated. How did you cope with that?

KING: Being 10 years old, I didn't really understand what was going on. Daddy was, in my mind, such a loving and caring person. I didn't understand why anybody would dislike him enough to kill him. I didn't really understand how significant he was to our society. And maybe now as an adult I still don't understand.

USA TODAY: How did the loss of your father affect you?

KING: Losing Daddy to some degree stunted my growth and development. Any child losing their father would suffer the same thing. It was my mother who helped me deal with it. She had already explained over the years how Daddy had been working trying to make this world a better place for all of God's children. I remember one day I was in school and a kid called Daddy a jailbird and a communist. Naturally I started crying.

USA TODAY: What did your mother say?

KING: She said: "Your father does go to jail quite frequently, but every time he goes to jail he makes it better for your generation. He is trying to make this a better place for all of God's children." Well, naturally, I acquired a new dignity. I went back to school the next day and no matter what this kid said to me it was not going to deter my faith in what my father was trying to do.

USA TODAY: How did your mother tell you that your father had been shot?

KING: Mother said to us, "Your father has gone home to live with God." We already understood that just by virtue of our going to Sunday school. We already believed that God was going to make a way no matter what happened. Certainly it hurt. The emotional part of it was still there for years and years. I don't know if you can ever get over that. It helped a lot that my mother was so strong and went on with the movement after my father's death.

USA TODAY: You found strength in family?

KING: I saw and felt a lot of strength. I saw Granddaddy say that he didn't hate anybody, that he loved everybody. That loving, strong, family network acted as a support system. I believe that is what made it possible for us to prevail. Even more important is that deep belief in God.

USA TODAY: As an adult, do you have a better sense of what happened now?

KING: It is much clearer. I believe now that God permits evil. And when God gets ready to intervene, God is going to intervene and change the whole situation.

USA TODAY: You sound like a preacher. Have you ruled out going into the ministry?

KING: I haven't ruled out anything. I do not feel at this time God is leading me in that direction. But if I do begin to feel that God is calling me to the ministry, then I will rise to the occasion.

USA TODAY: You are a leader in a new generation. How do you evaluate what has been done and what is still left to do?

KING: Integration helped immensely but integration created a liability within the minds of people. For example, prior to integration we had to patronize black businesses. We had no choice. We had to be communal. We could not stop or stay in the hotels. We could not stop and eat in the restaurants so when we traveled we had to pack lunches and just kind of go from house to house and hope that someone would let us stay for the night.

USA TODAY: Are you saying progress has its drawbacks?

KING: Once we became an integrated society, we became selfish and we tried to forget the past. If people do not remember their history they are doomed to repeat it, Daddy used to say. Somewhere along the line the children have not learned their history, our history. They are suffering from the "me" syndrome — I have mine and you get yours. Many of them even now don't know who Martin Luther King Jr. is. Had we not gotten a holiday, many more wouldn't have known him at all.

USA TODAY: What should young people know about black history?

KING: They don't understand what suffering took place or what the fight was really about.

USA TODAY: In your view, why did the changes of the 1960s happen?

KING: Everything that has happened was done

KING PROFILE

Born: Oct. 23, 1957, in Montgomery, Ala.

Family: Single.

Education: Bachelor of arts from Morehouse College, Atlanta.

On life: "In the 1960s many of us could not be in the political arena. It would take years to accomplish things that today might only take four votes. For example, the county commission can adopt legislation and sign bills into law at the stroke of a pen and help create opportunities for people. The political process is one that allows you to really help massive numbers of people. . . . But we have only begun to scratch the surface nationally."

Home: Atlanta.

Role models: His mother, Coretta Scott King; his father, Dr. Martin Luther King Jr.

MILESTONES

1968: Dr. King killed.

1974: Appointed a director of The Martin Luther King Jr. Center for Nonviolent Social Change, Atlanta.

1976: Consultant to President Jimmy Carter's election campaign; page on Sen. Edward Kennedy's Washington, D.C., staff.

1977: Technical adviser to and cameo role in the made-for-TV movie *King*.

1980: Consultant to President Carter's re-election campaign; staff aide to Atlanta Mayor Andrew Young; delegate to Democratic National Convention.

1982: Appointed to the board of directors of *Black Family* magazine.

1984: Fact-finding tour of drought-stricken areas in Africa, for The Martin Luther King Center for Nonviolent Social Change.

1986: Elected to the Fulton County, Ga., Board of Commissioners.

1987: Named vice chairman of National Labor Relations Committee of the National Association of County Officials.

in the interest of economics. They were not moral decisions. It's really been predicated on a large group of businessmen saying we are losing a large amount of revenue by not letting blacks come and shop downtown. If we had maintained our community spirit and then become an integrated society, it would be tremendous. We would probably be one of the most powerful ethnic groups in the world. Many of us have been programmed to hate ourselves. That is why we have the greatest homicide rate of any ethnic group. Something is wrong.

USA TODAY: Why is that hate surfacing?

KING: I believe the hatred has been surfacing for years. All our lives we have been told that we are nothing. A lot of it has been done over television. So I don't blame exclusively a white individual for being a racist. Society conditions him or her to be a racist. It is the system, not an individual.

USA TODAY: Is your father's message of love one way to counter racism and self-hate?

KING: That is one of the keys. It has to be love. Develop a true love for yourself. That means taking a hard look at yourself and writing down all the bad and good qualities that you have and eliminate the bad. Then say, "Even though I have these problems, I love me." You have really got to love yourself before you can even begin to love another.

USA TODAY: Do you feel the comparisons with your father are a heavy burden?

KING: Maybe unconsciously. I feel that some parts of the world are watching me because that has been programmed by people around me. I don't think the world is watching me. Not in the same sense that the world watches the Kennedy kids. I am a black American. I still believe that my destiny or my achievements can be unlimited. I believe that I can do whatever God wants me to do, whether it will be in politics or out of politics.

USA TODAY: Do you think there will ever be another man like Dr. Martin Luther King Jr.?

KING: Not for some time. I don't try to live my life trying to do what he did. If I did, I would have already flunked. Daddy at 28 was on the cover of *Time*. He was a national leader by the time he was 27. So I don't try to compare myself with Dad. I just hope God will allow me to enhance what he did.

SUGAR RAY LEONARD

Drive to win made him a champion;
he's passing on the secret to the young

LEONARD: 'You have to know you can win. You have to think you can win. You feel you can win. . . . Call it a plus.'

IMPRESSIONS

"Most defeat is in your brain," Sugar Ray Leonard said when I visited his training camp in Palmer Park, Md., shortly before his 1987 bout with Marvin Hagler. Watching him train, I knew that Hagler — who seemed so much bigger and more brutal — would destroy him. I even refused an invitation to the fight. I didn't want to see Leonard hurt. Because of his past eye injuries he was taking a tremendous risk. The next time I saw Leonard — after his victory over Hagler — we were both taking our sons to the movies, and he again told me that most defeat is in your brain. This time I didn't argue.

— **Barbara Reynolds**

Sugar Ray Leonard is one of the most celebrated boxers in history, winning professional titles in three weight classes. His April 6, 1987, victory over Marvelous Marvin Hagler for a purse of about $13 million is considered by many as the ring event of the decade. After winning an Olympic gold medal in 1976, he turned professional. His pro record: 34 wins, including 24 knockouts, and one loss. He avenged his June 20, 1980, loss to Roberto Duran five months later — on Nov. 25 — leaving Duran saying, "No mas. No mas," at the bout's end. A role model for young people across the USA, Leonard is known as generous, concerned and family oriented. Since retiring in 1987, he has helped train and manage young boxing hopefuls. An interview with Leonard appeared on the USA TODAY *Inquiry page Aug. 14, 1987.*

USA TODAY: You have won many titles in your career, knocking out numerous contenders. Do people ever tell you you cannot win?

LEONARD: Yes. Take the Marvin Hagler fight. People told me: "Ray, you can't beat him. It will be a defiance of history, logic and physics." The day before the fight I dedicated my winnings to a camp for terminally ill kids in New York. I did that because when people say you can't do something, you can't believe them. What my critics were telling me was the same thing people were telling those kids. That they didn't have a chance. But just as I had a chance, those kids have a chance. It's a matter of believing in yourself and trusting in God.

USA TODAY: Most people do not identify you with strong religious convictions.

LEONARD: My mother, my wife, my grandmother — we are all Baptists. If you don't think I am religious, why do you think I wear a crucifix around my neck? I always wear it when I fly. I do that because I am not one who loves to fly — you can't control what's going on up there.

USA TODAY: How do you convince yourself that you are a winner?

LEONARD: It is motivation and it is a matter of being a nonconformist. I had to take the negatives, the things that were in my way — like race, greed, money, ego — and transform them into positives. You have to know you can win. You have to think you can win. You feel you can win. So I had that feeling — that certain thing. I don't know what you call it. Call it a plus.

USA TODAY: As a fighter don't you often play mind games to destroy your opponent's confidence?

LEONARD: It is psychological warfare. It's a matter of diminishing another man's confidence. People don't realize that my psychology is based on a winning performance. I convinced Hagler, who was reigning champion for 11 straight years, to finally contemplate losing. Dealing with the opponent's persona is the biggest obstacle I face.

USA TODAY: How do people, blacks in particular, who have been put down, condemned and trivialized, convince themselves they are winners?

LEONARD: As blacks we fall prey to the myth, the stigma that we can't excel. We tend to use that as a barricade. I always have believed that you can be whatever you want to be if you are willing to sacrifice and dedicate yourself. So many of us say we want to be this, we want to be that, but we can't make it because of social and racial injustices. Those things can slow us down, but can't stop us.

USA TODAY: People see you as a wealthy boxer who can afford the best clothes, cars and homes. What did you sacrifice?

LEONARD: What you see is what materialized from hard work and dedication and belief. I always have said that what got me to this pedestal was giving up my social life. That sounds so insignificant now, but it wasn't back then.

USA TODAY: What kinds of social activities did you give up?

LEONARD: I would run to school instead of taking the bus. A lot of students laughed at me. They said, "This guy must be crazy." For gym, the coach would allow me to jump rope instead of requiring me to play basketball. I would jump rope for the entire class. I look back at myself and think that those who laughed at me had a good case. I might have acted like I was crazy. But it was the desire to win that drove me onward.

USA TODAY: When did you decide to box?

LEONARD: The idea started in junior high school in 1970 when I started winning local tournaments and would travel to places like Nevada, Florida and Wisconsin. It was an opportunity for me to grow, to go places I could not afford to visit on my own.

USA TODAY: Who was your hero?

LEONARD: My father, Cicero. He's a share-cropper's son from a hard and tough background. Whatever happened he always had to mentally smile and keep working. Just keep working. No matter what the dilemma, he just maintained. When I fight now, he cooks my meals.

USA TODAY: **Your family moved to Washington, D.C., from North Carolina when you were 3 years old. What was life like after the move?**

LEONARD: My parents came North looking for job opportunities. There were five children then. Now I have three brothers and three sisters. But back then we didn't starve. We just had the necessities. My mother and father worked incredible hours to fill the table for all of us. My mother worked as an LPN, a licensed practical nurse. My father worked at supermarkets for hours and hours at a time, from 11 p.m. to 11 a.m. or noon the next day.

USA TODAY: **Some fighters have won millions but, like Joe Louis, died penniless. How are you protecting yourself?**

LEONARD: Fighters are stereotyped as mismanaging money. I always felt that my money and what I do with it is no one's business but my own.

USA TODAY: **I see you are becoming angry!**

LEONARD: People don't ask Frank Sinatra that question, but they ask black fighters. I'm familiar with what happened to Joe Louis. I will always take that question as an insult. I'm glad you asked it though. I want people to know how I feel.

USA TODAY: **After making about $13 million on the Hagler fight, you retired. But we have heard that retirement song before. Will you fight again?**

LEONARD: This is it. I'm retired. I now represent other boxers. I have started a management firm and I have several guys under contract.

USA TODAY: **Many people worry about your eyes because you suffered a detached retina in 1982. Was your retirement based in part on a fear that someone would go for your eyes in the ring?**

LEONARD: No. If you ask every fighter, unless you really manipulate him, no one will say — well, go for Ray's eye. That is the last thing on their minds. The idea of just defeating me — that's their objective. I could go for *their* eyes. I could go for their noses. We go in there with the intention of defeating each other, not with the intention of seriously injuring anyone. There is a camaraderie fighters have. The barbaric image that boxing possesses is mainly because people have been watching too

LEONARD PROFILE

Born: May 17, 1956, in Wilmington, N.C.

Family: Married to Juanita Leonard; two children, Ray Jr. and Jarrel.

Education: Graduate of Parkdale High School in Prince George's County, Md.

On life: "I always have believed that you can be whatever you want to be if you are willing to sacrifice and dedicate yourself. So many of us say we want to be this, we want to be that, but we can't make it because of social and racial injustices. Those things can slow us down, but can't stop us."

Home: Glen Dale, Md.

Role models: His father, Cicero Leonard; boxer Muhammad Ali and Eddie Robinson, football coach of Grambling State University, Grambling, La.

MILESTONES

1975: Gold medal in boxing in Pan American games.

1976: Gold medal at the Olympic Games.

1979: Won World Boxing Council (WBC) welterweight title (147 pounds maximum weight) Nov. 30, ousting Wilfred Benitez.

1980: Lost WBC welterweight title to Roberto Duran on June 20. Regained title on Nov. 25, defeating Duran.

1981: Won World Boxing Association (WBA) junior middleweight championship (154 pounds maximum weight) on June 25, 1981, by defeating Ayub Kalue. Unified WBA and WBC welterweight titles by defeating Thomas Hearns on Sept. 16.

1982: Retired after detection of an eye injury, a detached retina.

1984: Returned to ring to fight Kevin Howard, knocking him out.

1987: Won middleweight title (160 pounds maximum weight) by defeating Marvelous Marvin Hagler by a unanimous decision on April 6.

many *Rocky* films.

USA TODAY: The boxing world does have its seedy side. What do you say to others to encourage them to steer clear of the drug pushers and other symbols of the fast life?

LEONARD: You must create an incentive at an early age for them to succeed. It is so easy to deviate from a positive role, from a positive goal because of the distractions, the influence of drugs and the illusion of grandeur they give. People see the guys on the street making it with illegal profits. You have to instill in them the fact that they have healthy bodies, valuable minds that they must utilize to the fullest. You have to talk to them and explain to them without being too domineering. It really takes a great deal of psychology. You can't lie and say you have never done wrong yourself. You have to play it straight. We've all done something at some time or another that was not right.

USA TODAY: How do you feel about yourself?

LEONARD: I feel I have reached a point where I have broken the color barrier. People don't see me just as black, but as an individual who has triumphed. When people come to you — elderly whites, elderly blacks and young kids — and say things like: "Hey man, I really love you! You have made a difference. You've given me that extra amount of confidence in myself to continue although my whole foundation has collapsed." Those types of things are so profound and they mean so much to me.

USA TODAY: Would you want your sons to follow in your steps?

LEONARD: If they really wanted to it would be fine. But I think it wouldn't be a good idea because they would be compared to their father. And kids have enough problems with peer pressure as it is.

JOSEPH LOWERY

His activism and ministry push the cause of equal opportunity, justice and peace

LOWERY: 'My job as a minister is to not only make heaven my home, but to make my home on earth sheer heaven.'

IMPRESSIONS

It was a tough job taking the helm of the Southern Christian Leadership Conference after the organization's founder — Dr. Martin Luther King Jr. — was assassinated in 1968. Joseph Lowery accomplished that in a way that commanded national respect. Lowery has made people see that his 20-year journey to maintain and enliven the dream of Dr. King is working. In 1987 he made me feel that I, too, was working on that dream when he handed me an honor I will always cherish — the SCLC's Drum Major for Justice Award.

— **Barbara Reynolds**

Joseph Lowery was named board chairman of the Southern Christian Leadership Conference in 1967 by Dr. Martin Luther King Jr. With a stellar history as a fighter in the civil rights movement, Lowery has kept King's dream alive through his work in the South and across the USA. A minister in the United Methodist Church, he has combined service to his church with the fight for the rights of others. Before he became a minister, he was editor of the Informer, *a black newspaper in Birmingham, Ala., that is now the* Mirror. *He has been pastor of Cascade United Methodist Church in Atlanta since 1986. An interview with Lowery appeared on the* USA TODAY *Inquiry page March 8, 1985.*

USA TODAY: You have virtually become Mr. Civil Rights, your involvement has been so long and arduous. When did you become involved?

LOWERY: I entered the civil rights movement when I was born. It was an action predetermined by white folks. I believe that all black folks live with the edict that they must enter the movement or perish. When I was 10 or 11 years old, I was a victim of an incident in an Alabama store. A big white police officer pushed me in the stomach with a billy club. Although I was almost out of the store, he said "Get back nigger, don't you see a white man is coming?" My father tried to protect me. He went to the chief of police who told him that there was nothing we could do. I knew then that something had to be done to free blacks from that kind of oppression. After I finished school, I edited a newspaper that crusaded against racial injustice. From the very beginning I knew that my ministry would reach for reconciliation, justice, love and peace. These are all components of the civil rights movement.

USA TODAY: When did you meet Dr. Martin Luther King Jr.?

LOWERY: When he came to Montgomery, Ala., to pastor. I was pastor of a church in Mobile. We were both leading movements against bus segregation. I raised some money in Mobile to support the Montgomery boycott and took it up there. I met him in Montgomery and we became friends. Later Rev. Ralph Abernathy, Martin, Fred Shuttlesworth of Birmingham and I would meet monthly in Montgomery to exchange ideas and discuss how we could support each others' movements.

USA TODAY: How was the idea for the Southern Christian Leadership Conference born?

LOWERY: It was out of those meetings that the idea to organize the entire South began. In early 1957 we met in New Orleans and founded SCLC.

USA TODAY: What other campaigns were important?

LOWERY: I was involved in a great many. The most exciting demonstration was a 1982 pilgrimage from Carrollton, Ga., to Montgomery, Ala.

USA TODAY: What prompted that march and what did you accomplish?

LOWERY: Two black women in Carrollton, Maggie Bozemann and Julia Wilder, were convicted of voting fraud. Their only crime was being black and politically active. By marching to Washington, we were able to tie their defense to the extension of the Voting Rights Act. We wanted to get the Voting Rights Act extended and to free Bozemann and Wilder. We got them out of jail. The Voting Rights Act was extended for 25 years.

USA TODAY: How many people participated?

LOWERY: We had a core of 100 who made the entire pilgrimage, but our numbers increased and decreased along the way. That was the longest march I had ever participated in, five states and 80 cities. It started in February and ended in June.

USA TODAY: You have told of the most exciting march. Which was the most dangerous?

LOWERY: The most dangerous march occurred in 1979 in Decatur, Ala. We marched on behalf of Tommy Lee Hines, a young black lad who was mentally retarded. He was accused of driving a car and raping a woman when he couldn't even ride a bike. The boy had no sense of motor control. In May 1979, the Ku Klux Klan attacked us while we marched in his defense. They shot three, four young people in the head. (All survived.)

USA TODAY: What happened next?

LOWERY: The Klan told us not to march again. We halted that march but went back a month later with about 5,000 people. The reporters told me that the Klan had issued an order to "get Lowery." Bullets whizzed over my head. But, thank God, they missed me. They also shot at my wife, who was riding behind me in a car. They shot in the windshield and just missed her.

USA TODAY: What became of Hines?

LOWERY: We got Hines free. Now he is under

medical care in a home for the mentally handicapped. He's not in prison.

USA TODAY: What are the goals of the Southern Christian Leadership Conference today?

LOWERY: Our goals have always been what we called the "beloved community" of justice, equal opportunity, housing, education and the reconciliation of all people as children of God. We want to redeem this world of America.

USA TODAY: How has the SCLC changed since the 1950s?

LOWERY: We are more international. We are involved in the South African struggle, in the Central American struggle and the struggle in the Middle East. But our goals have remained basically the same. Our major emphasis right now is on economic justice and the elimination of poverty in this country. To accomplish that we are challenging both the public and private sectors. Government has to set policies that lead to full employment, and the corporate community must put money back into the black community. Not only by hiring us in gainful positions, but by doing business with black-owned companies. That will enable black businesses to thrive. Black people must also develop lifestyles that will keep us free from dependency on any sources other than faith in God, love for each other and self-respect.

USA TODAY: Do you think that young black people understand what the movement did and continues to do?

LOWERY: I am afraid that today's young people do not realize how intense and how perilous our activities were. And perhaps many of them have grown up not knowing the tough, rugged pathway we had to pursue in order to achieve the measure of liberty we have now. Many think all the demonstrations were in the 1960s. But the Decatur, Ala., march was in 1979. The Carrollton-to-Montgomery pilgrimage was in 1982. The biggest demonstration I was involved in was when Coretta Scott King and I chaired the 20th anniversary march on Washington in 1983. That march involved nearly 500,000 people. These events are not a part of the school curriculums and they ought to be.

USA TODAY: What is the danger if young people do not learn about the civil rights movement?

LOWERY: If you don't know where you come from, it's difficult to assess where you are. It's even more difficult to plan where you are going.

LOWERY PROFILE

Born: Oct. 6, 1925, in Huntsville, Ala.

Family: Married to Evelyn Gibson Lowery; three children, Yvonne Kennedy, Karen Lowery and Cheryl Osborne.

Education: Attended Garrett Theological Seminary, Evanston, Ill., and Payne Theological Seminary, Wilberforce, Ohio.

On life: "If you don't know where you come from, it's difficult to assess where you are. It's even more difficult to plan where you are going."

Home: Atlanta.

Role models: Frederick Douglass, W.E.B. DuBois and Walter White.

MILESTONES

1950: Led civil rights movement in Mobile, Ala.

1957: Southern Christian Leadership Conference is founded; helped organize the Montgomery, Ala., bus boycott that was sparked by Rosa Parks' refusal to sit in "colored" section of a city bus.

1967: Named SCLC board chairman.

1977: Named SCLC president; led protest against Atlanta-based Southern Company for its contract to buy coal from South Africa.

1979: Became USA's first black leader to meet with Yasser Arafat in the Middle East; *Ebony's* Black Achievement Award for overall advancement of equality and religion.

1982: Organized march from Carrollton, Ga., to Montgomery, Ala.

1983: Met with Nicaraguan President Daniel Ortega; Co-chair of 20th anniversary march on Washington, D.C.

1984: Arrested in first anti-apartheid protest at the South African Embassy in Washington, D.C.

1986: Named pastor of Cascade United Methodist Church, Atlanta.

USA TODAY: Where did you get the courage to put your life and the lives of your family on the line for the sake of an idea?

LOWERY: I see it as part of my ministry. When I was called to preach, I felt a divine urge to spread the gospel and to pastor churches. I don't separate that from the movement. I think the Kingdom of God is a kingdom of love and justice and peace. I think it represents an end to hunger, an end to homelessness, an end to racial oppression and an end to poverty. None of those are detached from what I see as my ministry. My job as a minister is to not only make heaven my home, but to make my home on earth sheer heaven.

USA TODAY: What was your childhood like?

LOWERY: Compared to many of my companions and associates, my family was fortunate. We were not destitute, but we had hard times. My father worked for another man and he ran this little ice cream parlor, grocery store and pool room. He managed to eke out a relatively good living for us. I grew up in a very religious home. I had uncles and grandparents who were Methodist ministers.

USA TODAY: Who were your role models when you were growing up?

LOWERY: When I was growing up we didn't have many black heroes. But in history I read about Frederick Douglass, W.E.B. DuBois and Walter White. Those were men I felt were engaged in meaningful ministry. There were also several pastors who had influence over my life.

USA TODAY: What is your recipe for success?

LOWERY: Freedom from alien substances like drugs. Life is a secret lease from God and we should not allow ourselves to be bruised. Family life is our strength. It keeps us free from drugs, from sexual promiscuity. It helps us develop priorities that make maximum use of our resources for the future.

USA TODAY: What kept your wife and children going during the difficult times?

LOWERY: Faith in God. My children were movement children. They had to field all the nasty phone calls and bomb threats. They respected what we were doing. We gave them love. We gave them a sense of community responsibility, a sense of each-otherness.

MELBA MOORE

Music led her to be 'a rebel for a cause,' promoting the importance of family life

MOORE: 'If you study humility in your work, in your life, you will be studying the power of success.'

IMPRESSIONS

You can tell a lot about celebrities by the way they treat their fans. While we dined at an Arlington, Va., restaurant, Melba Moore's fans appeared from every corner, coming to our table for autographs. While her swordfish grew cold, she continued to sign, smiling, showing patience and care. She celebrates the good while still taking her role as Citizen Moore seriously. She has worked to help solve problems including abandoned babies, drugs, poor schools. As a spokeswoman for the National Council of Negro Women, she has made celebrating the strengths of the black family her vocation.

— **Barbara Reynolds**

A versatile performer, Melba Moore has crossed between stage, screen, television and nightclub. She has appeared in Purlie on Broadway and was the star of her own television series, Melba. A supporter of the black family and national efforts to strengthen family life in the USA, Moore also is active in unusual ways in her community, fighting drug trafficking, housing problems and more. An interview with Moore appeared on the USA TODAY Inquiry page Sept. 17, 1987.

USA TODAY: You have a history of being involved in social issues. You spray-painted the doors of some "crack houses" in Brooklyn, N.Y. Why did you get so deeply involved?

MOORE: It was my old neighborhood. We knew it would draw attention and perhaps set an example that the people who live in the neighborhood should not sit quietly and let the pushers take over.

USA TODAY: But why would you want to take on drug trafficking?

MOORE: I live in a very posh neighborhood in New York and yet I can look across the street and see people selling drugs. I'm not exempt. I'm also a mother. As much as I love and care about my daughter, when she's out on the street I don't know what she may fall victim to. So it is up to me to try to make the neighborhood safe. It is a personal passion. If you don't do something about it, it won't be done. It is your neighborhood. It belongs to you.

USA TODAY: What is the world of limousines and furs like for you?

MOORE: Interesting, but I never can forget that I'm a black person. When I don't have my chauffeur or my bodyguard and I'm out on the street trying to get transportation, I'm reminded very bluntly that I'm black when the cab driver passes me by to pick up a blond-haired, blue-eyed young lady. She gets the cab and I don't.

USA TODAY: What was your childhood like?

MOORE: The early part was spent in a broken family with a single parent, and violence both at home and in the neighborhood. A lot of damage had been done by the time I was 9 and my mother married. I was very sullen and sad and fearful. I was

withdrawn. I had trouble communicating verbally.

USA TODAY: Was the communication problem due to the turbulence in your life?

MOORE: I think it wasn't as important as being an only child and not having the joy that you get from relating to other children. I was left out of a lot of things. Being an artist, it became an extreme chore to learn how to communicate and to work at getting out of that shell.

USA TODAY: How did the violence affect you?

MOORE: I was not able to receive praise. I had no self-esteem. Still, there was this driving desire to sing and study music. I'm told I started singing around 3 or 4, that I always used to say I was going to be a singer, a star. I never really thought it was important to pay attention to your daydreams and desires. I didn't think mine were important. So I got my education because other people said that's what I should do. And I became a music teacher.

USA TODAY: Where did you teach?

MOORE: In the public schools of northern New Jersey. In the classroom I discovered I was a rebel for a cause. Music was an area that wasn't respected because it was just one of the arts. It wasn't math or social studies. I felt moved to show the young people compassion; many of them had suffered the same thing that I had. And I knew from experiences with my stepfather how the power of caring could cut through all of the hurt and pain.

USA TODAY: You have taken on another cause as chairwoman of the National Council of Negro Women's membership drive. Why?

MOORE: The council promotes the black family. I can offer something to that issue since I know from experience that the family and peace and the nurturing of love are vital. There is so much to celebrate. Everything we see in the papers, on TV is not indicative of the entire black community. Crime is a problem, teen-age pregnancy is a problem, AIDS is a problem, drugs are a problem, but they should not define who we are. We must bring the family together. We must go out and get the sick members and bring them back into the fold. Heal them. Teach them that nobody is wealthy or healthy or safe as long as this breach has happened.

USA TODAY: Has the gap between rich and poor — the haves and have nots — widened in minority communities?

MOORE: I think it's a love gap. I see a lot of people who have had success for themselves. They now can take time to look back and say: "Oh my God, I cannot leave them uneducated or unloved because they are going to kill me. And not only that, it's going to cost me everything that I've made — economically and psychologically."

USA TODAY: What should the black community do to begin healing itself?

MOORE: Start in the neighborhoods where we live. We have to look at our unborn babies, babies born to teen-age moms, our illegitimate babies as our treasure. People in the arts have not been committed. We find bandwagons to jump on. We make a big public issue out of it, but we have to go back into the communities. We have to set an example in our own homes. People like to sing message songs. It is not enough. You have to live the message!

USA TODAY: What part does religion play in your life?

MOORE: I want to know what God says for us to do. I'm interested in what the Scriptures say and in understanding it better. I want freedom to seek, but I don't really feel an allegiance to any one religious group. I believe I am a born-again Christian. I believe I have had — on a number of occasions — the personal experience that Christ is spiritually alive in me. I believe from experience that it is absolutely vital. When it comes to spirituality, we question it because we should question it. But when the proof is there, then I think you must make a choice.

USA TODAY: What did you mean when you said you almost self-destructed before embracing Christianity?

MOORE: You name it, I did it. Like any young person, I would experiment, try to do everything to extremes. I did not care who I was with or what I was doing. I really didn't have any order in my life. It wasn't just chemical self-abuse. It was a lack of caring. It was a lack of nurturing myself.

USA TODAY: What did you do to change?

MOORE: It occurred to me that it was such a struggle being unhappy and miserable. It was a habit. I decided I was just going to stop everything. There were some people in my life who were just helping my career along who weren't really managers. They were lawyers and accountants. We didn't have a formal arrangement but they turned out to be really bad and I came to the conclusion that I had to get these people out of my life immediately.

USA TODAY: When you look back, what was the most difficult challenge?

MOORE PROFILE

Born: Oct. 29, 1948, in New York City.

Family: Married to Charles Huggins; a daughter, Charli Moore.

Education: Bachelor of arts in music education at Montclair State College, Montclair, N.J.

On life: "A person coming out of an environment with a lot of violence and hatred needs to know what love is. I have seen some young people on TV and the news who were brought in for killing someone or some other violence and I could see in their little faces that they have never been loved. It is a scary thing to recognize that expression. I can imagine at one time my face looked like that. You can't teach that. They have to experience it."

Home: New York City.

Role model: Dorothy Height.

MILESTONES

1967: Taught music at Peshine Avenue Elementary School in Newark, N.J.

1968: Singer and pianist with Voices Inc.; backup singer for Frank Sinatra, Johnny Mathis and Harry Belafonte.

1968: Appeared in the rock musical *Hair.*

1970: Tony award-winning portrayal of Luttiebelle in the musical *Purlie;* appeared in the film *Cotton Comes to Harlem.*

1972: Host of *The Melba Moore-Clifton Davis Show,* a weekly TV musical-variety show.

1986: *Melba* television show debuts; fails after one episode.

1987: With Bill Cosby, co-chaired the National Council of Negro Women's second annual Black Family Reunion; chairwoman of the National Council of Negro Women's membership drive; Miss America pageant judge; hosted television special from Harlem's Apollo Theatre; her album, *Just A Little*, released.

MOORE: Overcoming the negative feeling of isolation. I praise God for music because in spite of those feelings I had some drive to go on. I said, "Why didn't somebody tell me that, first of all, I would be afraid, and that fear is not something that I should let stop me, no matter how terrible it is?" You should always try to do the good thing, the right thing. None of us really knows what that is. That is why we need each other. That is why we need the Scriptures, that is why we need laws. We all need to learn and study the work of love.

USA TODAY: How do you do that?

MOORE: A person coming out of an environment with a lot of violence and hatred needs to know what love is. I have seen some young people on TV and the news who were brought in for killing someone or some other violence and I could see in their little faces that they have never been loved. It is a scary thing to recognize that expression. I can imagine at one time my face looked like that. You can't teach that. They have to experience it. They can only experience it if you have given them that experience. If you have had love, give it.

USA TODAY: What do you think you'll be doing 10 years from now?

MOORE: Besides having established a good consistent career in films and continuing to put out good music and hopefully some theater, I would like to spend even more time with the National Council of Negro Women. This gives me a great deal of satisfaction. I feel like I'm living. I feel vital. I feel like my life is rich by helping to continue to find solutions and listen to problems. Be aware of what is going on in your community, with your race and with your country. Be a part of the solution.

USA TODAY: Some celebrities find success difficult to handle. Was it difficult for you?

MOORE: There is a lot that creates stress in people. One is the part that says they don't deserve success, the other part says they do. Ego is a killer. Humility is probably the greatest power that one can study, to understand that you didn't create anything here. God created it all. I can't make a person believe in God. I feel that if you study humility in your work, in your life, you will be studying the power of success.

ETHEL PAYNE

Her writing career has provided a forum for advocacy, protection and assistance

PAYNE: 'Age is not a handicap. Age is nothing but a number. It is how you use it.'

IMPRESSIONS

Years ago when my writings on black leaders were attacked, she defended my right to tell the truth, and the criticisms disintegrated. Ethel Payne fights for fairness. She has raised funds for Winnie Mandela, battled for government workers who have suffered discrimination and spotlighted the leaders and problems of Third World nations. A gourmet cook, she serves dishes that represent the countries she has visited. In 1982, Fisk University created a journalism chair in her honor. It was my honor to help initiate that token of our respect.

— **Barbara Reynolds**

The journalism career of war correspondent and social change activist Ethel Payne spans three decades. She has traveled with presidents and been honored by heads of state. An expert on Africa and black history, Payne has dedicated her life to improving the hopes of the poor and disadvantaged. Payne, who also has been a columnist, is a black pioneer in journalism and chooses to remain with the black press. Her dispatches stated clearly the dreams, fears and problems of black men in the military during the Korean and Vietnam wars. A column by Payne appeared on the USA TODAY Opinion page July 31, 1985.

USA TODAY: When did you decide to become a journalist?

PAYNE: I didn't have a thought of becoming a journalist. I had a talent for writing and my mother encouraged it. But my great ambition was to be a lawyer to defend the poor. I didn't realize I was poor myself. But I always had a desire to protect people. That grew out of the love for my brother who was three years older than I. He was a sickly child. He grew very fast and was kind of weak. He was always being picked on. I was always beating up on boys to defend him. Early on I had a sense of trying to protect people who couldn't protect themselves.

USA TODAY: You grew up in Chicago's Englewood community. What do you remember?

PAYNE: My father died when I was about 12. He had been a strong family person who supported the family. He was a Pullman porter. When he died my mother was left with six children. One of my two older sisters had gone to work for a dressmaking shop on Michigan Avenue and the other had finished teachers' college. She was ready to start teaching, but Chicago was in the midst of a financial crisis. We had to struggle. My mother was very proud; she would never consent to going on welfare so she did little domestic chores and everything to keep us together. We managed somehow because my mother was a religious person. We were African Methodist Episcopals. The church was very much an influence in our lives. It was a social center as well as a religious center.

USA TODAY: How did your family keep its spirit during that time?

PAYNE: We called frequent family councils and talked about what we were going to do with our lives. We decided that Ruth, my youngest sister, would be the first to go away from home to college. So we all worked together. I was doing part-time work doing all kinds of things. I worked in white folks' kitchens. I did factory piecework, which I hated. Anything to keep us together. We saved our little money and when she got old enough, sent her away to college.

USA TODAY: After attending Northwestern University evening classes for two years, you left for Japan in 1948 as a hostess for the Army Special Services, a major step on your path to journalism. What was your role?

PAYNE: I became the head hostess at the club. In June 1950 the Korean conflict broke out, and President Truman ordered the troops into Korea. This was a quartermaster depot that I was on. And, of course, the Army was still very much segregated. President Truman had issued an order to desegregate the armed forces, but Gen. Douglas MacArthur totally ignored it. Everything was segregated.

USA TODAY: What happened?

PAYNE: The black troops were ordered into the Korean conflict as backups, so many of them went into combat. That became controversial because they had not been trained for combat. I remember waving them off and crying because I had become so attached to them. I looked at some of them and something told me I would never see them again. Sure enough, they were among the first casualties.

USA TODAY: How did the troops respond to that unfairness?

PAYNE: Many blacks deployed on the front line were court-martialed because they mutinied. Some were tried and convicted right on the spot. Thurgood Marshall, then special council for the NAACP, came over to investigate. He stopped in Tokyo where we were and talked about his mission. He listened to our advice. By that time there were a number of black war correspondents who had come over. Marshall filed a voluminous report about the conditions. We always felt that was part of the reason President Truman finally fired MacArthur.

USA TODAY: You kept a dairy of those war experiences. How did your story end up in print?

PAYNE: One of the war correspondents asked for my diary and took it to the *Chicago Daily Defender*. There was a big red headline across the paper, "Army Service Club Hostess Says GIs Abused

Here." People wanted to know about what was going on with the GIs. How they were segregated. That was a sensation. The high command called me in. They accused me of disrupting the morale of the troops. I didn't realize then that this was an expose about the conditions there and about the flaunting of a presidential order (the order to desegregate the armed forces). What I had done was uncover a bag of worms. They threatened to send me home in disgrace. Thurgood Marshall heard about it and he included my particular situation in his report. They decided not to go forward, but they isolated me.

USA TODAY: Your "reporting" in Japan led to a 20-year career with the *Chicago Daily Defender*?

PAYNE: Yes. Louis Martin (then editor-in-chief of the *Daily Defender*) called me in Tokyo from Chicago and told me I had a job. So I went back home to Chicago in March 1951 and joined the staff as a feature writer. I had a natural flair for writing.

USA TODAY: The *Defender* sent you to Washington in 1953. You were the second black female White House correspondent. What were the press conferences like with President Eisenhower?

PAYNE: We used to meet in the old Indian treaty room, a very ornate place in the Executive Office Building. It wasn't air-conditioned or anything, and it was hot with all the lights. You had to be alert to get the president's attention. He was more democratic about recognizing the smaller newspapers than any other president I have known. When I got up and said, "Mr. President!" he recognized me.

USA TODAY: What was your first question?

PAYNE: It was about an incident that had occurred when the Republican Party held its annual Lincoln Day celebration. They had invited three choirs to participate: those from Duke University, Emory University and Howard University. When Howard arrived, they were turned back. I heard about it and asked the president.

USA TODAY: What was his response?

PAYNE: He said if, as I implied, there was discrimination involved, he would be the first to apologize. That was news. *The New York Times* carried the transcript of the press conference just as they do today with the names of the reporters who asked the question. My name got in *The New York Times*. That was a big achievement. People began to ask, "Who is that black woman?"

USA TODAY: You have been in journalism more than 30 years. What is your mission?

PAYNE PROFILE

Born: Aug. 14, 1911, in Chicago.

Family: Single.

Education: Attended Northwestern University, Evanston, Ill.

On life: "I didn't have a thought of becoming a journalist. I had a talent for writing and my mother encouraged it. But my great ambition was to be a lawyer to defend the poor. I didn't realize I was poor myself."

Home: Washington, D.C.

Role model: A. Philip Randolph.

MILESTONES

1955: Covered the Asian-African Conference, Bandung, Indonesia, for the *Chicago Daily Defender*.

1957: Attended Ghana's independence ceremonies in Accra.

1966: Covered black troops in Vietnam.

1970: Accompanied Secretary of State William Rogers on tour of Africa.

1971: Traveled to Lagos, Nigeria, to escort the remains of Whitney L. Young Jr., executive director of the National Urban League, to the USA.

1972: Covered Apollo 17 launch.

1976: Accompanied Secretary of State Henry Kissinger to six African nations.

1977: Visited China.

1978: Named a Ford Foundation Fellow in education reporting.

1979: *Roots, Rewards, Renewal*, a study of black colleges, published.

1982: Named to the Ethel L. Payne Professorship in Journalism at Fisk University, Nashville, Tenn.

1983: Attended Second Vienna Dialogue on Peace and Disarmament, Vienna, Austria; received Distinguished Service Award from Africare in Washington, D.C.

1987: Board member of Africare.

PAYNE: I started out as an advocate for the weak and I have used my role in that way.

USA TODAY: Your latest campaign is a fund to aid Winnie Mandela of South Africa. Why is she a high priority?

PAYNE: There is such a correlation between what is happening in South Africa and our experiences in this country. Mandela and others symbolize the whole struggle for human dignity, human decency. We have to be involved. I am trying to help in that struggle.

USA TODAY: What do you think is the state of the USA's black community?

PAYNE: In some ways the whole picture has changed. We don't have the great personalities we had in the '60s. Martin Luther King is gone. A. Philip Randolph is gone. Roy Wilkins. Julian Bond once put it very succinctly. He said: "In the '60s we had great leaders. In the '70s we have only ourselves." There are some very strong people emerging. Blacks gradually are becoming more sophisticated as individuals. They are producing more black elected officials and black personalities who are involved in the whole process. The climate has changed. We have retrogressed in some respect. But in others we have become smarter and wiser.

USA TODAY: At 76 you're still globe-trotting. Do you see age as a barrier?

PAYNE: Age is not a handicap. Age is nothing but a number. It is how you use it.

USA TODAY: What is it that keeps you moving all over the world?

PAYNE: The struggle continues. There are still challenges. As long as there are challenges I am involved. All the energy that I have goes into that. Until the day I close my eyes, I am going to be involved.

USA TODAY: How do you want to be remembered?

PAYNE: I would like people to remember me as someone who tried to alleviate the problems of the disadvantaged. I used whatever talents I had to write graphically about issues that affect people and to correct injustices. That's my great mission in life.

PHYLICIA RASHAD

After her work became worship, her work as an actress began to work

RASHAD: 'I'm a very simple person. . . . My goal never was to be famous nor wealthy. My goal was to be good.'

IMPRESSIONS

Her life story is like that of a rose opening bit by bit, revealing more beauty the more it unfolds. Phylicia Rashad travels peacefully, helped by a devotion to meditation. Her guru aids the journey. A picture of her spiritual leader, Gurumayi Chidvilasananda, hangs on her dressing room wall in the Queens studio where *The Cosby Show* is produced. Inside, Rashad is seated next to a white bassinet where her daughter, Condola Phylea, sometimes rests. Rashad is a controlled woman who cares deeply for causes and people. When I interviewed her, she revealed her beliefs. She is an exceptional person.

— **Barbara Reynolds**

Her road to fame and fortune has not been smooth, but Phylicia Rashad has weathered the worst and is riding the crest of stardom through The Cosby Show. *She's a dancer as well as an actress. She also devotes her time to lobbying for an improved lifestyle for the USA's elderly, particularly the poor elderly. An interview with Rashad appeared on the* USA TODAY *Inquiry page Nov. 20, 1987.*

USA TODAY: Besides acting, you have taken an active role in speaking out for the rights of elderly people. Why have you chosen this issue?

RASHAD: If you live long enough, you will be old. The aging process isn't something that anyone should ignore. It was the way I was reared. In my family, seniors were very much respected. Maybe that is why today I'm concerned with the condition of all senior citizens in America.

USA TODAY: When you reflect on your family life in Houston, what comes to mind?

RASHAD: My mother, Vivian Ayers-Allen, is a very creative person. She perceived potential in us when we — my sister, Debbie Allen, and my brother, Tex — were too young even to say the word. Everything she did with us she did against all odds. And we were very fortunate to have teachers who cared about us as human beings.

USA TODAY: You are a student of meditation. How did you start?

RASHAD: I went to see a play and the actress gave the most perfect performance I had ever seen. It was completely effortless and so right I couldn't stop watching her. Everybody on the stage was good, everybody was talented, but there was something very specific about her. I didn't know what it was so I went backstage to say hello. On her dressing room table was a picture of Swami Muktananda, her guru.

USA TODAY: How does meditation improve your life?

RASHAD: It's the power that leads you to your own truth. Everybody needs to be free. The main thing meditation frees you from is the idea of "do-ership," the thinking that "I am doing this." When you're free from the idea of do-ership then something else within you emerges. It is yourself. You don't have to have an ego about "I did this, or I did

that. I'm so rich. I'm so poor." It isn't something that can be explained, it's something that must be experienced. You have to contemplate it. It's written in the New Testament. That's all Jesus ever said: "I didn't do this, it's your faith that did it. That which I do, you can do also." If you contemplate the meaning of those words, you'll experience them. It's very simple.

USA TODAY: What message is *The Cosby Show* communicating?

RASHAD: It's a joyful look at human behavior. It touches that joy within the people who see it. People don't want to feel burdened, dark and ugly. People want to feel free, people want to laugh.

USA TODAY: What was the most difficult hurdle you had to overcome?

RASHAD: One difficulty I had to overcome was the idea that fame and fortune are corruptive. It isn't fame and fortune that are corruptive. I live a very simple life. I'm a very simple person. My great-grandfather was a farmer, my father was born on a farm and my mother was born in Chester, S.C. If you know about the Carolinas, you know it's a very sweet place where people are very natural with each other. Not highfalutin. My goal wasn't to be famous or wealthy. My goal was to be good.

USA TODAY: How did you make the leap to Clair Huxtable on *The Cosby Show*?

RASHAD: For years I was an understudy in the theater, on and off Broadway. I auditioned for commercials and for films that I did not get. All of this was good for me because I was growing. The turning point came with meditation. I understood work in a different way. I understood that I am not "the doer." And that work isn't done for the fruit of one's labors or for self-aggrandizement. It is for the worship of one's own self — and I'm not talking about personality. I'm talking about that divine presence within. I'm talking about that spark, that flame of God that exists in every human heart.

USA TODAY: How did you get the role of Clair?

RASHAD: I was at the audition, which lasted all day. I was sitting in a room and I remembered something that had happened to me in a meditation. All of a sudden I began to laugh out loud. I said: "Oh, God, you are so great. You are everything." I thought about the script and I said: "You (God) are the one who produces it, you are the one who directs it. You are the one who is chosen, you are the one who's not chosen — this has nothing to do with me." The door opened, the director walked in and said, "Come meet your new family." As I looked at them, I was very, very humble.

USA TODAY: Do you recommend meditation?

RASHAD: Yes. Young people are very good meditators because they don't have to work through the same stuff we do as adults. Tell a young person: "Just sit quietly and when the thoughts come up just watch them. Watch the colors rise and fall and then pay attention to who's watching the thoughts come and go." They can do it very well.

USA TODAY: Does your career conflict with family responsibilities?

RASHAD: It isn't easy. My son, Billy, has been the sweetest because he has gone through the thick and the thin, and he has always been very, very understanding — beyond his years. I had to give up a lot of time. I came from the school of actors that required time for preparation.

USA TODAY: What have you sacrificed to develop your talents and succeed as an actress?

RASHAD: I remember having to give up homecoming when I was a student at Howard University. I had to give up a lot of homecomings because we always had a play going on and you had to be there in the drama department, you had to be functioning. As a drama student you had to give your time. It wasn't like other courses. In later years, when I was working in professional theater, there came a time when I had to rededicate myself. Billy was 8 years old, and I was an understudy in *Dreamgirls*. I worked 10 or 12 hours, at least five days a week. I would say goodbye to my son in the morning and the next time I saw him he was asleep in bed. I had to give up a lot of his younger years. I can't go back and get that.

USA TODAY: Why did you leave *Dreamgirls* when you didn't have a job?

RASHAD: I knew that if I didn't leave, I would never have another job to go to. I didn't prefer the role that I was understudying. It wasn't that challenging. When I knew there was never going to be a song that I was going to sing any better, never a dance step that I was going to do any fuller, never a scene that I was going to play with any more realism, I said, "Now I've done this." It was as if I was the sun pretending to be a moonbeam.

USA TODAY: What did you do?

RASHAD: I meditated. It doesn't just make you quiet and soft, it makes you strong. I had the

RASHAD PROFILE

Born: June 19, 1949, in Houston.

Family: Married to Ahmad Rashad; two children, William Lancelot Bowles and Condola Phylea Rashad.

Education: Bachelor of arts from Howard University, Washington, D.C.; attended New York School of Ballet.

On life: "One difficulty I had to overcome was the idea that fame and fortune are corruptive. It isn't fame and fortune that are corruptive. I live a very simple life. I'm a very simple person. My great-grandfather was a farmer, my father was born on a farm and my mother was born in Chester, S.C. If you know about the Carolinas, you know it's a very sweet place where people are very natural with each other. Not highfalutin."

Home: Westchester County, N.Y.

Role model: Her mother, Vivian Ayers-Allen.

MILESTONES

1970: Performed off-Broadway in *To Be Young, Gifted and Black*.

1980: Danced in *The Wiz* directed by Geoffrey Holder.

1981: Understudy in Broadway's *Dreamgirls*.

1982: Worked with the *Negro Ensemble Co.*, appearing in *Puppet Play, Sons & Fathers of Sons, Zora, Weep not for Me* and *Upstate Motel*.

1983: Cast as publicist in daytime soap opera *One Life to Live*.

1984: Cast as Clair Huxtable on the award-winning *The Cosby Show*.

1986: Opened for Bill Cosby in Atlantic City, N.J.; performed to sold-out audience in New York City's Town Hall in a performance that fused American and East Indian songs.

1987: Spokeswoman for the National Caucus and Center on Black Aged.

strength to say, "This is it." People usually think that when you meditate you get all doe-eyed and you get all slurpy. No. You get peaceful. But when it's time to act, you perform the appropriate action at the right time because you're tuned in to the truth within yourself. There is no guiding force better than the truth within your being.

USA TODAY: How did you get by after you left *Dreamgirls*?

RASHAD: After that job, for the first time in my professional life I collected unemployment. That meant $125 a week. With a son. In New York. I didn't tell my father and I didn't tell my mother. I didn't tell my sister. I promised myself that with the money I collected I would have a voice class every week. I'm vegetarian so we ate very well. We had a comfortable place to stay. Billy didn't know anything about it. He thought it was great that I was home. And I never bothered to explain.

USA TODAY: What kept your spirits up?

RASHAD: I was inspired by Mahatma Gandhi. He wrote that if you could just accept what is given to you and not complain about it but just live through it, that it would get better. One day I did something that I've never done before and haven't done since. I took a solemn vow. I said, "I promise, by the presence of God within me, this is my last day here." And it was.

USA TODAY: What happened?

RASHAD: I got a job in the soap opera *One Life to Live*. The day I went for my audition I bowed my head to pray and said: "Lord, I'm not going to try to fool you because you know me better than I know myself. I would love to have this job. But more than that, I would love to have an experience of you in every moment." When they told me I got that job, tears welled in my eyes and I began to sing a song that we sing in meditation — *Kindle My Heart's Flame with Your Flame*. I understood. Here lie the treasures. Here are the riches. No one gave it to me. And no one can take it away. My work became worship and then my work began to work.

LOU RAWLS

Raising money to support black colleges is a passion, as are his songs about love

RAWLS: 'To enjoy life, you have to put something back. . . . Life ain't all barbecue, watermelon and potato salad.'

IMPRESSIONS

During the 10 years I spent in Chicago, Lou Rawls personified the Windy City. His raspy, bluesy voice that purred songs about the hawk and the eagle flying on Friday all hit home. But once I left Chicago, I saw another dimension. When we talked, he spoke of causes and of making a difference. He spoke of making things better. And music is his instrument of choice for getting things done.

— **Barbara Reynolds**

He launched his career singing gospel, but Lou Rawls changed course to become one of the top rhythm and blues singers in the USA. He sang with the legendary Sam Cooke in the 1950s. His Lou Rawls Live album crossed over into the mainstream pop market in 1966 and went gold. Though he did not have the opportunity to attend college, he has devoted his time and energy in the 1980s to raising funds for the USA's black colleges and universities through The Lou Rawls Parade of Stars. He is a spokesman for Anheuser-Busch. Rawls was interviewed for the USA TODAY Inquiry page on Nov. 12, 1987.

USA TODAY: Early in your singing career, an automobile accident outside Memphis, Tenn., changed your life. What happened?

RAWLS: I had been traveling with Sam Cooke, singing backup with him. There was a crash, everything went blank. In the ambulance on the way to the hospital, they pronounced me dead. Of course, I wasn't, but I stayed in a coma nearly six days. That incident made me realize that had I died at that time I would have been nothing but a speck of dust on a grain of sand in the Sahara Desert as far as what I would have contributed to the lives of others. Nor would I have received anything from life. I was in my teens. What I had experienced up to that time was nothing. Had I died, in about two weeks I would not even have been a memory.

USA TODAY: How did that change you?

RAWLS: I came to realize that, in order to enjoy life, you have to put something back into life. You just can't sit back and expect it all to come to you. Life ain't all barbecue, watermelon and potato salad. There is more to it than that.

USA TODAY: Where did you start singing?

RAWLS: In the junior choir at church. Then I formed a little teen-age quartet of my own. After that, I joined the Chosen Gospel Singers, then the Travelers, a gospel group from California. Next, I started working as a backup singer with Sam Cooke. We sang together as kids; he was my closest friend. Sam and I made the transition from the gospel field to rhythm and blues.

USA TODAY: Why do you think your music is so successful?

RAWLS: Maybe because I sing about love. Love is always going to be a predominant source of material — unrequited love, rejected love, in love, happy love, sad love — like the blues. It's just like the blues. We all have it.

USA TODAY: Where did you grow up?

RAWLS: I was raised on the South Side of Chicago by my grandmother. My mom went to Seattle to get a job. And my dad — he was somewhere — you know that story. My grandmother didn't live to see me become successful. But she lived to see me sing in the junior choir. As far as she was concerned, that was it. That fulfilled her dream.

USA TODAY: The South Side of Chicago has a reputation as a rough area. What helped you stay on the right track?

RAWLS: I got out of there. I had my grandmother's upbringing. I still remember her sayings like, "Every goodbye ain't gone."

USA TODAY: What are some of the biggest roadblocks you had to overcome?

RAWLS: One was a large amount of stupidity on my part. I used to think I was real slick. I was smarter than everyone else. I found out that slick ain't nothing but a word. It has nothing to do with reality and life.

USA TODAY: Since 1980 you have been a spokesman for the United Negro College Fund's annual telethon, which raises money for many of the nation's historically black colleges and universities. Yet you are not a college graduate.

RAWLS: My grandmother could not afford to send me, and I couldn't afford to send myself. It's funny because the reason for the United Negro College Fund is to assist kids that come from families that make less than $12,000 a year. And that would certainly have included me when I was growing up. You can't hardly get across the street now with $12,000 a year.

USA TODAY: What is the United Negro College Fund? Why is it needed?

RAWLS: It is a combined effort among the black educational institutions to try to turn out as near to perfect students as possible. When the schools were established more than 100 years ago, there were not many schools blacks could attend. But once those were established, supporting them was a real cut-and-dry issue.

USA TODAY: What do you mean?

RAWLS: Historically black colleges couldn't depend on support from students whose families were barely able to support themselves. They needed supplies, qualified teachers and good solid buildings. In recent years, no school has been able to rely on the government for support. The United Negro College Fund was and is a much needed thing.

USA TODAY: How did you become involved?

RAWLS: When I became a spokesman for Anheuser-Busch in 1976, August Busch II said to me: "Lou, you do a lot of community work. If we can get behind you on any of it let us know." I had seen a mini-telethon for UNCF with Nancy Wilson and Clifton Davis. I thought about that and I remembered having been on some of the black campuses. So I called Mr. Busch and I said: "Hey, I got a great idea. Why don't we do a real full-blown telethon for the UNCF and see what happens?" He said, "All right."

USA TODAY: Who actually gives to the United Negro College Fund?

RAWLS: Quite a cross section of people. People are becoming much more aware that education is the key to the majority of the problems that blacks are confronted with in today's society. In the beginning, the telethon was carried in only a few cities. We continued until we got it all across the country. The result has been tremendous. Since it began we have raised more than $50 million. In 1987 we raised about $13 million.

USA TODAY: Does the money go to the students or to the schools?

RAWLS: It goes to the UNCF, and the fund administers the money. Most of the money is used to restore the schools, to supply them with the teaching aids and faculty. A great portion of the money does go for tuition. Those who are away from home for the first time and living on campus receive some assistance as well. But the majority of the finances go for the maintenance and upkeep of the institution itself.

USA TODAY: Do people understand how hard it is for blacks and the poor to get an education?

RAWLS: Yes. They do understand. They are understanding more and more every day. That is why I was fortunate enough to be able to put this telethon together and make it work.

USA TODAY: Do students ever thank you for your help in sending them to college?

RAWLS: Yes. They realize that without the ef-

RAWLS PROFILE

Born: Dec. 1, 1936, in Chicago.

Family: Divorced; two children, Lou Jr. and Louana.

Education: Graduated from Dunbar High School, Chicago.

On life: "I was raised on the South Side of Chicago by my grandmother. . . .My grandmother didn't live to see me become successful. But she lived to see me sing in the junior choir. . . . That fulfilled her dream."

Home: Los Angeles.

Role model: His grandmother, Eliza Rawls.

MILESTONES

1953: Joined the Army and served with the 82nd Airborne Division.

1958: Toured with the Pilgrim Travelers, a men's gospel group.

1959: Performed at the Hollywood Bowl in a show produced by Dick Clark; led to first recording contract, with Capitol Records.

1966: Released first album, *Lou Rawls Live*, which became his first gold record.

1967: Won Grammy for *Dead End Street*.

1968: Won the *Downbeat* poll for favorite male vocalist, displacing Frank Sinatra.

1971: Won Grammy for *A Natural Man*.

1976: Became spokesman for Anheuser-Busch; first gold single, *You'll Never Find a Love Like Mine,* won an American Music Award.

1977: Grammy, Best Vocal Performance for *Unmistakably Lou.*

1979: Began *The Lou Rawls Parade of Stars* telethon for United Negro College Fund.

1982: Released *When the Night Comes;* began singing lyrics for Garfield the cat on CBS-TV animated specials.

1987: Released album, *Family Reunion.*

forts we put forth many people would not know that there are young blacks who are not rebels and dropouts and who really have the desire to be productive in our society. Most of our black politicians have come through these black colleges. Most of our black lawyers and doctors come through these schools. And these people are contributing something very worthwhile to mankind.

USA TODAY: What do you mean?

RAWLS: Take racial problems, for example. The only reason that you encounter any kind of racial problem is because the person that you are dealing with has no knowledge above and beyond their own areas, their own lives. Why is that? It is a lack of knowledge and education.

USA TODAY: How can you justify being a spokesman for Anheuser-Busch when alcohol abuse is a problem in black communities across the USA?

RAWLS: There's no more alcoholism in the black community than there is in the poor white communities. You go into a poor white neighborhood, you'll see just as many churches and liquor stores and bars as you will see in the black community. Now if you go into the affluent white communities, you won't see that. But you won't see it in the affluent black communities either. That's an issue that's left with the individual.

USA TODAY: Many entertainers of your generation have shied away from singing popular music. How do you manage to stay on the charts?

RAWLS: Consistency. When you are young and dumb and don't have enough of anything, you look for change. Once you reach your teens, you start to want to settle in for consistency. After you reach a certain age, change is not something that is exciting to you all the time. People always knew what they were going to get from me. Change for what? The only thing I'm going to change is my mind.

RANDALL ROBINSON

His knowledge of issues affecting Africa has spurred policy changes in the USA

ROBINSON: 'It is impossible to love ourselves without having an affection for Africa. And for me it is a romance.'

IMPRESSIONS

In the early 1970s I was among the journalists who depended on Randall Robinson for briefings on Third World issues. He would answer questions in his cramped TransAfrica offices for many hours. The concept of the Third World was confusing. His history and world political lessons helped a lot of us better understand and report about the struggles to shake colonialism, poverty and exploitation in the emerging "new" Africa. His passion for fairness led to the Free South Africa Movement, making Robinson the driving force to help a people's anti-apartheid movement catch fire in the USA in the 1980s.

— **Barbara Reynolds**

Africa's population is expected to double in the next 30 years, and Randall Robinson is committed to pushing U.S. power centers to respond with aid and trade. One of the architects of the anti-apartheid demonstrations that began in front of the South African Embassy in Washington, D.C., on Thanksgiving Day 1984, Robinson and his colleagues raised public consciousness. That helped spark the Anti-Apartheid Act of 1986. His leadership also has brought South Africa to the nation's campuses as a rallying point for student activism in the 1980s. Interviews with Robinson appeared on USA TODAY Inquiry pages Aug. 1, 1985, and Dec. 30, 1982.

USA TODAY: You have been one of the USA's foremost activists on Africa. Did this interest develop during your childhood?

ROBINSON: I knew very little then. From grade one through the end of college, I did not hear the name of an African country more than five times. But I knew all about tulips and wooden shoes and windmills. I knew about the Eiffel Tower, Big Ben and the Leaning Tower of Pisa. I knew about the lore of Europe. Who really knows the news of Africa, of Latin America, of Asia? A congressman told me that he did not think more than 20 of his colleagues could name at least five African nations.

USA TODAY: Do you feel obliged to espouse the African cause because of your ancestors?

ROBINSON: It is impossible to love ourselves without having an affection for Africa. And for me it is a romance. When I took my children to Senegal, we visited the island of Gore. We stood in the house where Phillis Wheatly was taken as a child alone and enslaved. We looked out the door where Wheatly saw the ocean for the last time. Then I understood how we came to America. History collapsed. As long as African-Americans see themselves as something disconnected from Africa, we never will be her heirs. We never will understand power in the world. We never will be free. We will remain millions of blacks among millions of hostile whites, disconnected from the fountainhead, the potential for our real power — a truly lost people.

USA TODAY: How does the USA's policy in South Africa affect you personally?

ROBINSON: When this nation supports apartheid, it contributes to the pain and suffering of black South Africa. It has an effect on me as a black American. So when the president responds by not only refusing to condemn the government but blames the victims for their massacre as President Reagan has done, he is sending a message to every American of African ancestry. We have a responsibility as Africans and as Americans — and as human beings — to salvage U.S. policy and make it comply with our ideals.

USA TODAY: How did TransAfrica evolve from the Congressional Black Caucus?

ROBINSON: Congressman Charles Diggs of Michigan was still in Congress and so was Andrew Young. Diggs, who I worked for as an administrative assistant, was a lonely soldier on the issue of Africa. In September 1976, Diggs and Young convened a meeting of about 130 black leaders to discuss Henry Kissinger's handling of the Rhodesian crisis. The meeting created a critical report known as the *Afro-American Manifesto on Southern Africa*. I chaired the planning group that followed that report. In July 1977, TransAfrica was incorporated in the District of Columbia.

USA TODAY: In those days, were you ahead of the rest of the country?

ROBINSON: It's important to say there were institutions that came before TransAfrica. It would not have been possible without the work done by people like W.E.B. DuBois, Marcus Garvey and many others. It's not as though we have broken new ground. We became the first black American institution solely concerned with the business of national foreign policy on a full-time basis. But it comes on the heels of efforts of previous eras.

USA TODAY: How would you characterize the USA's policy toward Africa?

ROBINSON: The United States claims to be sympathetic to Africa's development. But the facts would demonstrate something quite the contrary.

USA TODAY: Half of the world's refugees are African, yet they comprise only 2 percent of those admitted to the USA. Why?

ROBINSON: We like our refugees to be white and from communist countries. Our principal concern should be safety, but we turn Haitians away, lock them in prison camps and think nothing about it. But we would drag a Soviet ballerina off an airplane largely because she is white and we want to demonstrate that people want to leave the Soviet

Union. We spend about $3,000 helping a refugee from Eastern Europe and $20 on one from Africa. As the color of the refugee gets darker, the door through which he must enter gets smaller.

USA TODAY: How did the USA's African policy change between the Carter and Reagan administrations?

ROBINSON: The Carter policy was not what American policy ought to be, but it more nearly approached it than the policy of any administration before it. The Reagan administration has taken us to a new depth in callous disregard for human rights. The Reagan administration has unabashedly supported South Africa. They could find no money to raise the general level of African assistance but looked for money to buy arms for a country like Chad, which invaded Libya to accomplish American foreign policy objectives. They have put more money into arms in the Third World and less money into economic development. In that sense the Reagan administration has damaged dramatically African interests globally.

USA TODAY: What should the policy be?

ROBINSON: We ought not to have South Africa in the United Nations. We ought to have a realignment of American foreign assistance because our formula for assistance is inexcusably inequitable. It was inequitable under Jimmy Carter. It is more inequitable under Ronald Reagan.

USA TODAY: Why did you start the Free South Africa Movement, which picketed the South African Embassy?

ROBINSON: Not only did we picket, there were arrests every day for one year. Arrests at the embassy totalled more than 3,600 people, and nationally more than 5,000. We picketed with the understanding that to put an issue in the center of the American public policy debate, you have to dramatize the issue. You have to cause attention to be drawn to it. At the same time one has to move and accomplish some legislative results. That was our intention.

USA TODAY: What did protests accomplish?

ROBINSON: Increasingly, South Africa is being made to understand that the mood in the USA has changed. Our policy will be fundamentally different, partly because of those who took to the streets.

USA TODAY: What do you expect to happen in South Africa?

ROBINSON: After they begin to understand the real cost of pursuing the policies they've pursued to

ROBINSON PROFILE

Born: July 6, 1941, in Richmond, Va.

Family: Married to Hazel Ross-Robinson; two children, Anike and Jabari. A brother, Max, is a former ABC *World News Tonight* co-anchor.

Education: Bachelor of arts degree from Virginia Union University, Richmond; law degree from Harvard Law School.

On life: "From grade one through the end of college, I did not hear the name of an African country more than five times. But I knew all about tulips and wooden shoes and windmills."

Home: Washington, D.C.

Role models: His parents, Max and Doris Robinson; Nelson Mandela and Harriet Tubman.

MILESTONES

1970: Ford Foundation fellow, field research, Dar es Salaam, Tanzania.

1971: Staff attorney for Boston Legal Assistance Project, Roxbury, Mass.

1975: Staff assistant to Rep. William L. Clay, D-Mo., in Washington, D.C.; staff attorney for Lawyers Committee for Civil Rights Law, Compensatory Education Project, Washington, D.C.

1976: Helped found TransAfrica, the African and Caribbean lobbying group; aide to U.S. Rep. Charles Diggs, D-Mich.

1977: Named executive director of TransAfrica.

1978: Novel, *The Emancipation of Wakefield Clay,* published.

1982: Southern Christian Leadership Conference Drum Major for Justice Award.

1983: Humanitarian Award from Congressional Black Caucus.

1986: American Black Achievement Award from Johnson Publishing Co.

1987: Martin Luther King Jr. Distinguished Service Award.

the detriment of blacks and the nation as a whole, they will come to the table and begin the long process of reconciling differences with the black majority. But they won't do that until we enforce tough sanctions and a policy that will hurt.

USA TODAY: Hundreds of black children are killed and jailed in South Africa. Will this terror continue?

ROBINSON: If the government doesn't seize the diminishing opportunity to negotiate with the black majority while there's still time, you will have a blood bath in that country and tens of thousands of blacks will die. And the whole society will suffer.

USA TODAY: TransAfrica also lobbies for the Caribbean. What are your objectives there?

ROBINSON: They essentially are focused on better terms of trade. The American markets have to be opened to Caribbean products. That means tariff barriers have to be lowered. The problems in the Caribbean are more economic than political. We could have a dramatic impact if there was just the smallest will to do so.

USA TODAY: As a child, who did you admire most?

ROBINSON: My parents. They were my heroes. They were exceptionally strong and had exceptional principles. They proceeded through life in accordance with their own moral and political convictions. They both attended college. My father, Max Sr., taught history at Armstrong High School in Richmond, Va. He also coached various sports at the school. My mother, Doris Robinson, was active in church, and both of them tried to protect their children from the painful humiliation of segregation.

USA TODAY: Do you think it's important for children to have heroes?

ROBINSON: It is very important for children to have principles learned from those who are closest to them during the formation of their characters.

CARL ROWAN

His early reporting instincts led editors to change how black news was covered

ROWAN: 'Oh, racism never disappears. There are still editors who wouldn't carry my column because of my race.'

IMPRESSIONS

Long before I met him, I wished one day to become the female Carl Rowan. I wondered: What's the key to his endurance, to his longevity as a Washington institution? The Rowan answer: Hard work and integrity. Also, set a standard and don't change it to court popularity, convenience or favoritism. At the 1984 Democratic National Convention in San Francisco, USA TODAY provided a place to have photographs taken and placed on oversized buttons. With me on my button is Rowan. The button is one of the treasures that hangs above my desk at work.

— **Barbara Reynolds**

One of the USA's leading syndicated columnists, Carl Rowan also produces radio and television commentaries and documentaries. His daily radio commentary, Rowan Report, *can be heard on 60 radio stations across the USA. He took a break from journalism in the 1960s to serve in the Kennedy and Johnson administrations as deputy secretary of state, a delegate to the United Nations, ambassador to Finland and director of the United States Information Agency. He holds 42 honorary degrees. An interview with Rowan appeared on the* USA TODAY *Inquiry page Sept. 9, 1987.*

USA TODAY: Why did you go into journalism?

ROWAN: From my days in high school I knew I wanted to write. I had a marvelous English teacher, Betsy Quinn, who had me writing sonnets and believing that I could write them as well as Shakespeare. Growing up in a little town, I had no way of knowing how I could ever earn a dollar writing because there was no newspaper that would hire me because of my race. But when I got lucky and got into the Navy, I began to believe that sometime, somewhere, I might get a job as a newspaper man. I understood even then that the media influenced public opinion in such a way that black people could never go anywhere unless they could have some impact on the media.

USA TODAY: Did you have black newspaper people as role models?

ROWAN: There were no black newspaper people then. In fact, when I got my job at the *Minneapolis Tribune* in 1948, you could count on one hand all of the blacks in the entire United States who were working for a newspaper.

USA TODAY: Did you encounter discrimination in the newsroom when you began your career?

ROWAN: I was an extremely happy guy. I had a publisher who had a great social consciousness. I also had an editor who had come up to Minneapolis from Oklahoma. And he said to me the day I applied for the job, "Suppose I send you down to the Rotary Club to cover a luncheon, what do you think would happen?" I said, "If there is a story there, I'll bring it back." He said, "They say they don't want a Negro covering their luncheon." I said: "Well, either I am the *Minneapolis Tribune* reporter, or I am not. And if anybody can tell you who to send and who not to send, you are going to have trouble forever. But if they know that if I don't cover that story nobody is going to cover it, you'll never have any problem." He smiled and put his hand out and said, "We've got a deal." I did my first series of articles. They were a big hit. I didn't have any problems because the publisher and editor were thinking up new things for me to do that would glorify the newspaper.

USA TODAY: Of stories you've covered, which has the most personal meaning?

ROWAN: In 1951 I made a proposal to the *Minneapolis Tribune* and I went South and wrote on how far from slavery the nation had come. It brought in more mail than anything the paper had ever published. It changed the attitudes of a lot of newspapers that would only write about blacks if they had stolen a chicken or raped somebody. They began to write seriously about the social and economic place of black people in America.

USA TODAY: Did your accomplishments break stereotypical thinking about black reporters?

ROWAN: When the Soviets invaded Hungary and the British, French and Israelis went into Suez, the United Nations had emergency sessions of the General Assembly on those two issues simultaneously. I was the guy the *Minneapolis Tribune* sent to New York to cover those gripping sessions. This coverage helped to make a lot of editors understand that blacks could cover something other than race relations. I was intensely proud of that. I helped change their perspective.

USA TODAY: How did you become a columnist?

ROWAN: After I spent four and a half years in government and was about to leave, the syndicates started bidding for my services. I had contacts that I didn't have before coming into government. I could call a cabinet officer — and get him on the phone. When I resigned as director of the United States Information Agency, there were editors around the country who believed I knew things readers ought to know.

USA TODAY: Lyndon Johnson appointed you to the U.S. Information Agency. You took two trips around the world with him. What was your impression of him?

ROWAN: Lyndon Johnson is probably the most interesting president. There is nothing that you can say about Johnson that is so good or so bad that it wasn't true at some time or the other. Usually within the same half hour. He and I fought like dogs because Johnson had a habit of insulting his staff. I made it clear to him that I didn't play that game. If he tried to insult me he would get something back. I won his respect.

USA TODAY: How did your appointment play among Southerners?

ROWAN: There were several senators who didn't believe a black person could be the spokesman for America.

USA TODAY: Some people feel that the further your career takes you, the less you confront racism. Do you agree?

ROWAN: Oh, racism never disappears. There are still editors who wouldn't carry my column because of my race. I have had editors write to my syndicate suggesting that I not write about racial issues. I have had editors write and say they aren't interested in my views on Lebanon or the Persian Gulf, that I should only write about race issues. You get these stupidly contradictory viewpoints. I ignore them all. I write what I feel like writing.

USA TODAY: In the nation's capital, other than Carl Rowan, black journalists are rarely seen on network and syndicated talk shows. Why?

ROWAN: That's because white males still dominate the industry, and there's just no getting around that. We have broken up the white male club some, but there is a long way to go.

USA TODAY: You were born in Ravenscroft, Tenn., and grew up in nearby McMinnville. What was life like?

ROWAN: My daddy worked stacking lumber for 25 cents an hour, if he worked at all. We didn't have a clock, a radio. I almost never had a toothbrush. There was no running water, no telephone. I walked to the spring to carry water. There were days when we wouldn't have eaten but for going down to the river and catching a sucker out of that muddy water or hunting rabbits with my daddy.

USA TODAY: How did being poor affect your education?

ROWAN: An early crisis that I remember best was being at Tennessee State College as a freshman. I had worked for $1 a day at the hospital, but my money had run out. And I was about to leave Tennessee State after the first quarter because I didn't have the $20 to pay the next quarter's tuition. My buddy Joe Bates talked me into walking with him to

ROWAN PROFILE

Born: Aug. 11, 1925, in Ravenscroft, Tenn.

Family: Married to Vivien L. Murphy Rowan; three children, Barbara, Carl Jr. and Geoffrey.

Education: Bachelor of arts from Oberlin College, Oberlin, Ohio; master's from University of Minnesota, Minneapolis.

On life: "We've got to put a lot more emphasis on trained intelligence. We simply cannot go on with the percentage of school dropouts that we've got. We cannot have so many young women wrecking their future by having babies at 13, 14 or 15."

Home: Washington, D.C.

Role model: Jackie Robinson.

MILESTONES

1948: First black reporter at the *Minneapolis Tribune.*

1953: *South of Freedom* published.

1956: *The Pitiful and the Proud* published.

1957: *Go South in Sorrow* published.

1960: *Wait Till Next Year*, a biography of Jackie Robinson, published.

1961: Named U.S. deputy assistant secretary of state for public affairs.

1963: Named U.S. ambassador to Finland.

1964-65: Head, U.S. Information Agency.

1978: Named Journalist of the Year by The National Press Club.

1979: Received Ted Yates Award from Washington chapter of the National Academy of Television Arts and Sciences.

1985: Began writing autobiography, due to be published in 1988.

1987: Managing editor and correspondent for TV documentary *Thurgood Marshall the Man;* managing editor and host of TV documentary *Searching For Justice: Three American Stories;* founded Project Excellence, a scholarship program.

a greasy spoon where he could buy cigarettes. The restaurant was closed. As we turned to walk away, I looked in the weeds and there was a $20 bill. I paid my tuition. A few days later the Navy changed its policy and decided that for the first time in history it would give Negroes a chance to enter officers training school. I took the exam, passed, went to midshipman school and got a commission. That's lots of luck and faith.

USA TODAY: What must be done to make the USA's black communities progress?

ROWAN: We've got to put a lot more emphasis on trained intelligence. We simply cannot go on with the percentage of school dropouts that we've got. We cannot have so many young women wrecking their future by having babies at 13, 14 or 15. Somebody has got to put back an element of pride and pressure by saying: "No, you are not welcome in this house if you are robbing people, mugging people, if you are using or peddling drugs. If you make a baby, you have got to be a father and support that baby." It's not as simple as I put it. The social factors are so complex. There are a lot of things black people cannot control. But we can control dedication to trained intelligence, and that's why I am so proud of the response to my Project Excellence.

USA TODAY: What is Project Excellence?

ROWAN: I wrote a column deploring peer pressure that says, "If you speak good English, you are acting white, or if you get good grades, you are acting white." I proposed to give a few scholarships and I ponied up $10,000 myself to give scholarships to young blacks — high school seniors who are best skilled at using the English language, or those making the greatest progress. I talked in that first column about giving four $4,000 scholarships. But I expect I'll give 80. There has been an incredible outpouring of support. One couple said, "We allow $25 a month for charity, so for as far ahead as we can see, our $25 will go to Project Excellence."

USA TODAY: How do you want to be remembered?

ROWAN: I want people to remember me as a journalist who was never afraid to write or to say what he believes. A journalist who was willing to hold black public officials to the same standard that he held white public officials.

WILMA RUDOLPH

Determination, inspiration and drive
keep her moving the sports world ahead

RUDOLPH: 'It doesn't matter what you're trying to accomplish. It's all a matter of discipline. That's where a lot of people get confused.'

IMPRESSIONS

As a teen she raced the wind and won. But Wilma Rudolph began life sickly, hit with scarlet fever, pneumonia and polio. Many people thought she would be crippled for life. When I first met this woman of great physical, emotional and personal strength, I had to fight back the tears as I heard her story of triumph and victory. She talked freely of her Southern Baptist background and the love of family that is the cornerstone of her strength. Today she coaches young people in Indianapolis and offers proof that discipline, determination and motivation are keys to success and survival.

— **Barbara Reynolds**

She captured the hearts of the world when she was barely 20, winning three gold medals in track at the 1960 Rome Olympics. Wilma Rudolph's speed and fluid grace led the European press to dub her "The Black Gazelle." Before she could run she had to learn how to walk — with braces — because of childhood polio. Today she continues to run as fast and as hard as she can for the cause of women's athletics as director of the women's track program at DePauw University, Greencastle, Ind., and as president of the Wilma Rudolph Foundation, a non-profit amateur athletics and education organization. She had what she says was the best support in the world through it all — her family. An interview with Rudolph appeared on the USA TODAY *Inquiry page Aug. 6, 1987.*

USA TODAY: You grew up poor in Clarksville, Tenn., with 21 brothers and sisters. What do you relish most about your childhood?

RUDOLPH: We didn't look at it as being poor because you don't know you're poor until you actually get out into the world. The love and the family support overshadow that in my life. Coming from a large family is wonderful. But being near the bottom — I'm the 20th child — there was no way I could ever live with all of them. My sisters are old enough to be my mother. I have nieces and nephews my age. That's what made it so wonderful.

USA TODAY: You were very ill as a child. Few thought you'd ever walk. And no one imagined you would be the world's swiftest female runner.

RUDOLPH: I had a series of childhood illnesses. The first was scarlet fever. Then I had pneumonia. Polio followed. I walked with braces until I was at least 9 years old. My life was not like the average person's who grew up and decided to enter the world of sports. I didn't attend my first two years of grade school. I had what you call a homebound teacher. I missed an awful lot of my childhood.

USA TODAY: Why didn't you accept the prognosis that you would never walk without braces?

RUDOLPH: When my parents were away, I would take the braces off and try to walk without them. I have to attribute that motivation to my mother. She was instrumental in making me believe that you can accomplish anything if you believe in it. I would take my braces off and my sisters and brothers were there to help. I also come from a Southern Baptist background and God has always been in my life. Spiritually I have always felt good about Wilma. That's No. 1.

USA TODAY: When did you realize that you could not only walk, but could participate in sports?

RUDOLPH: I never really thought about the sporting world from that standpoint. It basically came about because of my sister who had played basketball before me. I discovered through my sister that there was a world for women in sports. There were four years between me and my sister who played basketball. My father insisted that his children were always chaperoned by one another. Because of that I was able to travel with my sister the first year on all of her basketball trips. I didn't play, but at least I was there. I was so amazed that women were allowed to participate in sports. I was determined to play basketball.

USA TODAY: When did you discover that you could run fast?

RUDOLPH: It's not something you discover overnight. It's something that takes years to develop. I had begun beating all the kids in my school but that was no guarantee. There's always a fastest somebody in the school you're attending. But from being the fastest somebody I had enough motivation to pursue running.

USA TODAY: You were first on the Olympic team in 1956. What was it like?

RUDOLPH: I went as a youngster, still in high school. It was my first experience traveling out of the United States. The Olympics that year were in Melbourne, Australia. I was the second youngest on the track and field team. I discovered all these wonderful people who were great athletes. They were written about in newspapers. People I never thought I'd ever have the chance to meet, I was on the team with them. And because I was so young they tended to look out for me.

USA TODAY: Was there a lot of drug use when you were participating in the Olympics?

RUDOLPH: I didn't know there was such a thing. Everything has become a lot more modern since the days when I participated in the world of sports. Even runners and sprinters using weights to develop the body — something as simple as that — it just wasn't done. We were thinking about being the fastest and the quickest. We weren't looking for the easy way out. We stuck with the basics: determination, inspiration and hard work. And years of hard work at that.

USA TODAY: How do you feel about steroids?

RUDOLPH: Anything you inject into your body, other than a medication from a doctor, is dangerous. I don't think anybody really knows the true outcome until years later. That's not what the world of athletics is all about.

USA TODAY: When will women's sports gain more visibility?

RUDOLPH: When large corporations start taking interest. They are the major sponsors. When the television stations and the writers and all those people start taking a more positive look.

USA TODAY: Much is made of the lack of blacks and women in coaching. What is the picture for women as coaches?

RUDOLPH: There are a lot of women coaches. Those women who are coaching have to be talked about, written about. We have to know where those programs are. I'm surely not saying it's nearly enough. There are some of us who are working very hard at it and making it.

USA TODAY: You have said your dream is to foster athletics through education. Do most people think it should be the other way around?

RUDOLPH: I was in athletics at an early age and it was before I discovered the academic part. I learned through athletics. A lot of people are just the opposite. They prefer it the other way. I'm sure there are a lot of kids in this world like me who have a great desire or a great ability in sports. Once they enter that world, they find out the beauty and the value and the emphasis that athletics puts on education. You must obtain one to have the other.

USA TODAY: Do your programs for youth stress academics?

RUDOLPH: I have designed my programs with both educational and athletic requirements. If they join the Wilma Rudolph Track Club or if they come into any of the programs at the Wilma Rudolph Foundation, they have to perform academically.

USA TODAY: How does that work?

RUDOLPH: A lot of them start that educational process because of their travel experiences. That leads back to the classroom.

USA TODAY: What types of classroom programs do you offer?

RUDOLPH PROFILE

Born: June 23, 1940, in Clarksville, Tenn.

Family: Divorced; four children: Yolanda, Djuana, Robert, Zurry.

Education: Bachelor of science from Tennessee State University, Nashville.

On life: "I had a series of childhood illnesses. The first was scarlet fever. Then I had pneumonia. Polio followed. I walked with braces until I was at least 9 years old. My life was not like the average person's who grew up and decided to enter the world of sports."

Home: Indianapolis.

Role models: Her mother, Blanche Rudolph; Jackie Robinson and Mae Faggs.

MILESTONES

1956: Won National AAU championships girls division, Ponca City, Okla.

1960: Won three championships in the AAU national indoor meet in Chicago; three gold medals at the Rome Olympics.

1961: Received James E. Sullivan Award.

1962: Retired from competitive track.

1973: Elected to Black Athlete's Hall of Fame.

1974: Elected to National Track and Field Hall of Fame.

1977: Autobiography *Wilma* published.

1981: Director of The Olympic Experience in Indianapolis, a federally funded program to teach children the importance of academics and athletics.

1982: Inducted into Greatest Sports Legends and Women's Hall Of Fame.

1984: Member of U.S. Olympic Committee delegation to Berlin.

1987: Received a Sammy, the United States Sports Academy's award for contributions to sports; named director of Women's Track Program and special consultant on minority affairs at DePauw University, Greencastle, Ind.

RUDOLPH: We offer reading and math programs. We plan to enhance those with courses like Honors English for seniors going to college.

USA TODAY: What does your victory over illness say to others wrestling with handicaps?

RUDOLPH: It doesn't matter what you're trying to accomplish. It's all a matter of discipline. That's where a lot of people get confused. They feel that because you're an Olympic champion, it is probably the only place you could excel.

USA TODAY: What do you mean?

RUDOLPH: You can take that same discipline, motivation and determination and put it anywhere. I just happened to be in the world of sports. I was determined, wanted to succeed and wanted to know what was beyond the street I was living on.

USA TODAY: Do you still get a lot of fan mail?

RUDOLPH: Yes. I'm told people look to me as a role model. I've worked very hard in my career and people appreciate the work I've done.

USA TODAY: What is your philosophy?

RUDOLPH: Treat people the way you would like to be treated. Don't do anything to anybody that you wouldn't allow to be done to yourself. I can disagree with someone and still respect them for how they feel. I always try to be objective.

USA TODAY: What do you hope to be doing 10 years from now?

RUDOLPH: I will probably be spending more time at my foundation because it is my legacy. It is the thing that I love doing most. We run a Wilma Rudolph track club and now that I am at DePauw University, I may be doing a program called Honors English. That will allow me to put the finishing touches on my team at DePauw and do some recruiting. I hope to be making speeches and, of course, spending a lot of time with my two grandchildren. I am sure I will have others.

DAVID SATCHER

Desire to make health care accessible
paved path of compassion and healing

SATCHER: 'I am more comfortable being in the struggle. Especially if I feel that I am making a difference.'

IMPRESSIONS

Becoming a doctor is an arduous assignment for anyone. For black people in the USA, it can be even more difficult. The proof is in the numbers: Black doctors account for only 3 percent of the USA's physicians. More than 40 percent of black physicians have graduated from Meharry Medical College, where David Satcher is dean. He is committed to working until the road to a medical career for blacks and other minorities is free of all obstacles. His example has helped reinforce the meaning of principle.

— **Barbara Reynolds**

A brush with death in the rural South set the stage for David Satcher's quest to become a healer. As president of Meharry Medical College, he now trains doctors who can make sure that health care for the poor and minorities, particularly blacks, steadily improves across the USA. A devoted family practitioner, he finds time for family pursuits as well. He has worked with young people each step of the way to help eliminate the burdens of poverty, illness and self-doubt. An interview with Satcher appeared on the USA TODAY *Inquiry page Oct. 8, 1985.*

USA TODAY: You came from a family of eight children reared in poverty on an Alabama farm. What was the most important factor in your climb out of poverty to become a doctor?

SATCHER: A combination of faith and drive. I have always had a lot of faith that I could accomplish anything. I wanted to solve problems and make a difference. I feel as though I have come full circle, from struggling to get health care in Alabama to leading a historically black college that trains doctors so others who are black and poor have access to medical treatment.

USA TODAY: Why did you become a doctor?

SATCHER: I grew up in Anniston, Ala., on a farm at a time when medical care was not readily available. My mother had 10 children — all delivered at home. Two died at childbirth. At 2 years old I became very ill with whooping cough that led to pneumonia. At one point they expected me to die. My dad, Wilmer, found a black doctor and persuaded him to come to the house to see me. He taught my mother, Anna, how to clear my chest but he told them that it was not likely I would make it. I made it. Having access to a doctor became very important to me early in life. I wanted to make a difference to people who are unable to get medical care when they need it.

USA TODAY: Was poverty or race the reason you, your brothers and sisters were born at home?

SATCHER: It was a combination. We were poor, but there was certainly discrimination in Alabama. Very few white physicians saw black patients. If they did, they saw them in a separate office. It has occurred to me that if it had not been for that one black doctor, I would have died. Blacks died at home then. They weren't taken to the hospital. Though I was only 2 years old, I remember all of the people coming around. When somebody was sick it was a big event. People came to offer support. If you were really sick, people would sit with the family as if they were waiting for you to die.

USA TODAY: When you realized you wanted to become a doctor, what did you do about it?

SATCHER: By the time I was in the eighth grade, I had made up my mind that I was going to do it and I started doing well in school. It paid off — I was valedictorian in a class of 70 where only three students went on to college. I went to Morehouse Medical College. That historically black college really set things in order for me.

USA TODAY: Why did you go to Morehouse?

SATCHER: From day one the attitude at Morehouse was: "You are somebody. We expect great things of you." Two weeks after high school was out I got a letter from Morehouse saying I had been admitted and had won a scholarship. I would just have to pay room and board. I was so scared. I spent the whole summer studying to make sure that when I got to Morehouse I could survive. I read everything. I took all those *Reader's Digest* tests to measure my word power.

USA TODAY: What happened after you began classes at Morehouse?

SATCHER: We spent the first week taking tests. Out of 240 students, I placed ninth and was put in an accelerated class. There were 24 students in that special class for the first year. I found myself in the accelerated class even though I went there worried about whether I would even be able to stay. And I think I have been benefiting from that ever since.

USA TODAY: After you graduated from Morehouse, you attended Case Western Reserve for your M.D. and Ph.D. degrees. What was it like going from a historically black college in the South to a predominantly white university in Cleveland?

SATCHER: There were a lot of things to deal with because there were only two black students in my class at first. There were four black students in the whole school. But I was ready for it. My development at Morehouse had not been just an academic one. It had been social, too. I was active in the civil rights movement and the sit-in movement during my years at Morehouse. My senior year I became leader of the campus sit-in movement and president of the student body. I was active in the community. I graduated at the top of my class.

USA TODAY: What do you mean when you say blacks at Case Western had to deal with a lot?

SATCHER: I hesitate to answer that because I think Case has dealt with a lot of these things now. But one of the things black medical students had to deal with was the segregation of patients — staff patients vs. private patients. Staff patients, who were usually black, were used for training in pelvic examinations. I refused to participate. The head of obstetrics and gynecology insisted I be put out of school. But the dean had to make the decision. He decided I would go back on the training cycle and the school would discontinue that practice.

USA TODAY: How many low-income people in the USA don't have adequate access to health care?

SATCHER: Somewhere between 25 million and 35 million people. We're talking about 15 percent of our population. And the number has been growing. In some states, 80 percent of the poor have no access to care because they are not eligible for Medicaid. Nationally, almost 50 percent of poor people don't have access to Medicaid. Two-thirds of women and children who are poor don't have access.

USA TODAY: What is the mission of Meharry Medical College?

SATCHER: Meharry was founded because there was no medical care for slaves and former slaves. Meharry's mission is to train qualified black physicians to provide good health care for all people — especially blacks. The college struggled because it took care of poor patients who many times did not have any way to pay. But there were many communities throughout the South — like the community I grew up in — that would not have had a black physician had it not been for Meharry.

USA TODAY: What were the important factors in your success?

SATCHER: My parents. Despite their lack of education, they had a lot of faith and drive. After all, they raised a family of eight during some very difficult times. But I could also talk about the help and support I received at Morehouse and the importance of black role models like Benjamin Mays, then the college's president.

USA TODAY: Are role models as readily available for young blacks today?

SATCHER: One of the things I worry about is whether young people are finding the kind of role models I had. Are they having the kind of close relationships with teachers that I had? I don't think so.

SATCHER PROFILE

Born: March 2, 1941, in Anniston, Ala.

Family: Married to Nola Satcher; four children, Gretchen, David L., Daraka E. and Daryl.

Education: Bachelor of science from Morehouse College, Atlanta; M.D. and Ph.D. from Case Western Reserve University, Cleveland.

On life: "I have always had a lot of faith that I could accomplish anything. I wanted to solve problems and make a difference. I feel as though I have come full circle."

Home: Nashville, Tenn.

Role models: His father, Wilmer Satcher; Benjamin Mays, Dr. Martin Luther King Jr.

MILESTONES

1972: Named director, Community Hypertension Outreach Program, Martin Luther King Jr. General Hospital, Los Angeles.

1976: Appointed professor and chairman of Department of Family Medicine at Charles R. Drew Postgraduate Medical School, Martin Luther King Jr. General Hospital.

1977: Named interim dean of the Charles R. Drew Postgraduate Medical School.

1979: Appointed professor and chairman of the Department of Community Medicine and Family Practice, School of Medicine, Morehouse College; served through 1982.

1980: Named outstanding alumnus in community medicine from Case Western Reserve University.

1982: Appointed president of Meharry Medical College, Nashville, Tenn.

1983: Counselor's Award from Golden State Medical Association, Los Angeles.

1986: Received Daniel Hale Williams Memorial award from Providence Hospital, Chicago.

1987: Community Leadership Award, National Conference of Christians and Jews.

One of the unfortunate things about integration is that a lot of black students are not seeing black role models as they go through school. As a student at Morehouse I remember the first day I met Benjamin Mays. I have dark skin and so did he. That has always been an issue among blacks.

USA TODAY: Why was skin color an important issue?

SATCHER: It had been an issue since I was young. I even had teachers who made an issue out of the skin color of their students. Such teachers assumed that students with dark skin would not do well in class. I had a complex about that. I just tried to show that I was as good as anybody else, sometimes going out of my way to do it. I think I have done that all of my life.

USA TODAY: How do you approach difficult situations?

SATCHER: I approach them head on because I think life is full of challenges. People struggle every day. People who are well educated can deny the fact that there is in this country — in this world — a constant struggle for medical care, for education, for economic parity. I am more comfortable being in the struggle. Especially if I feel that I am making a difference. The challenge is to become part of the struggle, to make a positive difference.

USA TODAY: Do you think that present and future generations of blacks will have to struggle as hard as previous generations?

SATCHER: One of the things that bothers me sometimes about some black children is they are not aware of the struggles it has taken for them to be where they are. They don't know about black history or the civil rights movement. I think it is our fault that they don't have the awareness. A lot of parents have tried to shield children from struggle. Some of us have worked two and three jobs to keep our kids from having to live through what we went through without realizing that positive things can come out of struggle. When those kids come face to face with a difficult situation, they are not prepared to deal with it.

NIARA SUDARKASA

She believes that understanding the past is the key to building a brighter future

SUDARKASA: 'When black people learn the realities of the past they can begin to understand the future they can have.'

IMPRESSIONS

We met in Nassau where Niara Sudarkasa delivered a paper on the international implications of single parenting. It is a topic that hits close to home as I am a single parent. She is a pivotal player in the Third World's movement to share culture and solutions to problems. Plagued by poverty, civil wars and colonialism, many nations with African roots have become islands unto themselves. But Sudarkasa, an anthropologist, seeks a new discovery, a coming together, a focal point for the Third World. In Nassau she was part of that spirit that calls people of color home to a special mindset of love.

— **Barbara Reynolds**

The challenge for Niara Sudarkasa is to make Lincoln University in Pennsylvania one of the foremost centers in the country for the study of nations, diplomacy and international business. She's president of Lincoln, one of the USA's leading black universities. An anthropologist, she has traveled extensively researching the roots of black people. Her vision for Lincoln is to make it an institution with an intercultural focus to help the USA move into the 21st century. An interview with Sudarkasa appeared on the USA TODAY *Inquiry page Oct. 12, 1987.*

USA TODAY: You are now a college president. But you started as an anthropologist. Why did you choose that discipline?

SUDARKASA: I studied anthropology at both Fisk University and Oberlin College. For the first time, I understood that African culture had made an impact on the Americas. If you went to Haiti and Jamaica and Trinidad and even to the southern United States, particularly to the Gullah islands off South Carolina, you could find real evidence of African culture in the music, in the religion, in the way people wove baskets and plaited their hair. That was exciting to me.

USA TODAY: Did that experience cement your decision to go into anthropology?

SUDARKASA: No. It was really cinched because of my maternal grandparents who brought me up. They are from the Bahamas. When I was growing up, my grandmother and a number of her friends had something called the Esu. It invoked my curiosity. Esu was a savings association. Every week each member would put in $10. Let's say there were 12 people. That would be $120 a week. Each week, one member got the $120. So it was a round-robin savings association. When I went to Oberlin, I found that the Yoruba of Nigeria were the originators of the Esu. The Yorubas had something called Esusu, and all over the Caribbean, African people, black people, had Esu or Esusu. If you go to Trinidad you can find it. You can find it in Jamaica. When I found out what my grandparents had was an African institution, and a Yoruba institution, I was determined to go to Nigeria and study.

USA TODAY: What did you study?

SUDARKASA: For my dissertation I went to Nigeria and studied the role of women among Yoruba. The women are very powerful in trade. They are the backbone of the markets in that part of the world. I did my study on the way those women were able to accommodate domestic life and demands of business activities.

USA TODAY: You were born in Fort Lauderdale, Fla. What were your early years like?

SUDARKASA: My grandparents raised me; my three brothers were farmers and longshoremen. My grandmother was a housewife. My mother never graduated from high school. All of her children were born when she was very young. My mother spent a good deal of her life as a single parent. None of my relatives had gone to college.

USA TODAY: What inspired you to go?

SUDARKASA: My grandmother said to me, "You can be another Mary McLeod Bethune." I was about 7 years old. I will never forget it. I have the image burned into my mind. I stood absolutely still and just stared at her. In Florida we all knew Mrs. Bethune as the greatest woman in the country. She and Eleanor Roosevelt were two women who were giants. For my grandmother to say that to me was awesome. I certainly didn't have any aspirations at that time.

USA TODAY: Could you afford college?

SUDARKASA: We were poor. My mother worked very hard in a cleaners in New York to send us to school. She left us with her parents in Florida when I was in the eighth grade. She left to find work that would enable her to take care of us. I went to college on a Ford Foundation scholarship. In those days it cost $800 a year to go to Fisk. My scholarship paid $500 and my mother had to find the other $300. It was a massive struggle to come up with that kind of money in 1953.

USA TODAY: How did you stick with it?

SUDARKASA: My relatives always would tell me, "You must find a way to go to college." I did well in school. I was a good student. So people expected that I would get scholarships that would enable me to go to college. They didn't want me to drop out. The main thing my teachers and my mother and my grandmother tried to instill in me was that I should not be waylaid. I should keep my eyes on the prize. I should not forget that I could do well if I persevered.

USA TODAY: Black colleges are losing students and are in financial straits. Why?

SUDARKASA: Most of the declining enrollments of blacks are at predominantly white institutions. In the '60s and early '70s, these institutions opened their doors to blacks on an unprecedented scale. In the last decade, most predominantly white institutions have lost ground in black enrollment. That decline is greater in predominantly white institutions than at historically black institutions. That doesn't say black colleges haven't had their share of problems. Financial woes are at the top of the list. Some have tottered on the brink of closure.

USA TODAY: How has Lincoln remained financially stable?

SUDARKASA: Lincoln is now a state-related institution. We get from 35 to 40 percent of our operating budget from the Commonwealth of Pennsylvania. This is an enormous help to an institution that has only a small endowment and depends very heavily on tuition and fees. We also have a faculty that seeks research funds from federal government sources and private foundations. That is an important income source for us.

USA TODAY: Are black students feeling isolated and alienated on white campuses?

SUDARKASA: When I left the University of Michigan, there was a series of incidents that highlighted this problem. We read about Dartmouth and Brown and many other institutions around the country where black students charged that there was a resurgence of racial incidents and attitudes among segments on campus.

USA TODAY: How are blacks affected?

SUDARKASA: There's no question that black students in many of these institutions have become dispirited. In some cases they have become alienated because they haven't felt that the institutions have reached out and tried to reflect the total student body or tried to incorporate some of their experience, their culture into the mainstream curriculum. Blacks too often feel they are marching into a foreign camp at some of these institutions.

USA TODAY: Black students' Scholastic Aptitude Test scores still trail those of white students, despite substantial gains. Do the rising scores for blacks make you optimistic?

SUDARKASA: I'm very encouraged by the closing of the gap. We must stress to students that they can do well. Expectations are very important. Motivation is very important. Marva Collins has proved that in Chicago. We have stressed that no

SUDARKASA PROFILE

Born: Aug. 14, 1938, in Fort Lauderdale, Fla.; name originally was Gloria Marshall.

Family: Married to John L. Clark; a son, Michael Sudarkasa.

Education: Bachelor of arts from Oberlin College, Oberlin, Ohio; master's and Ph.D degrees from Columbia University, New York City.

On life: "African culture had made an impact on the Americas . . . You could find real evidence of African culture in the music, in the religion, in the way people wove baskets and plaited their hair."

Home: Lincoln University, Pa.

Role model: Mary McLeod Bethune.

MILESTONES

1961: Research associate at Nigerian Institute of Social and Economic Research, Ibadan, Nigeria.

1963: Named Carnegie Foundation Fellow for the Comparative Study of New Nations, University of Chicago.

1968: Studied commercial migration in West Africa and Ghana.

1976: Received tenure as professor of anthropology at the University of Michigan, Ann Arbor; pilot project in the Caribbean studying the Yoruban diaspora in Trinidad, Guyana, Jamaica and Haiti.

1981: Named director of the Center for Afro-American and African Studies, University of Michigan.

1982: Senior Fulbright Research Scholar, People's Republic of Benin in West Africa.

1984: Associate vice president for academic affairs, University of Michigan.

1985: Chaired 25th anniversary of the Peace Corps.

1987: Named president of Lincoln University, Lincoln University, Pa.

single group has a monopoly on brains. Black students have the same capability as any other students.

USA TODAY: How do we nurture them?

SUDARKASA: We have to provide them with mentors. We have to provide them with the same kind of educational tools and equipment that other students get. You can't take students who have never seen a computer, introduce it when they become college age and expect they're going to be able to make the same kind of use of this important educational tool as students who have been using it since they were in first grade.

USA TODAY: What is the value of knowing your roots?

SUDARKASA: The Ashanti of Ghana and other people in West Africa have an icon. It is the image of a bird that looks backward and the feet of the bird are pointing forward. This symbolizes that a people must be rooted in their past if they are to move forward. How can you possibly know how far you can go if you have no sense of how far you have been? It is absolutely critical for our young black students to know the kinds of contributions to world civilization and world history that have been made by African people. If they don't know, they will assume the myths they have learned in America are true. Namely that black people have not achieved anything, that everything that they have was here when they came to these shores as slaves. I never talk about black people as slaves in America.

USA TODAY: Why?

SUDARKASA: I talk about them as enslaved Africans in America because when they left Africa they were free people. They were put in chains — albeit by Africans and Europeans — and brought here. For the entire time that Africans were in this country working on plantations, most of them were struggling to be free. When black people learn the realities of their past they can begin to understand the future they can have.

SUSAN L. TAYLOR

Having control of her own life gives her strength to keep moving others forward

TAYLOR: 'Thoughts have power. Thoughts are energy. And you can make your world or break your world by your thinking.'

IMPRESSIONS

If the glamour, polish and charm seen in *Essence* magazine could pour off the pages and into one individual, it would be Susan L. Taylor. As editor-in-chief she has become the personality of the foremost black women's publication in the USA. She is also the executive producer and host of the magazine's syndicated television talk show. Over a dinner of pasta and salad at her white-carpeted Manhattan apartment, she surprised me with the news that she is once again a college student — just like her 18-year-old daughter, Shana. Why? "I need more information."

— **Barbara Reynolds**

*F*inding her faith allowed Susan L. Taylor to find herself and her mission. She then quickly advanced from a free-lance writer to editor-in-chief of Essence *magazine, the nation's first magazine for black women. With a readership of 4 million people worldwide, her duties also include host and executive producer of* Essence, *a syndicated 30-minute television program that follows a magazine format. Taylor is a former actress and cosmetics firm owner. She also is a vice president of Essence Communications Inc. In 1985, she returned to the classroom as a night student at Fordham University in New York. Comments by Taylor appeared on the* USA TODAY *Opinion page July 24, 1984.*

USA TODAY: There was a time when you were a young actress, had a broken marriage, an infant daughter, a shortage of money and a car that wouldn't run. How did you move past all that?

TAYLOR: I had my daughter when I was 23. I was doing fine until I had Shana and my marriage fell apart. I found myself with a 6-week-old baby, no marriage, no man and no money. You know what happens when a woman has a child before she has her career and before she has skills that can be taken out there and marketed?

USA TODAY: What did you do?

TAYLOR: I wrote an article about it called *Coming To Faith.* It marked an incredible turning point in my life. I grew up in a Catholic environment. In those days no one ever said, "God is a living, breathing part of all of us." I thought Jesus was up on the cross or in the communion wafer. One day I called my ex-husband and asked him if he would come and get Shana because I had these tremendous pains in my chest. And I had only $3.

USA TODAY: What happened?

TAYLOR: He dropped me at the emergency room. I waited for hours. Finally, they X-rayed me. They told me I was fine so I left the hospital. It was a balmy October Sunday and some force that I can't explain pulled me into Reverend Ike's church. Reverend Ike wasn't even there. It was Rev. Alfred Miller — I will never forget his name. He started talking, "However hurtful your situation may be now, you can make things better if you change your mind." He was talking about how our lives are an

outgrowth of the kind of thoughts that we hold. It was the first time I had heard these concepts.

USA TODAY: So what did you do?

TAYLOR: I listened. I took home the little flyer. And I started believing and working on that. The point is if I had money I would have taken a cab and I would have passed that church as I had so many Sundays. If I had a man, I would have been in bed with him. I would not have been in that church. If I had not had the pain, I would not have gone to the hospital. If my car had been working, I would have driven past. So all of those forces had to be in concert for me to have that experience.

USA TODAY: Were you working then?

TAYLOR: I was working at *Essence,* but I was making only $500 a month.

USA TODAY: How did you feel when Ed Lewis tapped you to become editor of *Essence,* one of the nation's top magazines?

TAYLOR: I will never forget that evening. I came home, picked up the phone and called a person who I had greatly admired. My friend told me, "Black women need exactly what you have in your heart." I said, "They do." He said: "Oh, yes. You could do that job, and you will do it well." I just needed someone to tell me that.

USA TODAY: Why was *Essence* needed?

TAYLOR: Because there was no magazine for black women. There was nothing to tell us that we were beautiful. There was no mirror. It was a time when we were struggling with our beauty.

USA TODAY: *Essence* has evolved into a magazine for the total black woman. How did you shape that change?

TAYLOR: I wanted to create a product that would touch people, that would talk about some of the issues that I didn't feel any magazine was really looking at. Former executive editor Audrey Edwards and others were an incredible part of developing the new *Essence.* It was the first women's publication to really talk about AIDS. We were the first women's publication to send a writer to South Africa. What I wanted was a magazine that would speak to the whole person. We are going to tell you about fashion. We are going to tell you about beauty. We are going to tell you how to color your hair, if that's what you want to hear. We are also going to tell you that your size 16 body is fine. We are also going to talk to you about politics, about the plight of black America. We are going to talk about God.

USA TODAY: Is there a single philosophy that guides *Essence?*

TAYLOR: "Everything that's important to our forward movement." I have used that phrase over the years to dictate what goes into the magazine. Does it move black women, black people forward? If it moves black women and black people forward, then I want it in the magazine. If it doesn't, it's not in this magazine.

USA TODAY: *Essence* is a success but it still has problems getting advertising. How big a struggle has that been?

TAYLOR: It continues to be the major struggle. All black media really functions under that kind of constraint. Look at *Ebony, Essence* and *Black Enterprise.* Every ad you see, there's an editorial piece facing it off. But pick up *Vogue, Mademoiselle, Glamour.* You'll see 10 advertising pages back to back. If we ran two ads next to each other like that, we'd have to give both advertisers a free ad in a later issue. It's pure and simple racism. We're being disrespected by corporate America.

USA TODAY: Who has inspired you?

TAYLOR: My grandmother was a tremendous inspiration to me. I come from a long line of women who just took control of their lives. My great-grandmother, Susannah, who I'm named after, had a restaurant in the 1800s in Trinidad. My grandmother, Rhoda V. Weekes, came from Trinidad in 1916 by herself. She brought each of her six children over one at a time and finally her mother. At first she worked in a factory. It was right after the war. She started a number of businesses. She had a cleaners. I thought the house she lived in was a mansion. Then there was my mother. She didn't work outside the house because my father had a little business in Harlem. We lived upstairs from the business. My mother was in charge of her life. Nobody told my mother what to do. So I've always been around powerful women. I think that was a real inspiration.

USA TODAY: Who outside your family has inspired you?

TAYLOR: Angela Davis. She struggled and lived through a lot. When you meet her you see she's so soft and so gentle and so smart. I'm tremendously inspired by Shirley Chisholm. Women like Mary McLeod Bethune, who took $5 and started a school for girls in 1904. If she did that, I know I can do my work.

USA TODAY: You write an inspirational column called *In The Spirit* each month in *Essence.* Did

TAYLOR PROFILE

Born: Jan. 23, 1946, in Harlem, New York City.

Family: Divorced; a daughter, Shana.

Education: Attending Fordham University, New York City, with triple major in sociology, political science and economics.

On life: "I come from a long line of women who just took control of their lives. My great-grandmother, Susannah, who I'm named after, had a restaurant in the 1800s in Trinidad. My grandmother, Rhoda V. Weekes, came from Trinidad in 1916 by herself. She brought each of her six children over one at a time and finally her mother . . . She started a number of businesses . . . Then there was my mother. She didn't work outside the house because my father had a little business in Harlem. We lived upstairs from the business. My mother was in charge of her life. Nobody told my mother what to do. So I've always been around powerful women."

Home: New York City.

Role models: Angela Davis, Shirley Chisholm, Mary McLeod Bethune.

MILESTONES

1970: Understudy for Paula Kelley in *Dozens* on Broadway.

1971: Joined *Essence* magazine staff as free-lance beauty writer.

1972: Became fashion editor of *Essence* magazine.

1981: Named editor-in-chief of *Essence* magazine.

1983: Host and executive producer of *Essence,* a weekly nationally syndicated TV program with a magazine format.

1985: Began college studies at Fordham University.

1986: Elected vice president of Essence Communications, Inc.

you find your spiritual source through Reverend Ike's church?

TAYLOR: That never became my church. But I did take away with me the understanding that thoughts have power. Thoughts are energy. And you can make your world or break your world by your thinking.

USA TODAY: In 1987 your daughter was a student at Howard University and you were a night student at Fordham University. Why did you decide to return to school?

TAYLOR: I used to ask myself: "Are you serious, Susan, about helping to empower black people? Are you serious about really giving back to black America some of the gifts that have been given to you? You didn't start out to be a journalist. You didn't choose to be on any magazine." I asked myself, "Do you have enough information to really give people the kind of long-range, long-term guidance that is needed?" And the answer was "No."

USA TODAY: Is there any adage or saying by which you live?

TAYLOR: There are a few things. One is the first two words of the Lord's Prayer, "Our Father." And when I say them, I am comforted. It could only wish you good. You are protected. Our Father. I only need to say that much and I feel it's going to be all right, whatever it is.

USA TODAY: What was the most difficult thing for you to overcome?

TAYLOR: Lack of faith in myself and my own abilities. Not believing that I had talent or that I was good enough or worthy or able to do anything.

USA TODAY: What do you see for your future?

TAYLOR: I hope to start a whole-life institute for people who are in pain. If you need somebody to sit down and talk to, if you've got a drug problem, a problem with alcohol, if you want to stop smoking, if your man did you wrong — it would be a place where people can be healed.

CICELY TYSON

Her movie and television roles reflect positive and powerful images of black women

TYSON: 'What young people must learn is that nobody owes them anything. If they want it, they have to get out there and fight for it.'

IMPRESSIONS

While many people remember Cicely Tyson for *Sounder* and *Miss Jane Pittman,* I remember her for the roles she didn't accept. She always has been the actress who told Hollywood she would rather not work than degrade herself in roles that present blacks in a negative light. Her stance often meant no work at all, which says as much to me about Hollywood as an industry as it does Tyson as a lady. When we talked, I could see the rebel coming through. Tyson zealously guarded her private life, her private dreams. I thought: "Congratulations Cicely! Who says public people must tell all?"

— **Barbara Reynolds**

Her cornrowed hair has been her trademark, but it's the dedication coming from inside that has made her unforgettable. Cicely Tyson has been one of the nation's most active performers in the fight to improve the images of black people projected by the nation's television and movie industries. She wants those images to portray black people in a realistic way. Her most powerful roles have shown the strengths of black women through the lives of women like Miss Jane Pittman and Harriet Tubman. An interview with Tyson appeared on the USA TODAY Inquiry page Sept. 22, 1983.

USA TODAY: You have waged a one-woman protest against Hollywood's misinterpretation of blacks. Why did you fight back?

TYSON: As I traveled around the country and got an idea of what people were thinking, I was absolutely appalled at the ignorance about black women. I realized that I certainly did not want to be one to perpetuate the kinds of images that were being projected of blacks not only in this country but abroad. I made a very conscious effort that I would only accept roles that are true to my knowledge of blacks, particularly black women.

USA TODAY: What are those images?

TYSON: Those demeaning and degrading roles: pimps, whores, drug pushers and drug users, Barbie-type women and women of no substance. We were given a steady diet of these types of films. I said, "That's certainly not what I know of members of my race." We have made incredible contributions not only to this country but to the entire world. Those types of images need to be projected. Until *Sounder* came along, we were not given the choice. That is what I found most disturbing.

USA TODAY: Would it have helped your career to have taken some of those roles?

TYSON: I cannot do things just for money. I have to have some inner gratification. Otherwise I would become so ill that the money would probably end up in a doctor's hand.

USA TODAY: How did you get the role of Miss Jane Pittman?

TYSON: I had finished *Sounder*, a film that brought much acclaim and recognition. So when the producers who had the option on *Miss Jane Pittman* decided to make the film, they approached my agent about having me play the title role.

USA TODAY: Roles such as Miss Jane Pittman pay a powerful homage to black women. Is it by choice or accident that you have made such powerful statements with your acting?

TYSON: My interest was in learning my craft from the best possible source. Once I did that I needed to be able to execute whatever knowledge I acquired. I just began to work wherever I could possibly work secretly, without pay — just to have the experience of testing what I was trying to perfect.

USA TODAY: What impact did *Miss Jane Pittman* have on the industry?

TYSON: It did open the way for backing more serious dramatic films and films that deal with social issues. It is not easy to get backing for films that have black leads. The ratings surprised the industry because there were misgivings about who would want to watch an old black woman tell her life story. I am extremely grateful to Xerox for that because they sponsored it. I will be forever grateful to them and CBS.

USA TODAY: How can you tell when a role is right for you?

TYSON: When the role makes my skin tingle. That is how I determine what I do. When I read the script one of two things happens — either my skin tingles or my stomach turns. When my skin tingles I know that the role is right for me. When my stomach turns I just say, "Thank you, but no thank you."

USA TODAY: What has been the toughest obstacle you've had to overcome in your career?

TYSON: Just to be has been the most difficult thing because it is so difficult to be human. Because you are black, nine times out of 10 you are dealt with because of the color of your skin, not because of who you are. But I am not a quitter. I will fight until I drop. That is a strength that is in my sinew. It is innate in me to get up after being knocked down, to pick up the pieces and go on. And it is not easy. It is just a matter of having some faith in the fact that as long as you are able to draw breath in this universe you have a chance.

USA TODAY: You grew up in El Barrio on New York's East Side. What is unforgettable about that period of your life?

TYSON: Not too long ago I drove through the area, touching bases with all the places I knew as a child. It was such a nostalgic experience. I pictured my mother looking out of the window. I remembered schools that I went to in the area, some of the friends I grew up with. It still gives me goose bumps when I think about it. But the area has changed drastically. I recognized very little except a few of the houses where I lived as a child.

USA TODAY: You talk about your mother with love and respect. How did she influence you?

TYSON: My mother came to this country from Nevis in the Caribbean when she was 17 years old. She went as far as what is known as the 7th standard in the British educational system. She had an adage for everything. If I went out for an audition or interviewed for a job and it didn't work out, she said: "What is not for you, you'll never get. And what is for you, you'll get." Invariably something better would come along.

USA TODAY: Were you a model child?

TYSON: I was a rebellious child. If my mother said, "Walk," I ran. In retrospect I realize that my strength and my fortitude come from my mother.

USA TODAY: Are you religious?

TYSON: I was brought up in the Episcopal church. It dominated our lives as children. My mother felt it was the safest place for her children to be. So we went to church from Sunday morning to Saturday night. There was always some activity going on in the church. I sang in the choir, played the piano and the organ and taught Sunday school. Then there were all of those young people's meetings and the choir rehearsals during the week. On Saturdays we occasionally helped clean the church.

USA TODAY: Did your mother encourage you to become an actress?

TYSON: No. She thought the life of an actress was rather "tinsel." I became a secretary because my father wanted me to have a white-collar job.

USA TODAY: How did you become an actress?

TYSON: Purely by accident — or divine guidance. I was working in a social service agency as a secretary to an administrator. One day I became overwhelmed with the mechanics of banging on a typewriter. I pushed myself away from the desk and announced to the world that I was sure that God didn't put me on the face of this earth to bang on a typewriter for the rest of my life. Then I pulled myself back to the desk to continue typing the case history in my typewriter. I looked around and everyone was very quietly looking at me as if I had taken leave of my senses. And I suppose on a temporary

TYSON PROFILE

Born: Dec. 19, 1933, in New York City.

Family: Married to musician Miles Davis.

Education: Attended New York City public schools before studying acting.

On life: "I was working in a social service agency as a secretary to an administrator. One day I became overwhelmed with the mechanics of banging on a typewriter. I pushed myself away from the desk and announced to the world that I was sure that God didn't put me on the face of this earth to bang on a typewriter for the rest of my life. . . . I looked around and everyone was very quietly looking at me as if I had taken leave of my senses. And I suppose on a temporary basis, I did. I wasn't sure what else was out there for me to do, but I certainly was going to try to find it."

Home: Malibu, Calif.

Role model: Her mother, Fredricka.

MILESTONES

1961: Made stage debut off-Broadway, playing Virtue — a role she created — in *The Blacks*.

1963: Co-starred as Jane Foster in *East Side/West Side Story*.

1969: Co-founder of the Dance Theatre of Harlem.

1972: Starred as Rebecca Morgan, a sharecropper's wife, in *Sounder*.

1974: Won two Emmys for starring role in *The Diary of Miss Jane Pittman*.

1977: Starred as Coretta King in *King*.

1978: Starred in *A Woman Called Moses*, the story of Harriet Tubman.

1981: Starred in *Welcome to Success: The Marva Collins Story*.

1983: Starred on stage in *The Corn is Green*.

1987: Photojournalist assignment for *Ebony* magazine, covering the filming of the movie *Cry Freedom* in Zimbabwe.

basis, I did. I wasn't sure what else was out there for me to do, but I certainly was going to try to find it.

USA TODAY: What happened next?

TYSON: I wanted to make some money and then go on to college. I was very interested in the study of the mind so I was leaning toward becoming a psychologist. I was fascinated by that. But I wanted to work and earn my own money. And make my own way. Even if it required going to school at night and working during the day. Then my hairdresser asked me to participate in a hair style show. That led to modeling. Modeling led to acting.

USA TODAY: What is your message to young people who want success?

TYSON: What I see across the country as I speak in the various colleges is passivity, lethargy, no drive, no motivation, no desire, no pride. I'm not saying it is 100 percent, but what young people must learn is that nobody owes them anything. If they want it, they have to get out there and fight for it. And they have all the tools. They only need to have those tools sharpened. And they can be sharpened through education.

USA TODAY: What makes you happy?

TYSON: I was on my way back from running one day and there were some men working construction. As I passed I heard someone say my name. He said: "Cicely Tyson. What an exquisite bit of humanity. We are so glad we have you. God bless you." And I thought, "My God, he just made my morning." And the reason I bring that up is I am a very shy person. My tendency is always to avoid people. To go on the other side of the street. Not that I am being snobbish. It is just that it is difficult for me to face people sometimes. But if I had crossed the street, look what I would have missed.

MALCOLM-JAMAL WARNER

With sitcom stardom came his casting as a role model for USA's teen-agers

WARNER: 'I was taught to believe in myself. I had enough self-esteem not to feel that I had to do drugs to feel cool.'

IMPRESSIONS

Between rehearsals on *The Cosby Show* set, his long legs seem to wrap around corners before the rest of his body arrives. Malcolm-Jamal Warner dashes through the corridors greeting friends. He has definite ideas about how he can help Hollywood bring more positive images of minorities to USA movies and television. He feels that love of self and others is an answer to helping teens say no to drugs and other negative influences. Jovial and lovable, his personality and good manners no doubt have mothers crossing their fingers that their own children will turn out so well.

— **Barbara Reynolds**

His first love was basketball until Malcolm-Jamal Warner was enticed by a friend to take an acting class one summer in Los Angeles. Since that first acting lesson, he has performed in such Los Angeles stage productions as The Wizard of Oz. In 1983 he landed the role of Theo Huxtable, the son on The Cosby Show, and helped make that series one of the most popular on television. He is a role model for young people, encouraging them to stay in school and stay away from drugs. Warner was interviewed for the USA TODAY Inquiry page Nov. 6, 1987.

USA TODAY: You are quite a star today, but were things always so good? Were you poor when you were young?

WARNER: We didn't have a lot of money. But it was like the poor-rich kid. We were making it. I always had self-esteem. I always had love from both of my parents. Even though my dad didn't live in the same house, he was a vital part of my growing up. I was taught to care about other people, to care about myself.

USA TODAY: When did you begin acting?

WARNER: I've been acting since I was 9, but I wanted to be a basketball player. I had dreams of playing for the Los Angeles Lakers.

USA TODAY: So how did you get into acting?

WARNER: When basketball season was over, a friend of my mom's suggested I take an acting class, and I enrolled in a class in Inglewood, Calif., that put on stage productions. Acting held my interest. It was, "Well, maybe I'll stick with this, it's something I really like." Eventually I got an agent and did some television.

USA TODAY: When you auditioned for *The Cosby Show*, did any bells go off to say this is going to be big?

WARNER: No. But because it was a television series, it was something that I wanted. That exposure would be good for my career. I went in and I read with the casting director and that's when I met Bill (Cosby), and the director and the producers and the writers and everything. I read the script like you see on television. You see kids roll their eyes, huffing and puffing, just being little smart alecks. When I finished, I looked up and Mr. Cosby was there. He

said, "Would you really talk to your father like that?" I said, "No, I wouldn't." And he said, "Well, I don't want to see it in this show." I was able to go back and read the scene again. This time I did it. I went the opposite direction.

USA TODAY: What does the part mean to you?

WARNER: It means a lot. Being associated with the No. 1 show and a quality show like *The Cosby Show* is great for my career. It's also great to know that I'm part of something that is going to change the image of black Americans. Every time you turn on the television you see a black person who has to be part of a gang, who has to be a pimp driving a big Cadillac, carrying a gun in his pocket. On comedies you see black people as poor. And I think that is basically a reflection of how the American society views black people. To have a show like *The Cosby Show* that views black Americans as middle-class Americans who don't live in the projects, don't run around in big cars, aren't pimps, aren't street kids, aren't dope pushers, but are an all-American middle-class family — that starts to change the image.

USA TODAY: Has the show changed your lifestyle?

WARNER: All the bills are paid on time! That's the major thing. True, I have more money than back then, but I don't look at my career as a money-making vehicle.

USA TODAY: Who are your role models?

WARNER: My mom and my dad. They have always gone out and worked hard for whatever they wanted or whatever they felt they needed. They always worked hard for their family. I think that's very important because we see kids today who want to look to celebrities as role models. In actuality, your role models should be right there in your house.

USA TODAY: Do you seek to emulate anyone?

WARNER: One person that I really look to as inspiration is Ron Howard. He's doing what I want to do. He's the director. He was basically in the same position I'm in now. He started as a young child on *Andy Griffith*, then on *Happy Days* became a teen role model. He was able to make a transition from being a teen-age actor to adult director, actor, producer. That's what I want to do.

USA TODAY: Are you like Theo, your character in *The Cosby Show*?

WARNER: We're totally different because we have different backgrounds. Theo has four sisters, lives in a house, lives with both parents and has both parents as a safety net. I was basically raised as an only child. You learn more responsibility at a younger age because you have to. That makes Theo and Malcolm a little bit different.

USA TODAY: Are you more mature than Theo?

WARNER: I would think so.

USA TODAY: Are there any particular words that you use to sort of live by?

WARNER: A whole lot! Do unto others as you would have others do unto you. Love yourself. If you can't, who can? I think that's important because a lot of kids today have low self-esteem. That's the only reason you can explain the increase in drug abuse, the increase in teen-age suicide, because the kids aren't taught to believe in themselves.

USA TODAY: Have you been exposed to drugs?

WARNER: I was more exposed to drugs in junior high school in Los Angeles than I have been since doing *The Cosby Show*!

USA TODAY: How did you deal with that?

WARNER: I was taught to believe in myself. I had enough self-esteem not to feel that I had to do drugs to feel cool. My friends didn't do drugs. My friends weren't around drugs. I think that was good for me because I never had to be in that position. No one said, "Hey, man, if you don't take these drugs, you're not cool."

USA TODAY: What advice do you have for kids who are using drugs?

WARNER: Ask yourself why. Is it really necessary? Does it do more good than harm? I think it does more harm than good.

USA TODAY: Do you pray?

WARNER: When it comes to praying, I pray for everything! I pray for everyone — people I like and people I really don't like.

USA TODAY: What is it like to work with Cosby?

WARNER: I had heard he was really hard to work with, but I think people say that because Bill Cosby is a perfectionist. Ironically, that's the quality I admire most about him. Because *The Cosby Show* is his brainchild, he wants it to be perfect. The people who can't deal with that are the ones who say

WARNER PROFILE

Born: Aug. 18, 1970, in Jersey City, N.J.

Family: Single; lives with his mother, Pamela Warner. Father, Robert Warner Jr., lives in Chicago.

Education: Attends Professional Childrens School, New York City.

On life: "We didn't have a lot of money. But it was like the poor-rich kid. We were making it. I always had self-esteem. I always had love from both of my parents. Even though my dad didn't live in the same house, he was a vital part of my growing up. . . . I was taught to care about other people, to care about myself."

Home: Brooklyn Heights, N.Y.

Role models: Parents, Robert and Pamela Warner.

MILESTONES

1978: Performed in *The Wizard of Oz* at the Inglewood, Calif., Playhouse.

1979: Performed in *Alice, Is That You,* based on *The Wizard of Oz,* at the Inglewood Playhouse.

1983: Acted in PBS' *The Eye of the Storm.*

1984: Became Theo on *The Cosby Show;* served as national chairman for the Osmond Foundation's Miracle Network telethon, a fund-raiser for children's hospitals across the USA.

1985: Appeared on *NBC's 60th Anniversary Celebration;* named honorary youth chairperson for the National Parent Teachers Association.

1986: Acted in ABC TV special *A Desperate Exit;* appeared in *Motown Returns to the Apollo — Night of 100 Stars II;* was host of *Home Alone: A Kid's Guide to Playing It Safe on Your Own.*

1987: Honored by New York Mayor Ed Koch for encouraging young people to stay in school; played an orphan in NBC movie *The Father Clements Story.*

he's difficult to work with.

USA TODAY: Do you have advice for young people?

WARNER: Just basically to believe in themselves. Believe that they can overcome whatever problem is presented. Drugs are not the way. Suicide is definitely not the way. Life is not going to come easy. Life wasn't meant to be easy. Kids want to be famous. They want to be celebrities. That's not what it's all about. Instead of wanting to be a famous actor, they should be more worried about being able to make money. They look at all the glitz and glamour. The grass is always greener on the other side. These kids do not realize how much work it is. Truly, it is a lot of work!

USA TODAY: Are you a role model?

WARNER: Inevitably, I am. I can't get around that because kids relate to Theo Huxtable. Look around. There are no other black teen-agers in my position. So I know that I'm a role model and because I have that title, I'm going to do what I can.

HAROLD WASHINGTON

Inspired by his father, his life of service
helped break down barriers in Chicago

WASHINGTON: 'I want to be remembered as the catalyst who urged
people to include, to expand and to be fair.'

IMPRESSIONS

In 1979 I left Chicago. Racism and discrimination were among the reasons. Police brutality
was rampant. Housing and job discrimination
were standard operating procedure. I would not
have predicted an independent-minded black
man could have been elected mayor in 1983.
When Mayor Harold Washington took charge,
Chicago had a different feel. Streets in black areas were swept. The police found their mission
was to serve and protect. Minorities were no
longer treated like intruders in City Hall. When
we talked only a month before he died, he
shared with me his dream for a better Chicago.

— **Barbara Reynolds**

The election of Harold Washington as mayor of Chicago in 1983 was a major political event for the city and for the USA. The veteran politician spent most of his adult life representing the people of his hometown in the state Legislature or the U.S. House of Representatives or in City Hall. He ran unsuccessfully for mayor in 1977 in a special election, but six years later he became Chicago's first black mayor. He was elected to a second term as mayor in 1987. An interview with Washington appeared on the USA TODAY Inquiry page March 9, 1983. He suffered a fatal heart attack in his City Hall office Nov. 25, 1987 — a month after he was interviewed again for this book.

USA TODAY: When you ran in 1977 and in 1983, political analysts said the fight would be too tough for that racially divided city to elect a black man. Why did you try?

WASHINGTON: I always have been a rebel with a cause. I have always defied regimentation. I never have been satisfied with the norm. My attitude always has been "show me." Anyone who wants anything of me has the burden of proving to me that what they want is what I should do. I just don't take things for granted.

USA TODAY: Was there a time during the 1983 mayoral race when you believed that you would not be elected mayor?

WASHINGTON: I was convinced without any shadow of a doubt that I was going to be elected mayor. I knew I had the votes. During the last phases of the campaign, all I said was: "We can win. We can win." It never hit me that we had won until about a month after the election. One morning I was looking out my window drinking coffee and said, "Wow, I am the mayor of this damn city."

USA TODAY: What were the major obstacles standing in the way of your election?

WASHINGTON: I am aware of racism, how deep it is. I understand what greed and corruption are all about. I understand what duplicity means. But those were problems to overcome. I just kept moving, moving, moving. My election as mayor was not a one-person achievement. When people — be they Polish, Jewish, Asian, Hispanic, black — reach a majority in the population and decide to change things, they just go do it.

USA TODAY: Did race make a difference in what people expected from you in office?

WASHINGTON: No question about it. When you say a black, you are talking about a person with an orientation that justifies the reason people vote for him in the first place. If the mayor is a legitimate extension of the drive and the movement behind him, then race makes a definite difference. Whether you like it or not, whether you are good at it or not, you are a role model for black and white kids by virtue of your visibility. That visibility is assured by the very fact that you are a chief executive in this country. But in the role of the mayor of Chicago, you get a super abundance of visibility throughout the country and the world.

USA TODAY: What effect did your win have on the city's youth?

WASHINGTON: It is unbelievably potent to see. Any time I give a speech, children up to 19 years of age come up to me, saying: "I saw you yesterday on television. I read your speech." It goes on and on. Just by being there, you make an impact on the lives of young kids — both blacks and whites. And both groups are not used to seeing a black person in that role. People live through you. They cheer you on. They want you to do good because you represent them. The good will directed at you is unbelievable. Every day, women, primarily black women, tell me, "I am praying for you." I hear it so often that it's both comforting and frightening. It does something to you. It makes you want to be better and make better decisions.

USA TODAY: Who were your role models?

WASHINGTON: I don't have any heroes except my father or my grandfather. My father was a lawyer, a politician and then a minister. My grandfather was an AME minister too.

USA TODAY: What was your father like?

WASHINGTON: I had no confusion about who Santa Claus was. There was my father, Roy Washington. He came home every night, put his feet under the table and he said grace. I wanted to please this guy because he looked out for his family. He's the reason I wanted to become a lawyer.

USA TODAY: Has your being mayor helped change Chicago's reputation for segregation?

WASHINGTON: My being mayor forces a lot of people to face up to their biases, their narrowness. It probably has led to the hiring of more black middle class. Everywhere I go people say, "I got a promotion because of you." Or, "I got a job." There are also the more tangible results, such as neighborhood development. We put $12 million into neighborhood streets, roads and fixing faulty sidewalks. No one had tackled it before. We have done it.

USA TODAY: How has the work force changed?

WASHINGTON: When I came into office, blacks were in about 2 percent of the decision-making positions. Women represented about 3 or 4 percent. On paper, the percentage of Hispanics in those positions did not exist. Now blacks and women are each at about 40 percent of those decision-making positions. And Hispanics are about 12 to 14 percent of the decision-making positions. The whole face of government has been opened up.

USA TODAY: Your administration has helped many, but how do you feel when you see the homeless and the helpless?

WASHINGTON: I see a challenge. The process has failed them. After all, civilization is a veneer. You were not born with it. You have to be trained to appreciate getting along with people. We have got to try to do something.

USA TODAY: What has been the most serious crisis of your administration?

WASHINGTON: They all have been financial. When we came in we were $165 million short. That took us to the brink. We laid off some people. We got over that first fiscal crisis. The second major crisis was when we tried to get O'Hare airport expanded. They held up all the contracts. And we fought it out for about four months. Finally we worked out a compromise and we got O'Hare going. The third crisis: We wanted to start paving about 300 miles of streets throughout the neighborhoods for the first time in 50 years. The City Council had tried to hold it up. We went to the neighborhoods. We went out into the Polish, Irish, Italian communities. And the housewives wanted those streets paved. Bang! It happened. Our latest audit shows that our books are balanced and we have a surplus. We had our bond rating improved for the first time in 30 years.

USA TODAY: Wasn't your opposition on the City Council fighting you every step of the way?

WASHINGTON: That may be true, but we haven't lost a major battle since we started. Because we are so good? No. The law was on our side. Because we stuck to our guns. The bottom line? When we took it to the people, we won every time.

WASHINGTON PROFILE

Born: April 15, 1922, in Chicago.

Died: Nov. 25, 1987, in Chicago.

Family: Divorced; no children.

Education: Bachelor of arts from Roosevelt University, Chicago; law degree from Northwestern University, Evanston, Ill.

On life: "I am aware of racism, how deep it is. I understand what greed and corruption are all about. I understand what duplicity means. But those were problems to overcome. I just kept moving, moving, moving. My election as mayor was not a one-person achievement. When people — be they Polish, Jewish, Asian, Hispanic, black — reach a majority in the population and decide to change things, they just go do it."

Home: Chicago.

Role model: His father, Roy Washington.

MILESTONES

1939: Won Chicago's high school championship in 120-meter high hurdles.

1954: Started four years as assistant city prosecutor, Chicago.

1964: Elected to Illinois House.

1965: Served six terms through 1976 in the Illinois House of Representatives.

1972: Served 36 days in jail for failing to file federal income tax returns.

1976: Elected to Illinois Senate.

1977: Lost bid for mayor of Chicago.

1980: Elected to U.S. House.

1983: Elected Chicago mayor, defeating Republican Bernard Epton by about 45,000 votes out of 1.2 million cast.

1987: Re-elected Chicago mayor, winning by more than 130,000 votes; gained a majority political base on the City Council for the first time.

USA TODAY: So what does your election say about the democratic process?

WASHINGTON: As long as you keep the democratic process open, if you expand the franchise, you are saying, "New blood will come in because the door is open." As that happens, things continue to change for the better. New blood means new people, new ideas, new boldness, new thoughts.

USA TODAY: And if the door to the democratic process is closed?

WASHINGTON: You don't get the new blood. You just die out. A viable society must have new blood churning constantly. We should always be proud of the franchise, the right to vote.

USA TODAY: How would you like to be remembered?

WASHINGTON: As a man who changed the system, incorporated a sense of fairness based on a vision and plain common sense. I would hope that people would point to the 1980s and say, "We detected a different approach in that period." I would hope people would look at people like myself and say we succeeded to a great extent. I would hope that the bars of discrimination would continue to fall because talent is too important and limited to be wasted. I hope people who can see my vision also will see how I used the democratic process to change things.

USA TODAY: Describe your vision.

WASHINGTON: I am not talking about static goals but goals in progress. My vision for Chicago is to have a city where people strive to create more jobs, improve education, health delivery and housing services. We want a beautiful life. We want fine homes. But it's more than that. It's a constant push to achieve more and more equality. I want to be remembered as the catalyst who urged people to include, to expand and to be fair.

FAYE WATTLETON

Bombings, criticism haven't weakened her resolve to provide family planning choices

WATTLETON: 'Being black and a female adds dimension to my sensitivities as I carry out my work.'

IMPRESSIONS

Her reign at the helm of Planned Parenthood has not always been smooth. Family planning centers have been bombed. There has been pressure from those who want to shut down her organization. But Faye Wattleton isn't shaken by the storm. She is committed to cutting the economic drain on the USA caused by teen pregnancy. She has survived these trying times and helped me see that despite one's religious or political beliefs, the public has a right to choose. Without those choices, we abandon a right essential to the USA's well-being.

— **Barbara Reynolds**

When appointed president of Planned Parenthood Federation of America Inc., Faye Wattleton changed the declining organization into an aggressive proponent of reproductive rights. Her leadership of the non-profit educational, research and medical services organization has taken the group through years of expansion and controversy. A nurse by profession, she was director of nursing services for the city of Dayton, Ohio, before joining Planned Parenthood as a board member. She eventually became executive director of the Dayton chapter. She traces her interest in family planning and reproductive rights to her days at Harlem Hospital. Since taking over Planned Parenthood she has been at the cutting edge of shaping national policy to protect reproductive rights. An interview with Wattleton appeared on the USA TODAY Inquiry page Dec. 28, 1982.

USA TODAY: As a young nursing student in the '60s, you took care of a woman who died after an illegal abortion. Did that influence your decision to accept the helm of Planned Parenthood?

WATTLETON: This 17-year-old woman died as a result of her mother giving her a concoction of bleach and a well-known bathroom cleaning disinfectant to help her abort. She died from kidney failure; little could be done to save her. It was quite typical of the times. Many emergency beds were filled with women suffering from blood poisoning as a result of illegal abortions. I have seen this story printed many times as the reason I became involved in Planned Parenthood. But I was no less affected by the teen-age mothers for whom I helped to establish school programs, or by the battered and neglected children I saw as a nurse in a children's hospital. All of these things were very important.

USA TODAY: What did influence you to become involved in Planned Parenthood?

WATTLETON: I had to ask myself, "Is it better to continue trying to save these children and those people who are injured and vulnerable, or to work for a world in which these conditions don't occur?"

USA TODAY: How do you cope with the bombings of Planned Parenthood clinics?

WATTLETON: It is always important to keep a perspective on what your mission is and on what you want to achieve. I head an organization that has 183 affiliates in 47 states and the District of Columbia, has a $250 million budget, between 3,000 and 4,000 employees. I cannot permit myself to get caught in the fray and to simply spend my time addressing the attacks. It is incumbent upon me to remain constantly focused on the central purpose of our organization: to serve people who need us.

USA TODAY: What are the dangers of getting caught up in public debate?

WATTLETON: If I entered into every controversy and debated each critic, I would be in danger of losing sight of the more than 3 million who become pregnant in this country each year and who don't want to be. And the more than 1 million teenagers who become pregnant in this country every year. Those are the major dangers. I must maintain perspective and continue to provide the leadership that keeps the organization moving forward.

USA TODAY: Teen pregnancy is one of the burning social issues today. Has birth control availability caused teens to be more sexually active?

WATTLETON: There is no evidence of that. Teen-agers are normally sexually active 9 to 11 months before they seek any family-planning services. American teen-agers are no more sexually active than their European counterparts, but they are more likely to become pregnant.

USA TODAY: Why?

WATTLETON: American teens have the worst of all worlds. We do not educate our children well about their sexual development. Yet sex is widely exploited in this country. Our children are bombarded and confronted with sexual messages, sexual exploitation and all manner of sexual criticism. But our society is by and large sexually illiterate. Our children are perhaps the most vulnerable, the most likely to be damaged by these contradictions.

USA TODAY: Why are so many people who oppose abortion also opposed to birth control?

WATTLETON: In less than a generation we have gone from having few birth-control options to having a great many, including legal abortions. That has created a tremendous amount of anxiety and insecurity among some people who are not comfortable with change. They are people who may not understand that giving people choices enhances our capacity to attain dignity and reach our capacity as productive human beings.

USA TODAY: Has your race or gender added to the controversy surrounding Planned Parenthood?

WATTLETON: On the contrary, they have both been definite assets. Planned Parenthood was founded more than 70 years ago by Margaret Sanger and thereafter run by men. My appointment seemed a very bold step for the organization to take. As a black woman I have a deep and personal concern for the tragedy of unwanted children. I know that the burden of such conditions falls much heavier on blacks than on the white community. Being black and a female adds dimension to my sensitivities as I carry out my work.

USA TODAY: Your mother is a minister who wanted you to become a missionary nurse. How does she feel about your position?

WATTLETON: She and I have very different views on these issues. It would be very difficult for my mother not to recognize that I have accomplished a great deal. I am an only child who was raised in a very sentimental and a very religious family in the St. Louis, Mo., area.

USA TODAY: You mean your parents don't agree with your position on abortion?

WATTLETON: My parents' views on birth control and abortion are quite different from mine. But we all respect the right of individuals to hold views different from our own. I believe that the work I have chosen is perhaps the most fundamental missionary work one could have the honor to perform.

USA TODAY: What major obstacles have you overcome in your life?

WATTLETON: Being black in America and coming from very humble beginnings are major obstacles. I come from a family with distinctly middle-class values but without middle-class economic standings. Getting through college was an enormous struggle. Had I not gone to a university where school of nursing majors received room and board for clinical work in the hospital, I might not have gotten through college.

USA TODAY: How did you earn extra money?

WATTLETON: I worked part time on weekends to supplement what my parents gave me. In graduate school I received scholarships and stipends. Such programs allowed me to develop my intellectual capacity, work real hard and succeed. Others may be denied similar help because of government budget cuts.

USA TODAY: Who were your role models?

WATTLETON: My attitudes — and all that I

am — are the result of all my experiences. But my mother had an enormous influence on the shaping of my life and my attitudes about people. She taught me the need to understand and accept one's responsibility to make the world a better place. My mother had a tremendous amount of courage to become a minister when it was not fashionable for women. And my father was very supportive. So I gained a sense of courage from them.

USA TODAY: Why do you think success seems to escape so many blacks?

WATTLETON: It escapes many of us because we continue to live in a society in which doors are closed to the advancements and aspirations of blacks. We saw a reversal of these trends in the 1960s, but there has been a systematic effort to dismantle many of the structures created to help blacks achieve success and eliminate barriers. We have to look largely within the system to end the long-term effects of racism. But I think we also have to look within ourselves. We have to take the attitude that we will not be defeated by systematic barriers. If we would exercise that attitude collectively as a people, we would have the power to make political and economic changes. My hunch is that if Martin Luther King (Jr.) were alive today, he would recognize that the civil rights movement only took us so far.

USA TODAY: Did anyone advise you not to take the leadership of Planned Parenthood?

WATTLETON: There were plenty who said: "Planned Parenthood is in a terrible state. It has gone through two presidents in rapid succession. The organization is in turmoil. That's what always happens when an organization is on the skids — they turn around to look for a black to save it." I was in my 30s. In retrospect, accepting the position was a very courageous move. Sometimes we have to be willing to fail, although I have to say that I have not experienced much failure in my career. I have been enormously blessed to have led the organization during a period of tremendous success. The organization and I have grown together. We have met many challenges that were never anticipated when I was appointed.

OPRAH WINFREY

Years of tears and sorrow are gone;
her life is now glamour and contentment

WINFREY: 'In my life and in my work . . . the more I am able to be myself, the more it enables other people to be themselves.'

IMPRESSIONS

Wealth becomes her. Settled back in her white stretch limousine, Oprah Winfrey propped her cowboy boots on the seat, a sterling example of self-confidence, discipline and excellence. There was no doubt that she would hold on to her ratings as the USA's talk show queen. I only wished she had a bigger limousine, big enough to carry all the doubters, the "hemmers and hawers," those who depend on excuses so they could learn from her. When we stopped at a clothing store during the trip, Oprah swept through buying at will, not worrying about cost. Self-discipline and talent do have their rewards.

— **Barbara Reynolds**

*H*er professional and personal life combine a commitment to excellence seen by millions who watch The Oprah Winfrey Show *each week, or who saw her performance in* The Color Purple. *But she is also community minded. She offers herself as a role model for a small group of teen-age girls from Chicago's Cabrini-Green housing area. These young ladies from poor families join her regularly for slumber parties and conversation at her Chicago home. She has developed her own production company, Harpo, and hopes to produce movies. Comments by Winfrey appeared on the* USA TODAY *Inquiry page Feb. 10, 1987.*

USA TODAY: Success is often an illusive goal. What makes a person successful?

WINFREY: The universe has plans for your life, just as for my life. The way to succeed is to do what you do best. The way to ride around in a limousine and live where you want to live and buy the kinds of clothes and things you want to buy may not be the same way that I went. Listen to your own cues. If everybody did that, we would all be happy. Everybody would be in jobs they enjoyed. They would be fulfilled in their lives, instead of trying to do what Tom, Dick and Harpo are doing.

USA TODAY: What is the bench mark for you to determine when your show is successful?

WINFREY: It will be received well around the country. There is no reason for it not to be. It will succeed because I strive to show people the light in me. That is my goal. That is the only goal I have. My goal is for people to see the light. And you can define the light any way you want. I call it a loving energy that I try to maintain. It is up to you to discover at what level you have it. And once you discover it you continue to open up doors and let your love expand to more and more people.

USA TODAY: What do you mean by expand?

WINFREY: True expansion is when you reach a point where you no longer judge other people. I'm not there yet. I'm still striving for that one. I strive to walk in light and that is my goal. Because that is my goal, everything else comes to me. It was not my goal to become a millionaire. It just happened. And after it happened I said: "Well, I would like to become a multimillionaire now. OK, let's see how

that feels. I think I will like it."

USA TODAY: When you first entered the TV talk show arena, people touted you as a direct challenge to the king of talk, Phil Donahue. How did you handle that?

WINFREY: Isn't that fun? There is room for us all. I have nothing but respect for Donahue because if it wasn't for Donahue, there couldn't be an Oprah Winfrey show. He paved the way for morning talk shows and for letting the rest of the country know that women are really concerned about issues other than recipes. Donahue will certainly remain king. I would just like a part of the monarchy.

USA TODAY: You describe your show as spontaneous sharing. Is that what sets you apart?

WINFREY: I believe that good communicative television should be a give and take. You give something to the audience and they give back to you. It's reciprocal. So I expect my audience and my guests to be as open as I am. What I have learned in my life and in my work is that the more I am able to be myself, the more it enables other people to be themselves. That is why people tell me things on the air that they have not been able to tell their mother, their daughter, their brother.

USA TODAY: Do you have any examples?

WINFREY: On a show about children of divorced parents a guest chose to tell her daughter for the first time that she was ashamed of divorcing her husband 22 years ago. She said she had never found the words to say it, but because she was on *The Oprah Winfrey Show,* she was able to say it. On another show a woman admitted she had been having an affair for three years. Her husband didn't know. I thought, "Oooh, sister, you're in big trouble now."

USA TODAY: Is it fair for critics to say you are too emotional and subjective on your show?

WINFREY: I was a news journalist for 10 years. I don't consider myself a journalist anymore because I'm not objective and I am emotional. I do get involved, I allow myself to feel. I don't try to block the feelings or the flow. I tried for years to be a dispassionate journalist, and it made me really uncomfortable. I would be out on a fire assignment and I would begin helping people. So I got out of the non-feeling news business. I feel very, very comfortable doing what I do on television. And for those who complain, I do not let other people define for me what I think my life should be about.

USA TODAY: As someone who is neither pen-

cil-thin, white nor blond, you are trampling barriers that have hindered many in television. How have you done it?

WINFREY: My race and gender have never been an issue for me. I have been blessed in knowing who I am, and I am a part of a great legacy. I have crossed over on the backs of Sojourner Truth and Harriet Tubman and Fannie Lou Hamer and Madam C.J. Walker. Because of them I can now live the dream. I am the seed of the free, and I know it. I intend to bear great fruit.

USA TODAY: So you are saying you're secure in your ethnicity and you don't beat people over the head with it?

WINFREY: When I was younger I heard Rev. Jesse Jackson say excellence was the best deterrent to racism. And it is a motto that has become part of my own personal doctrine. Since race is not an issue for me, it is also not an issue for the people I interview. I do not try to remind people that I am black.

USA TODAY: You played a leading role in the movie *The Color Purple*, which was attacked for portraying black men as incestuous, sadistic philanderers. How do you feel about that?

WINFREY: It is such a stale argument. What upset me so much was going into the Oscars and seeing signs that said, "Ban *The Color Purple*." Then as I was coming out of the Oscars, the same people were carrying signs saying, "Why Didn't We Win?" I said: "People, please! Make up your minds!" The struggle should be to have more movies with black actors and actresses. The struggle should be to get more and different kinds of images on the screen, not to ban this one because it does not show black men in the most positive light. I want to tell people: "Shut up. Do something meaningful in your life."

USA TODAY: Why did you contemplate suicide over a broken relationship with a boyfriend?

WINFREY: That is why I am so joyous today, because I was down on my knees, saying: "Baby, please don't leave me now. Please, can we talk? Please, I promise I'll be better. I'll cook better meals. I'll have them on time." I did that. And when I look back to the woman that I was, it is enough to make me weep. I can't believe it.

USA TODAY: What was the old Oprah like?

WINFREY: Insecure. I was defining myself by things, defining myself by the kind of man I had in my life. I was one of those women who thought I was nothing without a man. I woke up when I was

WINFREY PROFILE

Born: Jan. 29, 1954, in Kosciusko, Miss.

Family: Single.

Education: Bachelor of arts from Tennessee State University, Nashville, Tenn.

On life: "True expansion is when you reach a point where you no longer judge other people. I'm not there yet. I'm still striving for that one. I strive to walk in light and that is my goal. Because that is my goal, everything else comes to me. It was not my goal to become a millionaire. It just happened. And after it happened I said: 'Well, I would like to become a multimillionaire now. OK, let's see how that feels. I think I will like it.'"

Home: Chicago.

Role models: Fannie Lou Hamer, Sojourner Truth, Eunice Kennedy Shriver and Maya Angelou.

MILESTONES

1976: Feature reporter and co-anchor for WJZ-TV, Baltimore.

1977-1983: Host of WJZ-TV's *People Are Talking*, which ran in competition with *Phil Donahue*, a national TV show then produced in Chicago.

1984: Host of *A.M. Chicago*, on WLS-TV, Chicago.

1985: *A.M. Chicago* renamed *The Oprah Winfrey Show*; played Sofia in the movie *The Color Purple*.

1986: *The Oprah Winfrey Show* goes into syndication on 128 stations across the USA; nominated for Academy Award for role in *The Color Purple*; received Woman of Achievement Award from the National Organization for Women; selected as one of *Playgirl* magazine's 10 Most Admired Women of 1986; started Harpo, her production company.

1987: Featured role in *Native Son,* a movie that was aired in theaters and nationally on Home Box Office.

28 years old and single and I wept all day. That is why I didn't have a meaningful relationship in my life or the kind of man who could give me the kind of support and love and kindness that I needed.

USA TODAY: Did being sent away by your mother, Vernita Lee, to live with your father, Vernon Winfrey, in Tennessee cause your former insecurity?

WINFREY: I was mischievous and kept getting into a lot of trouble. My mother could not handle it. I am grateful to my mother for sending me away. If she had not sent me to live with my father I would have taken an absolutely different path in life. My father is now a Nashville city councilman. At the time he was a barber at Winfrey's Barbershop where people still play checkers. He also owned a grocery store. I had to work in the store and I hated it, every minute of it. Hated it. Selling penny candy, Popsicles. But without him — even with all of this potential — I never would have blossomed.

USA TODAY: You have a company called Harpo, which is Oprah spelled backwards.

WINFREY: It's a production company that I started. I'm interested in becoming a mogul now.

USA TODAY: A mogul?

WINFREY: I have got to move on from millionaire to mogul. I would like to become what MTV has become to television. I want to produce movies for myself and for other people.

USA TODAY: Are you religious?

WINFREY: Going to church is a celebration for me, a way of fellowship and uniting in the spirit with other people. But I don't go to church because I feel I need direction. God talks to me all the time. We absolutely have an incredible personal relationship. And it is because of this "God-centeredness" that I am where I am. It is also because I fear nothing and no one.

USA TODAY: Some might call that arrogance.

WINFREY: No, it's an assuredness that I have. The more you praise and celebrate your life, the more there is in life to celebrate. The more you complain, the more you find fault — the more misery and fault you will have to find. I am so glad that I did not have to wait until I was 52 to figure this out, to understand the law of cause and effect — that divine reciprocity, reaping what you sow, is the absolute truth.

ROBERT WOODSON

His strong will and conservative philosophy help improve the USA's black communities

WOODSON: 'Despite the price of disenfranchisement . . . the true legacy of entrepreneurship still thrives in the black community.'

IMPRESSIONS

Black conservatives are not the most popular people, but Robert Woodson has gained widespread respect. He has proven he is not a creature of ideology. He dares to think. It doesn't matter to him if the solution sounds Republican or Democratic — as long as it works. On a special Black Entertainment Television interview, journalists pressed him for answers. He offered new approaches to education, neighborhood revitalization and a few observations on the need for more blacks to adopt black children. While I might not always agree with him, it is refreshing to hear his ideas.

— **Barbara Reynolds**

A *former fellow at the American Enterprise Institution, Robert Woodson started the National Center for Neighborhood Enterprise in 1981. He was among a group of black business and political leaders who met with President Ronald Reagan in 1985 to discuss economic development for the nation's black communities. Reflecting on his center, he says he has always hoped to establish a place where activists and thinkers could "join hands to uplift the poor." An interview with Woodson appeared on the USA TODAY Inquiry page Jan. 24, 1985.*

USA TODAY: As a Republican, it has taken a lot of courage to challenge the traditional thinking among blacks. You have done so and taken a lot of criticism. How did you develop such strong will?

WOODSON: I had a strong-willed mother, Anna, who raised five children when my father, Ralph, died. I was 9 years old. My father was a go-getter. He was the first black to drive a dairy truck in Philadelphia and he had to physically fight to keep his job. Unions were controlled by whites and my father was the first to break in. I remember his coming home telling about the struggles he had trying to keep his job. My mother also instilled in us a sense of ambition.

USA TODAY: How did she do that?

WOODSON: When I quit high school at age 17 and went to the Air Force, I came home after a year of being stationed in Florida. I spent my car fare back to Florida because I was so sure she would give it to me. But she told me to get back the best way I could. I hitchhiked a thousand miles, from Philadelphia to Cocoa Beach, Fla. It was rough. That incident helped to reinforce that my destiny is in my hands, that I can't rely on others to bail me out of my irresponsibility.

USA TODAY: You are one of the nation's best-known black conservatives. What helped you take on conservativism?

WOODSON: My mother had to raise four boys and a girl. She was helped by the Elks and the black institutions in our own community. They were substitutes for fathers. Our neighborhood was an extended family. We saw that what we needed was right within our community. My mother instilled in us how we could depend on ourselves from our own institutions. I feel today that white people may have been unfair, but still you have to get up.

USA TODAY: Was your childhood one of the reasons you became a self-help advocate?

WOODSON: I think so. Despite the price of disenfranchisement — lynchings, race riots, economic setbacks, misguided government programs, seething urban ghettos and the endurance of a thousand and one well-funded but meaningless studies on the pathology of poverty — the true legacy of entrepreneurship still thrives in the black community. Grass-roots organizations have blazed new trails across black America.

USA TODAY: Can you give an example?

WOODSON: There has been an explosion of black church-inspired community development programs. They are now taking hold nationwide. Examples include a collective banking and cash management program by the Congress of National Black Churches, church credit unions and 146 churches working to launch a major low-income housing program that will expand to 11 states.

USA TODAY: Is this a new direction?

WOODSON: For the first time denominations are putting aside religious rivalries and joining forces to attack poverty, unemployment, housing shortages and ignorance. Some 90 percent of these programs have been initiated with church resources. In addition to the traditional go-it-alone approach of the black church, many ministers automatically shy away from any fiscal arrangement with government agencies because of bad experiences. Red tape and loss of control are the main reasons cited for avoiding collaboration with city, state and federal agencies on community building.

USA TODAY: Does self-help lead to economic independence?

WOODSON: Yes. Rather than accept solutions parachuted in by middle-class professional service providers, black America must recognize and expand on indigenous self-help neighborhood efforts. The originators of these self-help programs have unique firsthand knowledge of the problems and resources within their communities. They have established track records for solving social problems by motivating their communities to develop innovative solutions to unemployment, substandard education, teen-age pregnancy, gang violence, day care and other sources of community travail.

USA TODAY: Why aren't blacks running more businesses in their neighborhoods?

WOODSON: Because blacks unfortunately have focused almost exclusively on civil rights for the past 20 years or so, as if applying civil rights solutions would somehow translate into economic equity. It does not. Most groups in this society didn't start off trying to achieve political equity. They went for businesses. In every other group the leaders of the community are business people. Once they have made their stake in business, then they go into politics.

USA TODAY: Are you saying economic power is underestimated compared to political power?

WOODSON: Yes. Let's say there were two revolutions going on in America: an economic revolution and a political revolution. If you're in the political revolution, that is the one that is televised. The economic one is not. One is seeking freedom, the other finance. If you have economic power, you vote every day with your money. If you have political power, you vote only once every two years.

USA TODAY: You are part of a black leadership group called the Council for a Black Economic Agenda that has met with President Reagan. Did you press him to change his administration's position on civil rights?

WOODSON: No. We said they had made some serious mistakes, such as supporting tax exemptions for Bob Jones University even though it discriminated against blacks. We told him we felt the president should move civil rights issues into the Oval Office, and the White House should play a more active role in formulating civil rights policy as other presidents have. But our main thrust was the black underclass.

USA TODAY: Your National Center for Neighborhood Enterprise has been applauded for novel approaches to helping the poor. What are some of those approaches?

WOODSON: People who are closest to the problem have the best chance of designing solutions. For example, we have found about 1.5 million people living in public housing. It's the absolute place of last resort and it's a billion-dollar industry. We have gone around the country and identified five locations where the residents took over and managed their own projects, organized themselves, took physical control of a public housing project and employed sanctions and incentives. The result of peers designing solutions for peers has been dramatic.

USA TODAY: Why do you argue that many

WOODSON PROFILE

Born: April 8, 1937, in Philadelphia.

Family: Married to Ellen Woodson; four children, Robert Jr., Ralph, Jamal, Tayna.

Education: Bachelor of science from Cheyney State College, Cheyney, Pa.; master's from the University of Pennsylvania, Philadelphia.

On life: "Rather than accept solutions parachuted in by middle-class professional service providers, black America must recognize and expand on indigenous self-help neighborhood efforts. The originators of these self-help programs have unique firsthand knowledge of the problems and resources within their communities. They have established track records for solving social problems by motivating their communities to develop innovative solutions to unemployment, substandard education, teen-age pregnancy, gang violence, day care and other sources of community travail."

Home: Silver Spring, Md.

Role models: Marcus Garvey, Arthur G. Gaston and Jesus Christ.

MILESTONES

1980: National Black Police Association Outstanding Service Award.

1981: Founded the National Center for Neighborhood Enterprise to give technical support and favorable publicity to grass-roots self-help organizations.

1983: Leslie Pinkney Hill Humanitarian Award, Cheyney State College Alumni Association.

1985: George Washington Honor Medal, Freedom Foundation at Valley Forge.

1986: Outstanding Public Service Award, The Georgia Coalition of Black Women.

1987: Speaking tour of Africa; editor of *On the Road to Economic Freedom: An Agenda for Black Progress;* author of *Civil Rights and Economic Power.*

agencies have a stake in poverty and no interest in relieving it?

WOODSON: Government has about 1,000 grant-in-aid agencies that distribute about $350 billion annually. You have thousands and thousands of professionals who make their living off poverty.

USA TODAY: What about the complaint that government helps Vietnamese more than blacks?

WOODSON: Blacks suffer from the victim mentality. The assumption is that if somebody is getting more than what they have, they must be receiving some outside help, that somehow people cannot obtain these things through hard work and discipline. The Vietnamese have established seed capital pools so other Vietnamese wanting to get in business can borrow money interest free.

USA TODAY: How do you respond to criticism that you want to supplant traditional civil rights leadership?

WOODSON: We want the black community to have more than one voice on issues of social and economic development.

USA TODAY: What do you think of today's civil rights leaders?

WOODSON: Their strategies are bankrupt. They are misleading people into believing that civil rights solutions will translate into economic gains. Racism could end tomorrow in America, but it would not reduce the mortality rate of black infants. It would not create a better health system. It would not mean more blacks would be employed. It would not increase our business formation rates.

USA TODAY: What's the answer?

WOODSON: We have to pursue non-romantic solutions instead of those that are compatible with our own ideological perception of the world. We can't believe that for every problem that exists, white folks are somehow responsible and therefore if they're responsible, the solution is for white folks to do something. Black leaders are responsible for perpetuating an attitude and an image to our black young people that their role is to be victims and that there is little they can do for themselves unless white people do it for them.

USA TODAY: Are you blaming the victim?

WOODSON: No. I'm saying the victimizer might have knocked you down but you cannot expect the victimizer to pick you up. The only person who is going to liberate you is yourself.

COLEMAN YOUNG

Meeting challenges he faced as a youth helped him make a difference in Detroit

YOUNG: 'You have to look at reality. . . . Once you cloud your vision with sentimentality, you are in trouble.'

IMPRESSIONS

On the bookcase in my study is the key to the city of Detroit. Mayor Coleman Young gave it to me in 1984 when I went to the Motor City to give the Founders Day Address for the Detroit Alumnae Chapter of Delta Sigma Theta sorority. His personality fits the city like a glove. He is tough, forward looking, not afraid of a challenge. He doesn't fear the aftermath of being honest. Known as a testy guy with a salty tongue, his life is a travelogue through decades of social change. He doesn't like talking to the press, but once he starts he is a leader whose words demand attention.

— **Barbara Reynolds**

The first black mayor of Detroit, Coleman Young has forged a coalition between business and the people of the city to correct the years of decline that followed the riot in 1967. A former union leader, he worked his way up through the ranks of state politics serving as state senator. He was elected mayor in 1974. He is controversial but effective in keeping the slow rebirth of Detroit on track. An interview with Young appeared on the USA TODAY Inquiry page Jan. 31, 1985.

USA TODAY: You have had tough times in your life. How did you learn to cope?

YOUNG: I believed in myself. I carried a burning anger in me at the advantage that people had taken of me — at the discrimination that I had suffered as a black person. Frankly, I find it difficult to understand why every black does not burn with that same rage. You could be sustained by that resentment. I know that sustained me. And I still have it. It makes you want to get wherever you have to get in order to improve yourself.

USA TODAY: Your family moved to Detroit after World War I. What was life like in the 1920s?

YOUNG: We came to Detroit in 1923 when I was five. We lived in Black Bottom. The area was a polyglot — Jews, Italians, Germans and other assorted Europeans. I can remember as a boy going in the German store on the corner. It smelled of rye bread, pickles and sauerkraut. Nothing was what it seemed to be. The tailor shop where I worked had a big crap game going on in the back room. Next door was the everyday shoe shine parlor with a poker game in the back room. On the other side was the city hock shop — the front for the local numbers headquarters. Next to the city hock shop was a confectionery, where they made ice cream. But in the back room they made corn liquor and I was a part of all that. I would collect the empty whiskey bottles and sell them back to the guy who made the corn for 2 cents each.

USA TODAY: What did your parents do?

YOUNG: Both graduated from college in Alabama. My mother from Stillman, in Tuscaloosa, where I was born. She taught school there. And my father attended Alabama A&M, in Norfolk, where he took up tailoring. In those days a two-year college was the most that black people got. My father was also a barber.

USA TODAY: Your father was an alcoholic?

YOUNG: That is true. My father hated white people. I think he retreated into the bottle. He is very light-skinned. And I guess he could have passed for white if he wanted to. He heard a hell of a lot more from white people than the average identifiable black would hear. He was always getting in fights out of his resentment. He was always kept back from promotions that he deserved because of his race. And, of course, he played poker. He was a very busy man.

USA TODAY: But you stayed on the right track.

YOUNG: There was never any choice. I was intrigued by guys with their diamond rings, but I was always challenged by anything that made you think — like some of the arguments I heard on social issues over at the barber shop. And in school I was very good at my studies. I devoured books, sometimes a book a day during summer vacation. I discovered new worlds in those books. I liked *The Three Musketeers*, especially when I found out that the author was black.

USA TODAY: Is there an incident of racism that sticks in your mind?

YOUNG: I earned a scholarship to a Catholic high school. I remember one brother over at De La Salle High School approached me as I was filling out the application. He said, "What are you, Japanese?" He just didn't believe there was a black person there. And I didn't know what the hell he was talking about. I said, "No, brother, I am colored." He put me out and unceremoniously tore my paper up. I will never forget it. I was about 12 years old.

USA TODAY: The labor movement was the stepping stone to your political career. How did you get involved in union activities?

YOUNG: I went to Ford Motor Co. when I came out of high school. I was an apprentice electrician. And here again I did not get the appointment because they gave it to a white guy, although I had much better marks. They were just beginning to talk about the union in 1936. I became active in the union after I was fired for fighting after a co-worker called me some names in 1937. After that, I was a volunteer organizer when the union organized Ford in June 1941. After I came back from World War II, the union I was promoting had organized the post office, so I worked for them as an international representative. In 1947 I was elected executive vice president of the Detroit CIO Council, which was the Wayne County CIO Council. It had over 400,000 members, the largest union council in the country. That was the highest position to which any black had been elected in the labor movement.

USA TODAY: During that time you met Paul Robeson and W.E.B. DuBois. What were they like?

YOUNG: They were the two greatest people I have ever known. DuBois was a remarkable intellectual. He also formed a connection with Winnie and Nelson Mandela in South Africa and across Africa with their African National Congress. We had the National Negro Congress here in Detroit. And DuBois was one of the organizers.

USA TODAY: What about Robeson?

YOUNG: Robeson was active in the labor movement. Right after an incident in which he was attacked in upstate New York and almost lynched, he made a tour of the country. Detroit was his first stop because he thought we had a strong enough labor movement to protect him. I was in charge of his security. He sang in the heart of the ghetto, and needless to say, no one threatening came within a mile of where Paul was.

USA TODAY: During that period many were being labeled communist. How did you handle this?

YOUNG: In Detroit we took these guys on. A congressional committee came here to look into claims that we had a lot of un-American activities going on. It was chaired by Rep. John S. Wood from Georgia. I did a little research on Wood and found that the majority of people in his district were black but they couldn't vote. I had the figures. So when he started questioning me about un-American activities, I challenged him on this. I said: "You are illegally represented. The majority of the folks in your district can't even vote. How the hell can you call me un-American?" So everybody took that tack in Detroit. And they left here in disarray.

USA TODAY: What did you do to become mayor of Detroit?

YOUNG: I had been state senator for about 10 years when I ran for mayor. I established a strong base in Detroit. When I defied that un-American activities committee in 1952 I developed a considerable standing. I was elected to the Constitutional Convention for the state of Michigan in 1960 and I discovered then that my strength was actually in Black Bottom where I had spent all my life.

YOUNG PROFILE

Born: May 24, 1918, in Tuscaloosa, Ala.

Family: Divorced; no children.

Education: Graduated from Eastern High School, Detroit.

On life: "I believed in myself. I carried a burning anger in me at the advantage that people had taken of me — at the discrimination that I had suffered as a black person. Frankly, I find it difficult to understand why every black does not burn with that same rage. You could be sustained by that resentment."

Home: Detroit.

Role models: Paul Robeson and W.E.B. DuBois.

MILESTONES

1941: Joined Tuskegee Airmen, the elite black flying unit of the Army Air Corps.

1945: Arrested with 100 others for demanding service in segregated officers' club at Freeman Field, Ind.

1947: Returned to job with the post office and resumed union activities.

1950: Joined the National Negro Labor Council and forced Sears, Roebuck and Co. to hire black clerks.

1960: Elected delegate to the Michigan state Constitutional Convention.

1964: Elected to the Michigan State Senate where he served through 1973.

1968: Became first black to represent Michigan on the Democratic National Committee.

1973: Elected mayor of Detroit, the first of four terms.

1981: Voters OK'd a 50 percent income tax hike to combat effects of recession.

1985: General Motors opened an $800 million assembly plant in city.

1987: Realized dream of making the police department resemble the community as force achieved 50-50 racial balance.

USA TODAY: What has been your greatest accomplishment?

YOUNG: Making the police department representative of the electorate. When I became mayor, less than 15 percent of the police department was black. No women at all. Today, in excess of 50 percent of the department is black. Women have gone up to about 12 percent. The chief of police is black and at least 50 percent of the top officers are black.

USA TODAY: Why haven't you been able to control the narcotics traffic?

YOUNG: I don't have the answer. If I did, we would have dried up the narcotics. The profits are so big that any kid would tell you they look down their noses at a job at a hamburger joint.

USA TODAY: There must be something more than the lure of money or you would have turned to crime in the Roaring '20s in Black Bottom.

YOUNG: You are right. The schools were good then. Both my parents were living and giving me some guidance. We have deteriorated. And we have developed a permanent underclass. About 50 percent of the kids in sixth grade will not graduate. They will drop out. All I can say is that we must fight it. And that is what I am doing.

USA TODAY: You have risen over so many obstacles. What's next?

YOUNG: People ask me: "Why don't you run for U.S. Senate? Why don't you run for governor?" It could never happen. You know we have a senator now from Michigan, Carl Levin, who is a bright young man. He was president of the City Council during the first term I served as mayor. I believe that I'm at my absolute height in terms of political aspirations. I don't think that Carl had any experience that was superior to mine or any knowledge that was superior to mine, but he could aspire to that which I could not. The truth of the matter is that racism is the reason.

USA TODAY: You sound pretty sad about that.

YOUNG: Sure, it is sad. But you have to look at reality. And you have to be able to see it like it is. Once you cloud your vision with sentimentality, you are in trouble.

USA TODAY: How do you want people to remember you?

YOUNG: I want to be remembered as a man who loved this city, who was devoted to his people and contributed to the progress of the city and of black people across the nation.

AND STILL WE RISE

'This book shows that black Americans have something special to contribute'

Coretta Scott King

I have always believed that the highest purpose of journalism is not merely to inform, but to inspire as well. Few books in recent memory have served these goals so well as *And Still We Rise.*

In these pages, Barbara Reynolds, surely one of the most dedicated and perceptive journalists we have, provides a remarkable testament to the power of faith, courage and determination to overcome adversity. Ms. Reynolds, herself an important role model for young people aspiring to a career in journalism, has brought many years of experience, expertise and commitment to these illuminating profiles in black achievement.

From the time the first black people arrived, bound and shackled, in America in the year 1619 on down to today, the black experience has been characterized by slavery, segregation and discrimination. Yet, somehow out of a terrible legacy of racism and suffering, a dynamic of faith and hope has steadily propelled black Americans forward in the quest for full human rights. Somehow we have survived the tearing apart of our families and the generation of poverty and brutality forced on us down through the centuries. Somehow, we have kept an unyielding belief in the promise of the American Dream.

"If the inexpressible cruelties of slavery could not stop us," said Martin Luther King Jr., "the opposition we now face will surely fail. We will win our freedom because the sacred heritage of our nation and the eternal will of God are embodied in our echoing demands."

This book shows that black Americans have something special to contribute to this country and the world, a strength and tenacity and a gift for compassion that has been finely honed and tempered in our struggle for survival and freedom. In exercising their rights and responsibilities with all of the proud history and wisdom of the black experience, the leaders profiled in these pages have shown that black Americans have a special mission as we move toward the new millennium.

Writers and artists, activists and scientists, scholars and athletes, business and labor leaders, black Americans from all walks of life must advocate a vision of a world where starvation and hunger will not be tolerated, where no child lives in fear of a nuclear holocaust. We must accept this challenge, not only to improve the lives of black Americans, but because we have a historic mission to provide the kind of leadership that can put things right in America.

The prominent black people profiled in this book can be appreciated as role models for the coming generations. But even more important is that we identify the common denominator that has made their success possible.

Although they represent many diverse fields, one could say that they share a commitment to self-discipline, a passion for excellence, a willingness to sacrifice and a determination to learn from mistakes. Knowing many of those interviewed in these pages, I would say that they also share a pride in their heritage and a commitment to help lift up those who have been left behind. But the key factor that has ensured their success has been the willingness to put heart and soul into their work.

And Still We Rise is not only a celebration of the contributions of black leaders in all walks of American life. The black experience is a vital part of our national heritage, belonging not only to black people, but to Americans of all races. A sense of appreciation for the struggles and accomplishments, the magnificent works and immutable contributions of different racial and ethnic groups provides a rich sense of the wondrous possibilities of the human imagination and spirit and the power of love and courage to overcome adversity.

AND STILL WE RISE

Commitment to equal opportunity helped make this book possible

Αnd Still We Rise was born of the work of many at USA TODAY and its parent, the Gannett Co. Inc.

Without the contributions of the editors, researchers and photographers from USA TODAY these 50 conversations with successful black men and women would not have been possible.

And without the commitment of USA TODAY and Gannett to serve all people of the USA, the Inquiry and Opinion page interviews that led to this book would never have been published.

For their longtime support for equal opportunity in general, and for support for this book in particular, special thanks go to Gannett Chairman Allen H. Neuharth, Gannett President and Chief Executive Officer John Curley, USA TODAY Editor and Gannett Chief News Executive John Quinn, USA TODAY Executive Editor Ron Martin, USA TODAY Editorial Director John Seigenthaler, USA TODAY Publisher Cathleen Black and USA TODAY President Thomas Curley.

I am deeply grateful to Nancy Woodhull, Gannett vice president/news services and president of Gannett New Media, publisher of this book.

And special thanks to those on the Opinion page staff with whom I work daily — especially Deputy Editorial Director Paul McMasters and Operations Director Diane Culbertson.

Also, a big debt of gratitude to Nikki Giovanni, the people's poet who first suggested this project to me; and to Carol Richards, former member of USA TODAY's editorial board, who reinforced the rightness of this idea.

Working side by side with me in producing this book were:

▶ Karen Howze, managing editor of USA TODAY's International edition, who was senior editor on my reporting and editing team.

▶ Norlishia Jackson, founding member of JFJ Associates, my publishing firm, who was one of the main editors and researchers. JFJ assisted in the production of this book.

▶ Gaynelle Evans, Gannett News Service reporter, who assisted in the editing of the interviews.

▶ Larry Brown, president of PONCHO Illustrations, who designed the cover.

Also, thanks to the Gannett New Media staff members who edited and published this book: Phil Fuhrer, Emilie Davis, Robert Gabordi, Randy Kirk, Lark Borden, Theresa Klisz Harrah, Theresa Barry, Victoria Everett, Tony Klimko, Carolynne Miller and Chris Singer.

And thanks to J. Ford Huffman, managing editor for features, graphics and photography of Gannett News Service, for his advice on the book's design.

Photographers whose work is featured include: Mary Ann Carter, James Colburn of Photoreporters, Tim Dillon, Paul Fetters, David Hathcox, Ken Hawkins, Joe Kennedy, Martha Leonard, Jeanne Marklin, Doug Menuez, Rob Nelson/Picture Group, Craig Molenhouse, Beverly Parker, Barbara Ries, Mario Riviz, Craig Ruttle, Howard D. Simmons, Christian Steiner, Mark Sennett of Gamma Liaison, Howard D. Simmons, David Tulis, UPI, Dixie Vereen and Ira Wyman.

Assisting with technical, production and administrative aspects: JoAn Moore, Candy Busey, Gina Porretta, Robin Jackson, Beth Goodrich, Judi Rice and Annette Jacobs. Providing assistance from the USA TODAY library were Dean Brown, Teresa Campbell, Clarencetta Jelks, Johnny King, Phyllis Lyons, Arabella Stewart-Stern and Letitia Wells.

Information for the Profile boxes was provided by USA TODAY research staff. The following sources also were used: The Negro Almanac, Earl Blackwell's Celebrity Register, Contemporary Authors, Contemporary Newsmakers, Current Biography Yearbook 1986, Encyclopedia of Black America, Marquis Who's Who in America, and Who's Who Among Black Americans.

Barbara A. Reynolds

ALSO AVAILABLE FROM *USA TODAY* BOOKS

USA TODAY Books is the imprint for books by Gannett New Media, a division of Gannett Co. Inc., with headquarters at 1000 Wilson Blvd., Arlington, Va.

USA TODAY Books produced its first self-published book in December 1987, titled *Bus-Capade: Plain Talk Across the USA*. Previous USA TODAY Books were produced in conjunction with non-Gannett publishing houses.

For more information or to order, write to USA TODAY Books, P.O. Box 450, Washing-ton, D.C. 20044 or phone 800-654-6824.

Portraits of the USA
Edited by Acey Harper & Richard Curtis
Pages: 144. Hardbound.

Glossy, high-quality coffee-table book. Features photos taken for USA TODAY, many of which are award winners. Photos are portraits of life in the USA, seen through the eyes of USA TODAY's photographers and selected by USA TODAY editors. Retail price: $29.95, shipping extra. ISBN: 87491-815-4.

Tracking Tomorrow's Trends
Anthony Casale with Philip Lerman
Pages: 268. Paperback.

Features charts and information based on USA TODAY polls and news research. Information written in USA TODAY's light, easy-to-read style. Trends and what is likely through the 1990s. Retail price: $8.95, shipping extra. ISBN: 0-8362-7934-4. Audio cassette interview with the author: $8.98, shipping extra.

The USA TODAY Cartoon Book
Charles Barsotti, Bruce Cochran, Dean Vietor
Paperback

Cartoons from the pages of USA TODAY's Life, Sports and Money sections. Funny, but filled with insight into our lives, our work and our play. Retail price: $6.95, shipping extra. ISBN: 0-8362-2077-3.

USA TODAY Crossword Puzzle Book
Volumes I, II and III
Charles Preston
Paperback

A series of puzzles from USA TODAY's crossword puzzle editor. Each volume contains 60 puzzles never before published in book form. Retail price: $5.95 each, shipping extra. Volume I ISBN: 0-399-52053-8. Volume II ISBN: 0-399-52055-4. Volume III ISBN: 0-399-52063-5.